THE GENTLE ART
OF COOKERY

THE GENTLE ART
OF COOKERY

WITH 750 RECIPES

by

MRS. C. F. LEYEL *and* MISS OLGA HARTLEY

With an introduction by

ELIZABETH DAVID

CHATTO & WINDUS

THE HOGARTH PRESS

1983

Published by
Chatto & Windus · The Hogarth Press
40 William IV Street
London WC2N 4DF

First published 1925
Reprinted 1942, 1947
First issued in the Phoenix Library 1929
Reprinted 1935
First issued as a Graham Watson edition 1942
Reprinted 1946
First issued in this revised edition 1974
Reissued in paperback 1983

British Library Cataloguing in Publication Data

Leyel, C. F.
    The gentle art of cookery.—Rev. ed
    1. Cookery
    I. Title   II. Hartley, Olga
    641.5   TX717
    ISBN 0-7011-1982-9

Printed in Great Britain by
Richard Clay (The Chaucer Press) Ltd, Bungay, Suffolk

CONTENTS

" Cookery means the knowledge of Medea and of Circe and of Helen and of the Queen of Sheba.

" It means the knowledge of all herbs and fruits and balms and spices, and all that is healing and sweet in the fields and groves, and savoury in meats.

" It means carefulness and inventiveness, and willingness, and readiness of appliances.

" It means the economy of your grandmothers and the science of the modern chemist ; it means much tasting and no wasting ; it means English thoroughness and French art and Arabian hospitality ; and, in fine, it means that you are to be perfectly and always ladies—loaf givers."

RUSKIN

INTRODUCTION

by
Elizabeth David

HOUSE-BOUND after a temporarily incapacitating illness during the early nineteen-sixties I enjoyed my compulsory leisure re-reading old favourites in my cookery library. Some of the books had been my earliest kitchen companions and it was instructive to discover which had survived the passage of time and my own changes of taste, increased knowledge, experience of writing and publishing my own cookery books, and my travels in search of gastronomic information.

Among the authors who came out as sturdy survivors were, predictably, Marcel Boulestin and more surprisingly, Mrs Leyel of Culpeper House fame.

It was partly that Mrs Leyel's writing still appeared fresh and alluring even if her recipes struck me as sketchy in the extreme, more relevantly the growing realization, as I read through *The Gentle Art of Cookery*, that the book was yet another manifestation of the English love affair with Eastern food and Arabian Nights ingredients.

During the 1939 war years, circumstances had landed me in Alexandria and subsequently in

Cairo. In my turn I fell under the spell of the beautiful food of the Levant – the warm flat bread, the freshly pressed tomato juice, the charcoal-grilled lamb, the oniony salads, the mint and yogurt sauces, the sesame seed paste, the pistachios and the pomegranates and the apricots, the rosewater and the scented sweetmeats, and everywhere the warm spicy smell of cumin. Because I had so often pored over Mrs Leyel's cookery book without quite realizing what she was putting into my head, the food of the Levant appeared more attractive than perhaps I should have found it without the background of that book. Come to that, I wonder if I would ever have learned to cook at all had I been given a routine Mrs Beeton to learn from instead of the romantic Mrs Leyel, with her rather wild and imagination-catching recipes.

Below is the tribute to Hilda Leyel which came out of my re-reading of her books. It appeared in the *Spectator* in July 1963.

*

Although Hilda Leyel is better known as foundress of the Society of Herbalists and the Culpeper House herb shops, and as author of some half dozen books on herbs and herbal medicine than as a cookery writer, *The Gentle Art of Cookery* is a book which should have its place as a small classic of English culinary literature. My own feelings towards *The Gentle*

Art, one of the first cookery books I ever owned, are of affection and gratitude as well as of respect.

One of the fallacies about the passing of judgement on cookery books is the application to the recipes of what is believed to be the acid test implied in the question do they work? A question which always reminds me of the Glendower-Hotspur exchange in *Henry IV*:

> I can call spirits from the vasty deep.
> *Why so can I, so can any man.*
> But will they come when you do call for them?

The question I should have wanted to ask Glendower would have been not so much whether he expected the spirits to turn up as whether he really wanted them to and what he intended doing about it if they did.

What one requires to know about recipes is not so much do they work as what do they produce if they do work? A cookery book which gives foolproof recipes for seed cake and pears bottled in crème de menthe and straw potato nests is a good cookery book only to those in whose lives seed cake, pears bottled in crème de menthe and straw potato nests play an important part. A book which tells you as Mrs Leyel's did that you can make a purée from fresh green peas and eat it cold and that a cold roast duck will go very nicely with the purée is not necessarily a bad cookery book because it does not tell you for how long you must roast the duck nor how many pounds of peas you will need for the purée. I am not now speaking from the point of view of an experienced cook whose path has been crossed by a great many roasted ducks (and by no means all of them perfectly done, no matter how much one may know about timing, temperatures, basting, or not basting) and who with a modest effort of memory is able to recall that twelve ounces of shelled peas make just enough peas for two and that to get twelve ounces of shelled peas you must pick or buy one pound of peas in the pod, or perhaps two pounds if they are small or even three if they are very small. No. I am recalling rather the reactions to Mrs Leyel's book of a young woman quite ignorant of cooking techniques but easily, perhaps too easily, beguiled by the idea of food as unlike as could be to any produced by the conventional English cook of the time; and at this distance it is not difficult to perceive that Mrs Leyel's greatest asset was her ability to appeal to the imagination of the young.

Lack of technical instructions and vagueness as to quantities were faults – if faults they were – which didn't bother me because I did not know that they were faults, did not suspect what I was up against and would, I think, not have believed anybody who had tried to tell me.

Allowing for questions of temperament as well as of taste the young and totally inexperienced will usually prefer a book which provides stimulus to one which goes into technical details,

makes strenuous efforts to keep the reader on
the straight and keeps to the main roads of
established cookery. At the age of nineteen one
is better off having a stab at Mrs Leyel's *marrons
glacés* in half an hour' than learning that the
confection of professional *marrons glacés* involves
no less than sixteen separate and distinct pro-
cesses and that to make enough for two people
is likely to mean a week's work.

Stimulus. That was the quality which Mrs
Leyel's book provided, and in plenty, for she
had the gift of making her recipes sound en-
ticing. Re-reading *The Gentle Art* and some of
those little books of Mrs Leyel's published by
Routledge under the collective title of *The Lure
of Cookery*, which includes *Meals on a Tray,
Picnics for Motorists, The Complete Jam Cupboard* and *Green Salads and Fruit Salads*, it has to
be admitted that Mrs Leyel suffered from in-
cipient jelly-mania – the incidence of dishes set
with gelatine and turned out of moulds is high
even for an English cookery book – and here and
there lost her head over a picturesque idea. A
picnic dish of hollowed-out lemons stuffed with
salmon mousse evokes an alluring freshness of
sharp scent and cool flavour; how many dozen
lemons I wonder would make enough containers
for say four people and would the mousse still be
in the lemons by the time you had driven the
picnic basket from London to, say, the top of
Firle Beacon? Small and carping criticisms,

these, compared with the positive virtues of Mrs
Leyel's attitude to cookery, the most attractive
of which, I now see, was her love of fruit, vegetables and salad and her treatment of them
almost as dishes to which meat and fish and
poultry were little more than incidental accom-
paniments or scarcely necessary adjuncts of a
meal. Indeed, *The Gentle Art* was notable for
the way in which the recipes were classified.
Appended to the vegetable chapter were two
separate sections dealing with mushrooms and
chestnuts respectively. How right of Mrs Leyel
to emphasize the strangeness of these foods by
separating them in the reader's mind from
potatoes and sprouts and beans. The fruit
chapter in *The Gentle Art* includes such rare
recipes as a compote of pomegranates, an orange
salad flavoured with sherry and lemon juice (a
tablespoon of each to four oranges – she did give
precise quantities when she knew that to overdo
a flavouring would spoil the dish) and strewn
with fresh mint leaves, a melon steeped in
maraschino-flavoured syrup then filled with
white grapes, white currants and pistachio nuts.
In a five-page section devoted to recipes for
almond creams, almond soups, almond puddings
and almond pastes was a recipe for a rice cream
to which ground almonds are added and 'when
cool pour into a silver dish and sprinkle with
powdered cinnamon and decorate with whole
almonds'. When I first had Mrs Leyel's book

nothing and nobody on earth could have sold me an English rice pudding, but a rice cream made with lemon and almonds and served in a silver dish, well, that gave one something to think about, silver dish and all.

Evidently much beguiled by the idea of Eastern cooking with its almonds and pistachio nuts, apricots and quinces, saffron and honey, rosewater, mint, dates and sweet spices, Mrs Leyel gave also in her book a little chapter of 'Dishes from the Arabian Nights' which, no doubt because of its vagueness and brevity contained the true essence of magic and mystery.

An Arabian way of cooking red mullet' – grilled in a sauce composed of tomatoes, onions, spices, shallots, salt, pepper, garlic, curry powder and saffron – sounded irresistible, so much so that even if you barely knew whether a red mullet was a bird, a flower or a fish you very quickly set about finding out. An hors-d'oeuvre called *munkaczina*, alleged by Mrs Leyel to have been brought from the East by Anatole France (maddeningly, Mrs Leyel gives neither chapter nor verse), is a salad of sliced oranges strewn with finely chopped onion which in turn is covered with a layer of stoned black olives, the whole to be sprinkled with red pepper, salt and olive oil. Mrs Leyel certainly took one very far away indeed from the world of grapefruit and Scotch eggs to which a bed-sitter cook so easily succumbs. Her book turned out to be almost the equivalent in cookery of Walter de la Mare's unsurpassed poetry anthology *Come Hither* which had enlightened my childhood. [1974]

*

Mrs Leyel died in 1957, and *The Gentle Art* had become hard to find when in 1974 Chatto decided to introduce it to a new public with a revised version of an article I had written in 1963. The book's charm still worked. From its pages still came potent whiffs of spices, mint and rosewater. Once again Mrs Leyel's dishes evoked those cargoes of exotic wines and fruit, gums and syrups and sugar carried to England in the Levant Company's sailing ships, once more the scents of my Alexandria and Cairo kitchens came tantalisingly back.

Now, nine years later, I find I am still much beguiled by Mrs Leyel's fresh and tempting ideas. Recipes for a delicate creamy mould of Jerusalem artichokes, cranberry cheese with walnuts and raisins, nasturtium salad, dandelion purée, eggs cooked with marigolds, little timbales of potatoes, geranium jelly, and ice cream of roses remind me afresh that somebody with imagination, flair, and a good garden, should surely attempt the creation of a restaurant providing really stylish dishes for vegetarians and non-meat eaters. What a welcome such a restaurant would now have in London. [1983]

PUBLISHER'S NOTE

IN preparing this new edition for press, as much as possible of the original character of Mrs Leyel's book has been retained. For example, her chapter at the end of the book, "The Alchemist's Cupboard", has been kept because, although it is outdated in parts, it is of real historical interest. But on the few occasions where her directions have become obscure, the recipes have been clarified or alternative ingredients suggested in parenthesis.

Throughout the book there are a number of recipes on which the reader may find some preliminary notes useful. Mrs Leyel appears, for example, to have had a wider range of bread roll than we have today, but her recipes work well with finger rolls and baps. Muffins can still be obtained, and Bermaline is a substitute for Veda bread, which no longer exists – it was basically a plain malt loaf.

In several recipes spinach juice is called for. This can be made by putting spinach leaves in the blender and then sieving if necessary. Similarly onion juice can be made by grating an onion over a bowl.

Some of the ingredients that are necessary for the success of a recipe are now only obtainable from the specialised grocer:

Harvey's sauce and mushroom ketchup (or catsup) for instance.

Nap is a cut from an ox, adjoining the foot, with approximately one pound of meat on it. See recipes for Calves Foot Jelly and Nap Pie.

Hominy is sometimes imported from America in tins, but the grits can be obtained at Fortnum and Mason.

Groult (see pp. 246, 248 and 275) is a French manufacturer of sago, tapioca and fecule (i.e. potato flour or starch).

Van Houten's cocoa is no longer exported from Holland, and Bournville is now the only brand generally available on the English market.

Isinglass can be ordered by most chemists.

Robinson's Patent Barley is manufactured by Reckitt and Colman, and is stocked by many chemists.

In the recipe "Mushrooms under Glass" fire-proof glass covers are called for. These are still being made and can be obtained from Ferrari's of Wardour Street, London w1.

Mrs Elizabeth David has very kindly supervised the revision of this new edition: her help is gratefully acknowledged.

PREFACE

THERE are seven ways in which this cookery book differs from all others :

(*a*) A great many more recipes than is usual are given for things that are obtainable all the year round, such as eggs, mushrooms, potatoes, apples, oranges, etc.

(*b*) The recipes are arranged in the only practical way, that is, under their principal ingredients, because it is more economical to do as the French do, shop first, and then arrange the dinner according to what is most plentiful in the market, than to go out and buy what is necessary for a pre-arranged menu.

(*c*) A whole chapter is given up to recipes for cold Sunday Supper Dishes.

(*d*) Another chapter contains a unique collection of flower recipes, all of them delicious and easy to make, bringing within everybody's reach things at present only obtainable at shops like Hediard's in Paris. This chapter also contains the newest information about Chinese scented teas.

(*e*) In the " Arabian Nights " Chapter, a whole Arabian Nights Dinner is given, with the real recipes for actual dishes mentioned in the stories.

(*f*) A chapter is given to children's cookery, giving recipes for things that will peculiarly appeal to children either to eat or to make for themselves.

(*g*) A list is given of the best materials to buy and also information as to where unusual ones may be bought.

The book has been made as modern as possible ; there are a great many recipes for cooking vegetables and fruit, because the tendency of to-day is to eat less meat. Though all the good French recipes are included, the book is not exclusively French, but contains the best American and cosmopolitan dishes. The original names have been used as far as possible. Many of the most famous dishes are quite old, though variations of them appear in many modern books under fanciful names. In every case recipes have been carefully compared and the best chosen. Recipes have been taken from old family recipe books and from a unique library of the cookery books of every country. Recipes that are very extravagant or only interesting archaically have not been included, nor have recipes been given for any dish that cannot be made perfectly from written instructions—for instance, omelettes and soufflé potatoes can only really be learned by practical demonstration, and are therefore not included.

This is not intended to be an elementary handbook on cookery, but has been written for those who appreciate the fact that good cooking is one of the attainable amenities of life if extravagance is eliminated.

I
SAUCES

" I detect the hand of an artist ; the shredded lamb, the chick-peas, the pine-kernels ; the cardamon seeds ; the nutmeg ; the cloves ; the ginger ; the pepper ; and the various aromatic herbs. I taste them as a whole, and I taste them separately, so exquisite is the blending."

CHAPTER I

SAUCES

A FRENCHMAN once said : " On devient cuisinier, on devient rotisseur, on est né saucier." The old definition of genius— " an infinite capacity for taking pains," will make a " Saucerer."

All sauces should be made in a double saucepan, the convenient equivalent of the " bainmarie," which derives its name from a famous Jewish woman alchemist of the fourth century called " Marie," who invented this method of boiling her concoctions.

Most of the famous sauces are many centuries old (the Sauce Robert probably dates back to the days of the Normans), and the compiler has chosen as far as possible the old recipes, which are better and simpler than the elaborate modern versions, spoilt by being drowned in vinegar and wine.

If the directions are carefully followed, all the following sauces can be made as well by an amateur as by a chef. A large number are given because it is in the sauce that one dish differs from another, and most made dishes take their name from their sauce.

It is not true that the English have only one sauce, but it is true that in England sauces are very often badly made, badly mixed, and not flavoured at all. The " white sauce " prepared in many kitchens would be useful for pasting scraps in albums on a wet day, but is not fit for eating. Yet it is perfectly easy to prepare a good sauce, and as the success of any made dish depends upon the sauce that gives it its name, it is important that the first principles to be observed in sauce-making should be understood.

Before a sauce is flavoured the foundation of the sauce must be of the right consistency and perfectly smooth, and neither too thick nor too thin. The general rules for ensuring the right consistency apply to all sauces.

The usual roux for thickening sauces is made of flour and butter ; as the quality of butters and flours vary it is not possible to lay down the accurate proportions of each. Some butters will take less flour than others, but the flour must be added to the melted butter very gradually and worked into the liquid butter over the fire with a wooden spoon until the paste is absolutely smooth. For the white roux the mixture must be cooked just long enough to cook the flour ; cooked slowly, not boiled. For a brown roux the roux must be cooked till it begins to turn brown. A sauce made with flour must simmer for ten or fifteen minutes after the flour is added to it or it will not be cooked. If milk forms part of a sauce it should be boiled first to avoid all risks of curdling, and strained into the sauce to keep out any skin that may form.

Remember that water in which macaroni, or rice, or vegetables, or mushrooms, has been cooked should not be thrown away, but be used for sauces in preference to plain water (if the sauce does not require meat stock).

When the roux for the sauce is mixed into a smooth paste, add the liquid gradually, stirring it well over the fire all the time, but do not let it actually boil until all the liquid has been added. The sauce won't thicken till it boils, and mustn't thicken until all the stock has been added. If when it boils it is too thick, a little more liquid must be stirred in carefully. If it is too thin, there are several ways of thickening it. The best way of thickening is by evaporation ; continue to cook it until the liquid reduces itself. The sauce thickens and improves in flavour, as it concentrates. Alternatively, a little flour, cornflour, chestnut flour, potato flour, or arrowroot may be sifted in : one ounce will thicken one pint, and some sauces or purées are thickened with the yolks of eggs, breadcrumbs or butter added at the last moment.

Anyone can make a plain sauce by following these directions carefully, and anyone who can make a plain sauce can make any of the following sauces, for their secret lies in their flavouring.

Beurre manié is often used to thicken sauces. This is a small quantity of butter mixed to a paste with an equal quantity of flour, and added uncooked to the hot sauce at the last moment before serving.

The recipe given for Sauce Béarnaise explains a most useful process of reducing vinegar. This method can be employed in other sauces that require sharpening or flavouring. Too much vinegar will make a sauce too thin ; by boiling the vinegar down the flavour is condensed.

ALMOND SAUCE FOR TURKEY

℄ Blanch some almonds ; dry two ounces of them, mince them very finely. Melt in a small saucepan a pat of butter (about half an ounce), and put the almonds into this, stirring them until they colour brown. Then sift in a heaped dessertspoonful of flour, a quarter of a pint of stock, or the soup that the giblets of the turkey have been cooked in. Flavour it with a pinch of salt, a pinch of mace, and a pinch of sugar. Bring it to the boil and keep the sauce hot in a bain-marie.

Do not strain this sauce, and before serving stir a tablespoonful of cream into it.

SAUCE BÉARNAISE

℄ The peculiar flavour of this sauce is obtained by reducing two tablepoonfuls of good vinegar to a teaspoonful by boiling it. In the vinegar should be boiled a teaspoonful of chopped

shallots. Strain the vinegar into a double saucepan and add two tablespoonfuls of cold water
into this. Mix slowly the beaten yolks of four
eggs and a quarter of a pound of butter. Divide
the butter into six portions and stir in one at a
time over a very slow fire. The sauce must be
stirred continuously till it is as smooth as thick
cream and of the same consistency. At the last
moment mix into it a little tarragon chopped
very finely—not more than a teaspoonful.

Béarnaise Sauce must not boil, and will
curdle if it is allowed to get too hot.

*To be served with a Châteaubriand or a Tour-
nedos of beef, or any hot fillet of steak.*

SIMPLE BÉCHAMEL SAUCE
*This Sauce is named after the Marquis de Béchamel, who was
maître d'hôtel to Louis XIV*

❦ When a sauce is made with flour it must be
allowed to simmer from ten to fifteen minutes
after the flour has been added, otherwise the
flour will not be cooked and the sauce will not
be at all good.

To make a Béchamel sauce, melt a piece of
butter the size of an egg in a double saucepan,
stirring into it, over very gentle heat, two tablespoonfuls of flour. Into this add gradually half
a pint of milk, stirring it steadily with a wooden
spoon over a slow fire for a quarter of an hour.
When it is perfectly smooth and of cream-like

consistency, remove it from the fire ; add salt and pepper, and mix in another smaller piece of butter.

This sauce is the basis of all white sauces.

BÉCHAMEL SAUCE

℃. Three-quarters of a pint of white stock, half a pint of milk, two ounces of butter, one of flour, six peppercorns, a carrot, an onion, parsley, a bayleaf, salt and pepper.

Boil the stock with a little sliced onion and carrot, half a bayleaf, a piece of parsley, and six peppercorns for twenty minutes, or till it is reduced to half a pint ; strain it into a bowl.

Melt the butter in a saucepan, work the flour into a smooth paste, heat the milk, and gradually add the hot stock and the hot milk to the butter and flour, stirring it well. Add salt and pepper to season.

Béchamel Sauce can be served with nearly all vegetables, with eggs and chicken, etc.

BLACK BUTTER

℃. Two ounces of butter; parsley, two tablespoonfuls of lemon juice.

Take a handful of small sprigs of parsley freed from their stalks. Put the butter in a frying pan and make it hot. Fry the parsley in it until crisp and brown. When the sauce is brown without being burnt pour it into a very hot sauceboat.

8

Boil the lemon juice, and just before serving the sauce pour it into the black butter and parsley.

This sauce invariably gives its name to the dish with which it is served—œufs au beurre noir—raie au beurre noir.

BREAD SAUCE

This is one of the sauces we make better in England than in France, for the French don't have bread sauce at all—a great mistake on their part, for properly made it is excellent, not only with birds but with many kinds of fish. Cold bread sauce ought always to be served with cold roast chicken.

℀ The secret of making good bread sauce is to flavour the milk before adding it to the bread. The bread crumbs should be stale, dried in the oven and then pounded.

First boil a small onion for five minutes. Then put half a pint of milk into a saucepan and add to it the boiled onion cut into pieces, a dozen peppercorns, not quite a level teaspoonful of salt, and either a good pinch of nutmeg or a leaf of mace, or half a dozen cloves. Watch the milk to see that it does not boil, and let it simmer over a gentle fire until it has time to absorb the various flavourings in it. Every time it begins to bubble, move it from the fire to cool down a little. As this process reduces the milk a little more must be added.

9

Then strain the milk into another saucepan, bring it to the boil, remove it from the fire and stir into it the breadcrumbs.

A tablespoonful of cream added at the last moment improves the sauce.

To get the right consistency the crumbs must be added to the milk, the milk must not be poured over the crumbs. The sauce must be made with milk and not with milk and water.

CELERY SAUCE

℘ Two or three celery heads, half a pint of milk, two ounces of butter, flour.

Slice the celery thinly, and put it into a double saucepan with a little sugar, the butter, pepper and salt to taste. Stew it till it becomes a purée, but do not let the celery brown. Add sufficient flour to thicken half a pint, and when it is smooth put in the milk. Let it simmer for twenty minutes and then strain it.

A little cream added at the last minute is an improvement.

To be served with boiled turkey or pheasant or stewed partridges.

CHERRY SAUCE

℘ Half a pound of cherries, a quarter of a pint of red wine, a quarter of a pint of water; sugar, cinnamon, lemon peel, a spoonful of arrowroot.

Stone the cherries, break the stones and add the kernels to the fruit. Pound the fruit and the kernels ; put them in a small saucepan with the wine and water, a spoonful of sugar, a little cinnamon, and a piece of lemon rind. Boil it till the cherries are cooked. Put them through a sieve and back in the saucepan. Mix a spoonful of arrowroot to a smooth paste with a little cold water, stir it into the sauce and bring to the boil. Add some fresh cherries from which the stones have been removed, and serve.

CHERRY SAUCE FOR TONGUE

℄ One tablespoonful of red currant jelly, a wineglassful of port or claret, a little chutney, a spoonful of Harvey sauce, and of Worcester sauce, the juice of three oranges and one lemon, cayenne pepper.

Melt the above ingredients together and boil till they are reduced to half. Add some glacé cherries and serve.

CRANBERRY SAUCE

℄ Make a syrup of sugar and water and stir it over the fire until the sugar is dissolved. Let it boil for about ten minutes and then add to it half a pint of cranberries. Put the lid on the saucepan and let them all simmer very gently until transparent, but do not allow the cranberries to burst and spoil the appearance of the sauce (quick cooking will do this). Remove any scum that may arise. When the berries are tender the sauce is ready—do not overcook it.

This sauce is improved by being made the day before. Serve cold with cold roast turkey.

A SIMPLE BUT EXCELLENT CUMBERLAND SAUCE

❦ Put into a saucepan as many tablespoonfuls of red currant jelly as are required, and to each tablespoonful add a dessertspoonful of Lea and Perrin's Worcester sauce, and a teaspoonful of Harvey sauce, also a very little nutmeg and the juice of half a lemon.

Mix all together, make them very hot, but do not allow it to boil.

This sauce is excellent with all kinds of hot meat and with jugged hare.

CURRY SAUCE

❦ Six onions, two ounces of butter, a tablespoonful of curry powder, a pint of gravy or stock, flour or arrowroot.

Peel and slice six large onions. Put two ounces of butter into a pan, add the onions and let them stew without browning ; add a good tablespoonful of curry powder and mix them all together. Then moisten them with a pint of gravy or stock and stir the mixture for twenty minutes. Rub it through a sieve and thicken it with flour or arrowroot if necessary.

Three apples sliced and added to the onions is an improvement.

This sauce is used for curried vegetables and fish.

COLD DEVIL SAUCE

¶. One and a half ounces of butter, three ounces of red shallot, half a pint of stock, a quarter of a pint of claret, a tablespoonful of green ginger, a table-spoonful of chutney, sugar or red currant jelly.

Melt the butter in a small stewpan over a moderate fire ; put into it the finely minced shallot, fry gently, adding the minced skin of two green chillies or of one fair-sized capsicum, and a teaspoonful of rasped green ginger. When the shallot has browned slightly, moisten it with half a pint of good stock, a quarter of a pint of claret, and a tablespoonful of chili vinegar ; stir in while this is heating a tablespoonful of chutney and a teaspoonful of sugar or red currant jelly. Boil it up, skim it, let it simmer for fifteen minutes, and strain it.

When cold remove any scum that may have risen and serve.

SAUCE ESPAGNOLE

℃. Three carrots, one onion, butter, scraps of game, meat or veal, flour, stock, herbs.

Cut up three carrots and one onion ; put them into a pan with a little butter, and add any scraps of game, meat or veal. Put the lid on and cook them over a slow fire till a pale brown, then stir in one tablespoonful of flour and enough hot stock to moisten it ; then stir it till it thickens ; add a bouquet of herbs and let it simmer for about an hour. Strain it and serve.

It will keep for some days if put into a covered jar.

GARLIC SAUCE

℃. Oil, almonds or other nuts, garlic.

For one gill of olive oil, blanch, peel and pound thirty almonds or nuts ; add finely chopped garlic to taste, and stir both into the oil.

GREEN SAUCE
To be served with eggs, boiled fish, or chicken.

℃.Take a handful of very green parsley and another of chervil, also some tarragon leaves and some spinach, and scald them all in boiling water. Pound them in a mortar; add to them two gherkins and two spoonfuls of capers. Pound all together with a piece of butter and pass through a sieve.

Mix into a white Béchamel (see page 7).

GREEN GOOSEBERRY SAUCE
To serve with grilled mackerel.

℃ Half a pint of green gooseberries, a wineglass of spinach juice; butter, nutmeg, sugar, pepper and salt.

Boil half a pint of green gooseberries and drain away the water. Pass them through a sieve and put the purée into a stewpan with a wine-glassful of spinach juice or raw green sorrel ; add a little butter and season with nutmeg, sugar, pepper and salt.

Make very hot and serve.

GUBBIN'S SAUCE
This sauce should be made over boiling water.

℃ One ounce of butter, one dessertspoonful of vinegar, one tablespoonful of cream, two teaspoonfuls of made mustard, half a dessert-spoonful of tarragon vinegar.

Melt the butter and stir into it the mustard ; then stir in a dessertspoonful of vinegar, half that quantity of tarragon vinegar, and a table-spoonful of cream. Season with salt, black pepper, and cayenne.

To be poured over grilled fowl, turkey, pheasant or game, just before serving. It is good with any grill.

SAUÇE HOLLANDAISE

℄ Two ounces of butter, the yolks of three eggs, one lemon, a little parsley, a little nutmeg, a little vinegar, salt.

Beat up the yolks of the eggs with a little salt, grated nutmeg, chopped parsley, and a dash of vinegar. Melt the butter in a double saucepan, add the beaten eggs slowly ; stir all the time, but do not let the sauce boil. When the sauce is smooth and well mixed, add the juice of a lemon and stir it in.

Serve the sauce very hot, but never let it boil.

To be eaten with asparagus and other vegetables and all fish.

COLD SAUCE HOLLANDAISE

℄ A Hollandaise Sauce should be made with butter and eggs, but to be served cold the butter must be left out. Therefore a custard must be made with the yolks of three eggs and half a pint of milk, seasoned with salt and pepper. When this is cold add the following :

Boil a quarter of a pint of French vinegar with a little salt and a teaspoonful of chopped onion until there is little more than a tablespoonful left. Strain this, and when it is cold stir it very gradually into the cold sauce.

HORSERADISH SAUCE

℃ Horseradish, stock, almonds, vinegar, sugar.

Grate two roots of horseradish in a cupful of white stock or milk, and add to it two lumps of sugar, a teaspoonful of ground almonds, and two tablespoonfuls of vinegar. Let it boil, and make it an hour before it is served.

If it is to be used cold do not boil it.

To be eaten with roast beef.

Another Recipe for
HORSERADISH SAUCE

℃ Horseradish, castor sugar, vinegar, salt, cream.

Grate a young horseradish root as finely as possible, and add to it a dessertspoonful of castor sugar, a tablespoonful of vinegar, and salt to taste. Stir into it a quarter of a pint of cream, and if it is for hot meat heat it by pouring it into a jar and standing it in boiling water.

Oil can be used instead of cream, and then it should have grated orange rind in it.

MAÎTRE D'HÔTEL BUTTER

℃ Butter, parsley, lemon juice, nutmeg, salt and pepper.

Melt an ounce of butter in a pan, and add the same quantity of parsley chopped finely, a good squeeze of lemon juice, nutmeg, salt and pepper to taste.

The lemon juice should be added gradually to the butter and parsley.

If a " Maître d'Hôtel Sauce " is required, these ingredients are added to a simple Béchamel (see page 7).

To serve with vegetables and fish, grilled kidneys, etc.

MAYONNAISE SAUCES

℟ All Mayonnaise Sauces are made in the same way, and varied with different flavourings. It is important to keep all the ingredients for a cold sauce as cool as possible. Oil kept in a hot kitchen in the summer will be almost tepid, and then no amount of whipping will thicken it properly. Mix the sauce in a cool place—the larder if necessary, and in hot weather cool the oil by standing the bottle on ice for a few minutes, or in a basin of cold water.

PLAIN MAYONNAISE SAUCE

℟ Eggs, salad oil, salt, vinegar.

Stir the yolks of two fresh eggs in a basin with a little salt. Stir with a silver spoon, and add the salad oil very slowly, a drop or two at a time. When the yolks begin to thicken, the oil may be added a spoonful at a time. Two yolks will thicken half a pint of oil. To this quantity add only a tablespoonful of vinegar.

An egg whisk may be used after the sauce has begun to thicken, but should not be used till then.

GREEN MAYONNAISE

℀ To half a pint of plain mayonnaise sauce add the following mixture :

Boil half an ounce of parsley, watercress and chervil in salted water for seven minutes ; drain it and pulp it through a fine sieve. It is then ready to turn the yellow sauce into a pale green one.

RED MAYONNAISE

℀ A plain mayonnaise may be changed into a red one by the addition of a tablespoonful of the flesh of ripe capsicums pounded to a purée ; or if capsicums are not available, and the sauce is being used for lobster, the coral of the fish will colour it.

TARTARE MAYONNAISE

℀ When making the sauce as for a plain mayonnaise, add a level teaspoonful of dry mustard powder, and add to the sauce when finished one tablespoonful of mixed parsley, watercress, chives and chervil, all finely minced after being scalded and dried.

MAYONNAISE À LA RÉMOULADE

℀ To half a pint of plain mayonnaise sauce add a tablespoonful of made French mustard. Then add parsley, watercress and chervil, exactly as for Green Mayonnaise, with three or four chopped pickled gherkins as well.

MAYONNAISE AU RAIFORT

℃ Grate very finely two tablespoonfuls of horse-radish, and add this to half a pint of plain mayonnaise sauce.

CAZANOVA MAYONNAISE SAUCE

℃ Place the yolks of three eggs in a basin with a little pepper and salt; add drop by drop about half a pint of salad oil and one-eighth of a pint of tarragon vinegar. Add to this sauce, which should be of the consistency of thick cream, four finely shred truffles or mushrooms, a pinch of shallot, the whites of three hard-boiled eggs shredded finely, and the sieved yolks of three. Mix and serve.

SAUCE MORNAY
A Cheese Sauce.

℃ Prepare a white sauce (see page 7), and without letting it boil, stir in gradually two tablespoonfuls of grated Parmesan cheese and one ounce of butter, added in small pieces.

The sauce must be made very hot, but must not boil.

SAUCE MOUSSELINE

℃ Take equal parts of cold Sauce Hollandaise and whipped cream, and whip them both together until the sauce is light and frothy.

Serve with cold asparagus.

MUSHROOM SAUCE

℄ Put a dozen mushrooms into a small stew-pan with a glass of mushroom catsup and half a pint of good brown gravy. Boil it for ten minutes.

To serve with fish or meat.

MUSTARD SAUCE

℄ Melt one ounce of butter in a double sauce-pan, stir into it a dessertspoonful of flour till it is smooth, add a teaspoonful of vinegar, salt and pepper, a tablespoonful of dry mustard and a spoonful or two of water.

Stir this over a slow fire till it thickens.

To serve with grilled herrings.

Another Recipe for
MUSTARD SAUCE

℄ One tablespoonful of made mustard, one tablespoonful of Chili vinegar, two tablespoon-fuls of butter, one cup of boiling water, one squeeze of lemon, one teaspoonful of anchovy sauce, two tablespoonfuls of flour.

Melt and mix together the butter and flour, add the cupful of water and stir all the time till it boils, then add the mustard, vinegar, lemon and anchovy. Stir altogether, and serve.

CHRISTOPHER NORTH'S SAUCE
To be served with goose, duck or pork.

℃ Two tablespoonfuls of Harvey Sauce, one tablespoonful of lemon juice, one dessertspoonful of mushroom ketchup, one glass of port wine, one dessertspoonful of sifted sugar ; salt, cayenne pepper.

Put into a jar a dessertspoonful of sifted sugar, a saltspoonful of salt, and rather more than that quantity of cayenne. Mix it well, and add by degrees two tablespoonfuls of Harvey Sauce, a dessertspoonful of mushroom ketchup, a tablespoonful of lemon juice, and a large glass of port. Place the jar in a saucepan of boiling water and let it remain till it is almost boiling. It must *not* quite boil.

ONION SAUCE
To serve with Roast Mutton.

℃ Three onions, butter, one dessertspoonful of flour, a teacupful of milk.

Drain and chop three onions after boiling them in salted water till they are tender.

Put a lump of butter in a pan with a dessertspoonful of flour ; beat them till they are smooth and add, stirring all the time, a teacupful of milk. Add the onions and stir it till it boils. Season it to taste, and just before serving stir into it another piece of butter.

To make Soubise Sauce, pass this sauce through a strainer, add two tablespoonfuls of cream and a little grated nutmeg.

Soubise Sauce is served with stewed pheasants, grouse or rabbits.

HOT ORANGE SAUCE

℧. Two oranges, one lemon, stock, brown sauce, salt and cayenne.

Cut the very thin rind of an orange into long strips, and pour boiling water on it ; cook it for five minutes, then drain it.

Add to the drained peel the juice of two oranges and one lemon, and a cup of rich brown gravy, made of brown roux and stock, pepper and salt to taste. Stir it till hot.

Serve with wild duck or game.

PAPRIKA SAUCE

℧. Bacon, onion, paprika, milk, flour, pepper and salt.

Fry some small pieces of bacon with a chopped-up onion until it is brown ; season it with paprika.

Take a pint of sour milk and let it boil till it becomes thick ; mix it with a little flour, pepper and salt, and add the onion and bacon.

Strain and serve very hot.

Serve with hot mutton, beef or tongue.

SAUCE PIQUANTE

❦ This requires one ounce of butter, two onions, one carrot, two cloves, two shallots, a sprig of thyme, a bay leaf, parsley, and chives ; a tablespoonful of flour, a little stock, and a tablespoonful of vinegar.

Chop up all the vegetables and herbs ; put them with the butter into a double saucepan. When the butter is melted and turning brown, sift in the flour, stirring all the time ; add a little stock and the vinegar ; season it with salt and pepper.

Boil the sauce up slowly and put it through a sieve.

Serve with calf's h̄ad, brains, grilled trout, or braised cutlets.

SAUCE ROBERT

This is one of the simplest, oldest, and most famous of all the French sauces. It is mentioned as early as the thirteenth century, and may be of Norman origin.

" Robert " is supposed to be derived from Roebuck Sauce.

This is considered the best recipe for Sauce Robert : —

❦ Take four large onions and cut them into small pieces ; sprinkle them with flour. Put some butter into a frying pan and brown the onions in it ; moisten them with a little stock and finish cooking them. Season them with mignonette pepper and salt, and French mustard. After the mustard is added the sauce should not be cooked any more. English mustard mixed with tarragon vinegar, can be used as a substitute for French mustard.

Serve with vegetables, fish or meat.

TOMATO SAUCE

℃. One and a half pounds of tomatoes, two ounces of onions, one clove of garlic, a little butter, a little dried basil, a teaspoonful of sugar, black pepper, salt.

First of all put the basil and the clove of garlic in a little muslin bag, as it must be cooked in the sauce but removed before serving The tomatoes must be ripe, and well dried after they are washed. They must be sliced. Use the whole of the tomatoes, with skins and seeds.

Melt a spoonful of butter (about an ounce) in a pan, and in this fry two ounces of chopped onion for five minutes. Then put in the sliced tomatoes, with the muslin bag containing the flavourings, the white sugar, and pepper and salt to season. Put the lid on the pan and let it stand for about twelve minutes before bringing it to the boil. Let it boil for a few minutes to thicken the sauce, stirring it well. Then strain it through a hair sieve.

Put it back in the pan (without the muslin

bag), add a tablespoonful of " beurre manié " (made of equal parts of butter and flour kneaded to a paste), bring it to the boil and it is ready for serving.

To serve with macaroni, fish or cutlets.

TOMATO SAUCE TO BOTTLE

❡ Eight tomatoes, two onions, half a pound of white sugar, six cloves, salt, grated nutmeg.

Boil the sugar till it candies, then put in the onions cut into pieces ; when they are brown add the tomatoes, salt to season, the cloves and a little nutmeg. Boil it quickly. Pour it into bottles when cool, and keep it well sealed in a cool, dry place.

WELSH RABBIT

❡ A quarter of a pound of Cheddar cheese, one gill of milk (or cream), a good teaspoonful of made mustard, one ounce of butter, pepper, a slice of bread, a little vinegar.

Have a hot dish ready. Toast a whole round of bread half an inch thick on one side, butter it and lay it on the hot dish, the untoasted side uppermost.

Well butter a small iron saucepan, put the milk into it, then the mustard, the butter divided into small morsels ; plenty of pepper, a dash of vinegar, and the cheese. Stir the mixture on the fire till the cheese is melted, then quickly pour it on the bread and servê at once. Beer can be used instead of milk.

This is often poured over fish such as halibut and used as a sauce.

SAUCE FOR WILD DUCK

Put some gravy into a saucepan, and squeeze into it half a lemon ; add a wineglassful of port or claret, and cayenne pepper to taste.

POULETTE SAUCE

⁋ Make a Béchamel sauce by the recipe on page 8, and add to it the juice of half a lemon, some chopped parsley, and a few mushrooms.

II
VEGETABLES

" . . . . In my garden ground,
Let still the esculents abound ;
Let first the onion flourish there,
Rose among roots, the maiden fair ;
Wine-scented and poetic soul
Of the capacious salad bowl.
Let thyme the mountaineer (to dress
The tinier birds) and wading cress,
The lover of the shallow brook
From all my plots and borders look.

Nor crisp and ruddy radish, nor
Pease-cods for the child's pinafore
Be lacking ; nor of salad clan
The last and least that ever ran
About great nature's garden beds.
Nor thence be missed the speary heads
Of artichoke, nor thence the bean
That, gathered innocent and green
Outsavours the belauded pea."

CHAPTER II

VEGETABLES

"POINT de légumes, point de cuisinière," says the French proverb, and indeed vegetables are the *pons asinorum* of the kitchen, the dividing line between good and indifferent cooking. French cooks treat vegetables as respectfully as the dormouse did its watch, and use the best butter, which makes a dish of green vegetables scientifically a perfect food, fit to be served as it is in France as a course by itself.

The repugnance of many English children for green vegetables is explained by the dishes of stringy, watery, tasteless, tough green leaves that are sent up for the nursery dinner, a relic of the Victorian days when grown-up people ate far too much meat, and when butter was regarded as a superfluous luxury for children brought up almost exclusively on starch.

The method of stewing vegetables in water and then throwing away the water containing the most valuable properties is not only stupid, it is not economical. It is wasting good material for stocks and sauces. No other nation treats vegetables quite so casually as the English do—except, of course, the Scots, Welsh and Irish. No other nation makes a " melted butter " sauce out of flour and water and pours it over an unfortunate half-drowned cauliflower or vegetable marrow, with the optimistic object of invigorating it ; and in other countries the seasoning of vegetables, and of other dishes too, is done by the cook for the diners, not by the diners for the cook. It is " the English habit " to have salt, pepper and mustard on the dinner table ; in private houses abroad they are superfluous, and to ask for them is to insult the cook. On the other hand, there are English cooks who are insulted if they are requested to treat vegetables with a little more consideration. One excellent English cook of our acquaintance, asked to fry vegetable marrow, flatly refused ; she amiably softened her firmness by giving a reason for her obstinacy. She explained that it was " against nature " for a vegetable marrow to be fried, naturally the only way to deal with it was to boil it.

But as doctors are more and more insisting upon the virtues of vegetables, more variety in the ways of cooking them is called for. Although we are told to eat uncooked food, very few vegetables, except lettuce and cucumber, are palatable raw. Very young, tender carrots, carefully washed and rubbed clean, are excellent as a salad, sliced finely with mayonnaise sauce. And the white hearts of young spring cabbage, very finely shredded, can be eaten with lettuce in a salad. But most vegetables must be cooked to be digested.

ARTICHOKES

ARTICHAUTS À LA PROVENÇALE

℃ Take young and tender artichokes ; remove the outside leaves, trim the others with scissors and rub each artichoke with lemon to prevent it blackening. Sprinkle them one by one with good olive oil, and put salt and pepper between their leaves. Put them into a saucepan with some olive oil, enough to soak the artichokes, and then pour in enough cold water to cover them. Put the saucepan on a very hot fire so that the oil and water may boil quickly. In twenty minutes the artichokes will be cooked.

Serve the artichokes on a very hot dish, pouring over them the boiling oil which is left. They should be eaten off very hot plates.

The whole of the little artichokes are eatable when they are cooked in this way.

Fresh water should be drunk after eating them ; wine will seem acid, while water will have a delicate sweet taste.

ARTICHOKE SALAD

℃ Artichokes, fresh or preserved, minced parsley, lemon juice, oil, salt and pepper, and fennel.

Put the *fonds* of the artichokes at the bottom of the dish in which the salad is to be served, and cover them with a mayonnaise made of oil, salt, pepper and chopped parsley, a very little fennel chopped, and a little lemon juice.

Let it stand for a few hours before serving.

Another Recipe for

ARTICHOKE SALAD

⁋ Six artichokes, cold asparagus, one lemon, two tablespoonfuls of almonds, and a few table-spoonfuls of cream.

Boil the artichokes ; free the *fonds* from the leaves and the choke, and slice them. Add an equal amount of the heads of cold cooked asparagus. Pound two tablespoonfuls of chopped salted almonds, add to them the juice of a lemon, pepper, salt, and the cream. Mix the artichokes and asparagus together, and serve with the salad dressing poured over them.

ŒUFS AU FONDS D'ARTICHAUTS

⁋ Fresh artichokes or tinned *fonds* d'artichauts, eggs, Parmesan cheese, salt, pepper, and butter.

After boiling the artichokes remove the leaves and the chokes, leaving only the *fond*. Scrape the edible part of the leaves with a silver knife, and make into a paste with butter, pepper and salt.

Poach as many eggs as are required, and very carefully lay each egg on a *fond* of artichoke.

Lay the paste already prepared on the eggs, sprinkle with Parmesan cheese, put a tiny piece of butter on each, and serve very hot.

PALESTINE SOUP

℃. Take one pound of Jerusalem artichokes, one pint of milk, three good-sized onions, one stick of celery, salt and pepper, three pints of water.

Chop up all the vegetables and boil them all together in the water with the milk and pepper and salt to taste, for three-quarters of an hour. Strain into the tureen and serve with croutons of fried bread.

FRIED JERUSALEM ARTICHOKES

℃. Sixteen Jerusalem artichokes, boiling fat, salt and pepper.

Peel and cut up the artichokes into thin slices ; throw them into cold water for a minute ; dry them, and when the fat is boiling throw them in and fry a pale brown.

Drain, and sprinkle with salt and black pepper, and serve.

ARTICHOKE CREAM

℄ One pound of Jerusalem artichokes, two eggs, half a pint of milk, salt and pepper, three tablespoonfuls of whipped cream.

Boil the milk, beat in the eggs to make a custard and let it cool. Boil the artichokes and pass them through a sieve. Then whip together the artichoke purée and the custard, and add the whipped cream, with salt and pepper to taste. Steam in a buttered mould for forty minutes, and serve, turned out with tomato sauce poured over it.

ASPARAGUS

Asparagus should never be laid down flat and boiled. It should be tied together in bundles, the stalks cut even and stood upright in enough salted water to come half-way up the bundle. In this way the delicate, tender heads are steamed and retain their full flavour, and the tougher stalks are boiled for longer than they would be if the whole were boiled, and are therefore more tender.

The best sauce for serving with asparagus is either black butter sauce, or plain melted butter flavoured with a pinch of salt and pepper and a drop or two of lemon juice.

Sauce Mousseline is served with cold asparagus.

ASPARAGUS MOULD

¶ A bundle of young green asparagus, two ounces of butter, one pint of simple Béchamel sauce, the yolks of two eggs, stock.

Make a pint of Béchamel sauce. Chop up thin young green asparagus into small pieces ; boil for five minutes in salted boiling water, then drain. Melt the butter, add pepper and salt. Stir into it the Béchamel sauce and let it simmer. Add a little stock, and stir in the beaten yolks of two eggs and the asparagus. Pour it into a buttered mould. Stand the mould in a pan of hot water and cook it ; then let it get cold and turn it out to serve.

ASPARAGUS IN FRENCH ROLLS

¶ Take as many French rolls as there are people. Scoop out the centres and fry the rest in butter a golden brown.

Prepare a Béchamel sauce, and into it put the heads of some cooked asparagus. Add these to the sauce and make it very hot.

Pour the boiling mixture into the rolls and serve at once.

AUBERGINES
GRILLED AUBERGINES

¶ Split the aubergines, remove the seeds and slice them ; salt and pepper the slices and sprinkle with a little good salad oil.

AUBERGINES AU BEURRE
An old French Recipe.

℃. Cut the aubergines lengthways, put them aside for half an hour, covered with salt, between two plates. The salt will bring out drops of water, which must be wiped off. Put the slices of aubergines in a saucepan with a piece of butter, and sauté them.

When they are cooked and browned on both sides, sprinkle them with chopped parsley, and serve.

AUBERGINES À LA PROVENÇALE

℃. Prepare the aubergines in the same way as for Aubergines au Beurre, only cook them in oil instead of butter. Then cover them with the following mixture :

Two chopped onions, one tomato, a little parsley, a slice of bread steeped in bouillon and a clove of garlic. Cook all these together with a little butter, pepper and salt. When cooked, spread over the slices of aubergine, breadcrumb them, and bake them in the oven for half an hour. Put a little butter on the top before serving.

BAKED AUBERGINES

℃. Six aubergines, six tomatoes, two cloves of garlic, a few spoonfuls of veal stock.

Skin the aubergines and cut them in slices lengthways ; skin and slice the tomatoes, fry them both in butter, with two cloves of garlic, which must then be taken away.

Butter a fireproof dish, arrange the aubergines and tomatoes in alternate layers, with salt and pepper. Moisten them with a few spoonfuls of thick veal stock ; cover them, and bake them in a moderate oven for two hours. Then remove the lid, sprinkle them with grated Parmesan and breadcrumbs, and brown for five minutes. Serve hot.

AUBERGINES FRIED IN BATTER

℆ Peel the aubergines and cut them in slices. Make a frying batter with flour, water, one egg, salt and olive oil instead of butter.

Dip each piece of aubergine in batter, and fry them in boiling fat.

BEANS

Beans are vegetables with a history. The Greeks voted with them at their elections, with a helmet for ballot-box. Possibly this tradition is the origin of the modern slang expression, " Give him beans "—invented with the irony which is the peculiarly English form of humour. On the other hand, the Romans regarded beans as emblems of ill-omen, probably because their augurs used beans in their occult séances. Oddly enough, this habit of attributing abnormal intelligence to beans—and broad beans too !—

still lingers in rural districts in England. One summer during the war, in a remote Shropshire village the broad beans in some of the village gardens were discovered to have grown their " eyes " on the wrong side of themselves ; this, said the villagers with unanimity, meant that the war would be over by Christmas. For the benefit of the superstitious, it must be recorded that those Shropshire beans were quite mistaken.

French beans, or their English green brothers known as scarlet runners, should never be cut with a knife ; they should be broken up by hand into halves if young and tender. If they are old they must be broken into small pieces, and the skin and tips and stringy filaments removed.

Beans should be cooked in an earthenware casserole, and so should peas ; never in a tin-lined saucepan. An iron saucepan or frying pan is better than a tin one.

Haricot beans are sometimes improved by being cooked with a pinch of carbonate of soda, for in some water haricot beans refuse to cook properly ; but soda should never be used with green beans.

When the broad beans are young it is a great mistake to throw away the pods. As long as they are tender they are as good to eat as French beans, and should be treated in the same way. Broken up into small pieces and cooked with the beans, they make an excellent and most economical dish.

HARICOT BEANS À LA
MAÎTRE D'HÔTEL

℘ One pint of beans, two ounces of butter, lemon juice, chopped parsley, pepper and salt.

Parboil some young beans, then add salt and a little butter. Drain them well, and finish cooking them in another pan, with butter, chopped parsley, lemon juice, salt and pepper.

HARICOT BEANS À LA ROMAINE

℘ One quart of fresh beans, three small onions, one lemon, two anchovies, grated nutmeg, pepper and salt.

Cook the beans. In another pan cook the onions, cut into small pieces. When they are brown add them to the beans, with pepper and grated nutmeg to season, and the anchovies finely minced and passed through a sieve. Moisten with good brown stock. Cook the beans until they have absorbed all the stock.

Squeeze lemon juice over them, and serve hot.

HARICOT BEANS À L'ITALIENNE

℘ One quart of beans, a quarter of a pound of butter, one ounce of flour, stock, the yolk of an egg, half a lemon, parsley.

Parboil the beans, then drain them and finish cooking them in a pan with melted brown butter.

41

Stir them well, and serve with the following sauce poured over them :

Melt the butter, stir in the flour till it is smooth, add enough hot stock to make a sauce, and bring it to boiling point. If necessary strain the sauce and put it back on the fire. Stir in the beaten yolk of an egg, the juice of half a lemon, and a spoonful of finely chopped parsley.

Serve very hot.

HARICOTS VERTS À LA BRETONNE

¶ Cut a few small onions into dice and fry them in butter. Moisten them with some meat jelly from the bottom of a bowl of stock, and add sufficient stock to cover the beans, which should already be prepared for cooking. Season the stock with salt and pepper, stir and cook it till you have a smooth, thick sauce.

Put the beans into it, and let them simmer for nearly half an hour.

SALAD OF FRENCH BEANS

¶ One pound of French beans, one small onion, an anchovy, a beetroot.

Boil the French beans and drain them. When they are cold put them into a salad bowl, with shreds of anchovy, a little chopped onion (the onion must be boiled first), and some slices of beetroot.

Make a salad dressing of pepper, salt, oil and vinegar.

DUMAS' WAY OF COOKING
BROAD BEANS

℃. Wash and put into a casserole with some water and a piece of butter some freshly shelled beans. Let them simmer, and when they are half-cooked pour a glass of cold water into the casserole. Let them go on cooking till tender.

When they are cooked put into another casserole a quarter of a pound of butter, with parsley and shallots, salt and pepper.

Drain the beans and put them into the melted butter. Sauté them and add a squeeze of lemon juice.

BROAD BEANS STEWED WITH WINE

℃. One small onion, two ounces of butter, one quart of broad beans, two ounces of chopped ham, one ounce of flour, mixed herbs, two ounces of sugar, a quarter of a pint of white wine, a little stock.

Brown the onion, chopped small, in the butter in a casserole. Add the beans, ham, flour, a bunch of herbs, and enough stock to moisten, and stew them ; then add the wine and sugar, and serve.

BROAD BEANS AU BÉCHAMEL

℃. Half a peck of young broad beans, butter, stock, sugar, black pepper, salt, one tablespoonful of chopped parsley.

43

Shell half a peck of young broad beans ; put them into an earthenware casserole with a piece of butter, and toss them for a few minutes in the butter, then sprinkle them with flour, and moisten with a little water or stock. Season them with black pepper, salt, a pinch of sugar, and a tablespoonful of chopped parsley. Let them simmer till cooked.

Make a white sauce, and add to it the yolk of an egg.

Pour it over the beans, and serve.

HARICOTS AU LARD À LA VILLAGEOISE
(Dumas' favourite way of cooking haricot beans.)

❡ One quart of haricot beans, one pound of bacon ; water.

Soak a quart of haricot beans. Cut a pound of good bacon into slices, and mix well together with the beans. Cover the beans and bacon with the right amount of water to cook them, so that none need be added during the process nor any poured away.

The whole secret of this dish's success is that the beans should be cooked slowly enough to absorb all the flavour of the bacon and all the juices without being reduced to pulp.

HARICOTS ROUGES À L'ETUVÉE

❡ This recipe does equally well for red or white haricot beans or French beans.

Take beans, bacon, small onions, butter, flour, mixed herbs, a glassful of red wine.

Cook the beans in water with bacon and small onions. If they are fresh beans, put them into boiling water ; if they are dried, into cold water. When they are cooked, put into a casserole a piece of butter, a pinch of flour, mixed herbs ; add a glass of red wine. Boil for half an hour, and serve with bacon and small onions.

The red beans need less water to cook them than white or green beans.

HARICOTS À LA CRÈME

℄ Haricot beans, a little butter, a little grated nutmeg, a little celery, cream.

Soak the haricot beans well, and boil in salted water. When they are nearly cooked drain them, and finish cooking them in a little butter, with a little grated nutmeg. Just before serving add a few spoonfuls of cream.

Serve hot, sprinkled with shreds of fried celery.

BROWN HARICOT BEANS

℄ One quart of beans, a quarter of a pound of butter, three tablespoonfuls of flour, one small onion, salt and pepper.

Boil the beans for thirty minutes. Melt the butter in a pan, stir in the flour smoothly, add a small onion finely chopped and fry it. Then pour in a little brown stock to make a brown sauce, adding salt and pepper to season. Drain the beans, add them to the sauce, and cook together for ten minutes. Serve very hot.

RED BEANS STEWED IN WINE

❡ In this recipe you can use either fresh or dried beans of any colour. If dried, they must be soaked overnight.

Put as many beans as are required into a saucepan, with a few onions, a quarter of a pint of red wine, a quarter of a pint of water, a few mushrooms, salt, pepper, and a little nutmeg. Let them boil very gently for nearly three quarters of an hour. Serve with their gravy.

BEETROOT

BEETROOT SOUP

❡ Three beetroots, one head of celery, one pint of milk, water.

Bake the beetroots in water in a fireproof dish for three hours, adding more water as necessary. Peel them, chop them up with a head of celery. Stew them in a pint of milk and a pint of water till they are soft. Pass the soup through a sieve, add a little butter or a spoonful or two of cream. Heat again, and serve with croutons of toast.

FRIED BEETROOT

¶ Take a large cooked beetroot and cut it lengthways into long slices. Make a mixture of one egg, one tablespoonful of white wine, a tablespoonful of flour, pepper and salt to taste, and a very little nutmeg. Dip each slice in this, cover with breadcrumbs and chopped parsley, and fry.

Drain, and serve very hot with slices of lemon.

DEVILLED BEETROOT

¶ Half a beetroot, an onion, a tablespoonful of flour, three tablespoonfuls of milk, three table-spoonfuls of cream, a little mustard, a little Harvey sauce.

Fry a little piece of chopped onion in butter. Put into half a teaspoonful of Harvey sauce a pinch of salt and a pinch of dry mustard ; mix it with a teaspoonful of flour ; stir it to a smooth paste with the milk ; add the cream ; put it over the onion and boil for a few minutes. Then add the beetroot sliced.

Serve cold.

WINTER SALAD

¶ One beetroot, celery, two or three spoonfuls of cream, a little chopped onion and parsley.

Make a sauce as follows :

To each tablespoonful of cream add a teaspoon-ful of tarragon vinegar, a little sugar, and a pinch of cayenne. Cut up the beetroot and the celery into small pieces. Arrange in a dish in alternate layers, sprinkle a teaspoonful of finely chopped onion and one of parsley over the whole, and pour the sauce over it.

BRUSSELS SPROUTS

CHOUX DE BRUXELLES AU CITRON

ℭ Brussels sprouts, butter, flour, lemon juice.
Wash the sprouts and cook them for twenty minutes in salted water, meanwhile making a sauce of four ounces of butter and two table-spoonfuls of flour, and a little broth ; boil it, keeping it well stirred, season and add the juice of two lemons. Pour the sauce over, and serve.

CREAMED BRUSSELS SPROUTS

ℭ One and a half pounds of sprouts ; salt, pepper, nutmeg, a quarter of a pint of cream.
Clean and cook the sprouts in boiling water for seven minutes ; drain and cool them in cold water. Drain them well, and place them in a *sauté* pan with a little brown sauce, one tea-spoonful of salt, half a teaspoonful of pepper and the same quantity of nutmeg, finely grated. Add half a cupful of cream, heat them for five minutes (do not boil), tossing them frequently.
Serve at once.

PURÉE OF BRUSSELS SPROUTS

℗ One and a half pounds of Brussels sprouts, two tablespoonfuls of cream, one and a half pints of milk, one and a half pints of white stock or water; salt and pepper.

Boil the sprouts in boiling salted water till tender, and pass them through a sieve. Boil the milk and stock together, and when boiling add it to the purée. Season it and mix in the cream. Put it back on the fire and heat it until nearly boiling. It must not quite boil.

Serve with sippets of fried bread.

If too thin, an ounce of cornflour can be added to the stock in the early stages.

FRIED BRUSSELS SPROUTS

℗ Sprouts, butter, salt and pepper, nutmeg.

Boil the sprouts in boiling water with the lid off till they are tender, then thoroughly drain them and fry lightly in boiling butter or oil. Season them with salt and pepper, and sprinkle them with nutmeg before serving.

This makes a good luncheon dish with poached eggs served on the top.

SCALLOPED BRUSSELS SPROUTS

℗ Twenty sprouts, one and a half ounces of butter, one and a half ounces of flour, one and a half pints of milk, two heads of celery, breadcrumbs, salt.

Cook the sprouts in boiling salted water till they are soft. Drain them. Chop up the celery and put it in a saucepan with the melted butter ; salt to season, sift in the flour, and add the milk (which must be hot) very gradually. Lastly, put in the sprouts and turn the whole into a buttered fireproof dish, cover them with breadcrumbs and morsels of butter, and bake.

BRUSSELS SPROUTS AND CHESTNUTS

¶ Two pounds of Brussels sprouts ; chestnuts, one ounce of butter ; salt, pepper, a little gravy.

Boil the sprouts for fifteen minutes. Peel and boil the chestnuts separately. Drain the sprouts and put them under the cold-water tap. Then put them in a pan with an ounce of butter, pepper, salt, and a little good brown stock or gravy. Stir them, and add the boiled chestnuts. Cook them together for a few minutes, shaking the pan, and serve hot.

CABBAGE

AN EXCELLENT CABBAGE SOUP

¶ One pound of streaky bacon, two quarts of boiling water, two large cabbages, two onions, one carrot, one turnip, one head of celery, one pint of dried peas.

Put the bacon into a saucepan with the boiling water, also the cabbages (from which the stalks have been cut off) cut into pieces, the onions, carrot, turnip, celery, and dried peas (previously soaked). Let the whole boil very slowly for four hours. Remove all the fat and the bacon, and season with pepper and sugar.

Put at the bottom of the soup tureen slices of French roll or bread, and pour the soup over it.

CLEAR SOUP
with
BRAISED CABBAGE

℃ Choose a nice cabbage—the ones with curling leaves are best. Blanch them and cut them into quarters, then braise them in brown stock for a few hours, adding plenty of seasoning.

Prepare a clear soup. Serve it very hot with the braised cabbage cut in quarters in the tureen. One quarter should be served with each plate.

BRAISED CABBAGE

℃ Put a young spring cabbage into salted boiling water for ten minutes ; then take it out of the water and drain it. Put it in a fireproof casserole with a little butter, pepper and salt, cover it, and braise it for an hour. It wants neither water nor stock.

51

PURÉE OF CABBAGE
with
HARD-BOILED EGG

℄ One cabbage, half an ounce of butter, one tablespoonful of flour, two tablespoonfuls of vinegar, salt, pepper, one hard-boiled egg.

Boil the cabbage well, drain it and chop it small, and pass it through a sieve. Melt the butter in a frying pan, stir in the flour ; then add the cabbage, season with salt and pepper, moisten with the vinegar, and stir it over the fire for ten minutes. Pat it down smooth in the dish it is served in, and garnish with rounds of hard-boiled egg.

CHOU À LA CRÈME

℄ One cabbage, half a pint of milk, one ounce of butter, one ounce of flour, salt, black pepper.

Boil or steam a fresh cabbage. Make a smooth white sauce with half a pint of milk, a roux of the butter and flour, and the salt. When the cabbage is nearly done take it out of the water, chop it, and finish cooking by simmering it for ten minutes in the white sauce. Flavour it with ground black pepper at the last moment.

CABBAGE AS COOKED IN BUDAPEST

℄ Cabbage, breadcrumbs, half a pint of sour cream, butter, salt, and paprika.

Wash the cabbage, cut it in quarters, and boil

it in salted water. Well butter a pie dish and lay the cabbage in it, with the cut part upwards. Cover each layer of cabbage with sour cream and sprinkle it with breadcrumbs, on which place small dabs of butter.

Bake until brown.

CHOU MARRONÉ

ℂ. One cabbage, a dozen chestnuts (large), a dozen small sausages, stock.

Blanch a cabbage in boiling water, skin and boil in salted water a dozen large chestnuts, and fry a dozen little sausages, which should not be larger than the chestnuts. Cut out the heart of the cabbage, and in its place put the chestnuts. Tie up the cabbage, and braise it in stock. Cook it well, skim off the fat.

Drain and cover with sauce à l'Espagnol, and serve with the sausages round it.

POLISH RED CABBAGE

ℂ. One red cabbage, one sour apple, one onion, butter, brown sugar, cinnamon, powdered cloves, vinegar.

Cut up a red cabbage into fine pieces ; put it into a saucepan with the apple peeled and cut into slices, a chopped onion and a lump of butter, with just enough water to prevent it burning. When cooked, season with brown sugar, cinnamon, powdered cloves and vinegar.

STEWED RED CABBAGE

¶ One cabbage, one ounce of butter, one tablespoonful chopped onion, a saltspoonful of salt, a pinch of cayenne, a little grated nutmeg, one dessertspoonful of sugar, two tablespoonfuls of of malt vinegar.

Slice and soak a red cabbage in cold water ; put the pieces in a saucepan with the butter, chopped onion, salt, cayenne, and nutmeg. Put the lid on and cook till the cabbage is tender. When ready add the sugar, vinegar, and cook it another five minutes.

CARROTS

POTAGE LORRAINE

¶ Nine good-sized carrots, one onion, two heads of celery, a quarter of a pound of butter, five ounces of haricot beans, three pints of stock.

Slice the carrots, celery and onion ; put them in a saucepan with the beans and butter, and let them simmer for an hour, stirring occasionally. Add the stock and boil for an hour and a half ; pass it through a sieve.

CARROTS AU BÉCHAMEL

¶ Six carrots, two ounces of butter ; sugar, half a pint of white stock or milk ; lemon juice, flour, pepper and salt.

Scrape and slice the carrots after scalding them. Boil them in hot water with a lump of sugar and a little butter till tender, and drain them. Make a sauce by mixing the flour and butter with salt and pepper over the fire, and add to the sauce the milk and a little lemon juice. Add the carrots to this and heat all together, but do not let them boil.

Serve very hot with fried sippets of toast and fried chopped parsley.

CAULIFLOWERS

Cabbages and cauliflowers, which have been defined as " cabbages with a college education," should be plunged head first into strong salt water and left there for a quarter of an hour ; this disturbs any caterpillars. They should be cooked head downwards, too, to prevent them being discoloured by the scum that rises. The water they are boiled in should have a good pinch of carbonate of soda in it, half an ounce of salt to every two quarts of water, and a teaspoonful of sugar. Preferably, cauliflowers should not be immersed in water and boiled at all, but cooked in a steamer, with salt sprinkled over the leaves.

All bruised leaves should be removed when the cauliflower is trimmed, and the stalk should be cut squarely so that the vegetable will sit up straight.

CREAM OF CAULIFLOWER SOUP

❦ One good-sized cauliflower, one pint of milk, two pints of good white stock, two ounces of butter, one stick of celery, one ounce of flour, a little onion, one bayleaf, salt and pepper.

Cook the cauliflower in boiling water with salt for twenty minutes. Cut it in half. Put aside half the white flower, and put the rest of the cauliflower through a coarse sieve. Chop up the celery and the onion and fry it in the butter for five minutes. Take out the bayleaf, and stir in the flour. Warm up the stock, and put the celery, etc., into it, stirring well. Boil the milk, pour it on to the cauliflower purée, stir well, and add it to the stock. Add salt and pepper to taste. Strain it, and put in the pieces of cauliflower.

Heat it up again, and serve with croutons of fried bread.

CAULIFLOWER AU BEURRE

❦ One cauliflower, two ounces of butter, one tablespoonful of white wine, vinegar, salt and pepper.

Steam the cauliflower. When it is nearly cooked, sprinkle it with salt, pepper, and put an ounce of butter on it. Finish cooking, and serve with the following sauce poured over it :

Mix one tablespoonful of vinegar with one ounce of melted butter, pepper and salt.

CAULIFLOWER BORDIGHERA

℃. One cauliflower, three-quarters of a pint of milk, two ounces of butter, two tablespoonfuls of flour, a bayleaf, chopped parsley, pepper and salt.

Boil the cauliflower, then drain it dry and put it in a baking dish.

Make a sauce by melting the butter, stirring in the flour to a paste, adding the milk and stirring till it boils. Add the bayleaf, a spoonful of chopped parsley, salt and pepper, and cook for ten minutes. Remove the bayleaf. Pour the sauce over the cauliflower and sprinkle grated breadcrumbs on it and put morsels of butter on the crumbs. Bake in a hot oven till the crumbs are brown.

CAULIFLOWER AUX BOUQUETS
with
CHEESE

℃. Take the white flowers of a cauliflower, separate them from the green leaves ; put them into hot milk, with enough salt to season, to cook till they are tender. Arrange them in the dish they will be served in. Melt grated cheese in the milk they have been boiled in, and pour this sauce over them, dust a little freshly grated cheese over the dish, and serve hot with croutons of fried bread.

CHOUX-FLEURS EN PAIN

℄ Cauliflower, bacon, veal, beef suet, parsley, shallots, mushrooms, salt and pepper, three eggs.

Take one large or two small cauliflowers, wash it and half-boil it, rinse it in fresh water and put it aside on a sieve to drain.

Take a small saucepan, the same size round as the plate upon which you are going to serve the cauliflower, cover the bottom of it with slices of bacon, and put the cauliflower in next, head downwards, stalks uppermost.

Make good forcemeat with veal, beef suet, parsley, shallots, and mushrooms, season with salt and pepper ; add three well-beaten eggs, but neither cream nor stock. When this forcemeat is mixed and seasoned, put it in between the cauliflowers, pushing it into place with your fingers ; cook it with good stock seasoned to taste.

When the " pain de choux-fleurs " is cooked and it has absorbed the sauce, turn it out carefully into the dish in which it is to be served, remove the slices of bacon, pour over it a good gravy with a little melted butter, and serve as an entrée.

CAULIFLOWER À L'ITALIENNE

℄ One cauliflower, one small onion ; two anchovies, a little butter, half a pint of stock, a teaspoonful of minced mixed herbs, a dash of vinegar.

Boil the cauliflower and serve it hot with the following sauce poured over it :

Chop the onion and anchovies very small, and cook in one ounce of butter with the stock, the herbs and a few drops of vinegar.

CURRIED CAULIFLOWER

℃ Cauliflower, curry sauce, rice, butter.

Partly boil the cauliflower ; drain and cut it up into small branches. Lay it in a hot curry sauce, and let it simmer for about an hour.

Serve with rice handed separately.

The curry sauce will be found on page 12.

Cabbage can be curried in exactly the same way ; the cabbage being chopped small.

CAULIFLOWER AU GRATIN

℃ One cauliflower, half an ounce of butter, half an ounce of flour, one gill of milk, one ounce of Parmesan.

When the cauliflower is boiled, put it in a fireproof dish. Make a smooth sauce with the milk, flour and melted butter ; add the cheese grated, boil it, and pour over the cauliflower. Place a little butter over it, and bake till it browns.

CAULIFLOWER SALAD

℃ Cauliflower, beetroot, cucumber, gelatine.

After boiling the cauliflower, break it into small branches.

Prepare a thick mayonnaise sauce, which can be made extra thick by the addition of a little dissolved gelatine.

When the cauliflower is quite cold, dip each branch into the mayonnaise and lay in the dish in which it is to be served.

Pour the rest of the sauce over and decorate with slices of beetroot and cucumber.

CAULIFLOWER SALAD

❦ One cauliflower, two shallots, minced parsley, half a pint of mayonnaise sauce.

Boil a cauliflower, plunge it into cold water ; drain it. When it is quite cold and dry, break the white part into pieces and put them in a salad bowl with two chopped shallots ; sprinkle with pepper, salt, and minced parsley, and pour the sauce over it.

CELERY

RICE AND CELERY SOUP

❦ Two tablespoonfuls of rice, one head of celery, one and a half pints of white stock.

Boil the rice with the chopped celery a good many hours on a slow fire in enough water to prevent it burning. Add one and a half pints of white stock and boil it. Strain into the soup tureen. Serve with croutons of fried bread.

CREAM OF CELERY

℄ Celery, white stock, milk, flour, butter, salt and pepper, two tablespoonfuls of cream ; nutmeg.

Parboil a head of celery, cut in short lengths, in boiling salted water. Drain and put into a saucepan with enough white stock to cover, and cook till tender. Add a little milk and thicken the stock with flour and butter in the usual way. Season with salt and pepper, add two table-spoons of cream, sprinkle with nutmeg, and serve with the sauce poured over.

If a richer dish is required, the yolks of two eggs can be added to make " Celery à la Poulette."

RAGOUT OF CELERY

℄ Well wash the celery and blanch it in boiling salted water ; put it under the cold water tap and drain well. Chop it up and let it simmer in a casserole with a piece of butter for ten minutes, then add to it a good brown sauce and let it cook very slowly for about an hour. Season to taste.

Chicory is good cooked in the same way.

CUCUMBERS

CUCUMBER CREAM SOUP

℄ Two cucumbers, two pints of white stock, two onions, quarter of a pound of butter, five or six tablespoonfuls of cream ; breadcrumbs.

Cut the cucumbers in small pieces, removing the peel and seeds. Boil them in water with salt and vinegar for three minutes. Drain ; put them in a saucepan with the butter ; add the stock when the butter is melted, and about a small teacupful of the crumbs of bread soaked in milk ; also the onions cut up, salt to season, and a pinch of sugar. Bring it to the boil, then let it simmer, stirring occasionally and skimming it. Strain the soup ; heat it up again, and before serving stir in the cream.

Serve with croutons of toast.

PAPRIKA OF CUCUMBERS

¶ Peel and cut a large cucumber into small squares. Butter a baking dish and put a layer of cut cucumber at the bottom. Season them with grated onion and lemon juice, and then put a layer of breadcrumbs, and place on them pieces of butter. Season well with paprika and celery salt. Repeat these layers until the dish is full, finishing with crumbs and butter. Cover and bake for an hour, until brown.

A sauce piquante can be served with this dish.

CUCUMBER PURÉE

¶ Quarter of a pound of onion, two ounces of butter, one cucumber, one ounce of flour, two level tablespoonfuls of arrowroot, quart of milk or one pint of stock, a little chervil and water-cress, pepper and salt to season.

Chop up and fry the onion in butter ; slice half a good-sized cucumber very finely into the pan with the onions. Do not skin the cucumber. When the cucumber begins to colour sift in the flour. Add gradually one quart of milk or one pint of stock and one pint of water. Season with pepper and salt. Simmer till the cucumber is quite soft.

In the meantime cut the rest of the cucumber into small cubes, and when the soup is nearly cooked add these to it, also the leaves of the watercress and chervil, which must be first boiled for three minutes and then pounded into a green paste with a piece of butter the size of a walnut. Mix the arrowroot with a quarter of a pint of the soup, and add it gradually to the soup to thicken it.

Serve with croutons of fried bread.

CUCUMBER À LA CRÈME

℃. One cucumber, two ounces of butter, one teaspoonful of minced parsley, half a pint of stock, pepper, salt, flour, and vinegar.

Peel and cut the cucumber into half-inch slices, and leave them for fifteen minutes covered with a mixture of salt and vinegar. After drain-ing them, put them into a casserole with the butter ; fry them without letting them brown ; sprinkle them with flour, and add the stock, and boil gently.

Heat and serve on slices of fried bread, sprinkle with lemon juice and chopped parsley.

BAKED CUCUMBERS

ℂ. Cucumbers, breadcrumbs, grated onion, butter, salt, cayenne pepper. —

Peel one or two cucumbers, split them lengthways and take out the seeds. Mix the breadcrumbs with grated onions, melted butter, salt, and cayenne pepper, and with this mixture stuff the cucumbers. Put them in the oven in a baking tin with a little stock, or water and melted butter, and with this baste the cucumbers from time to time.

CUCUMBER FARCIES

ℂ. Two large cucumbers, three eggs, one and a half pints white sauce, a little cold boiled rice, a spoonful of grated cheese, bread, a little stock.

Cut the cucumbers in lengths of three inches ; take out the seeds with a vegetable cutter. Make a little stock hot in a saucepan. Stand the pieces of cucumber upright in it, to simmer for at least a quarter of an hour. Hard boil the eggs ; keep one yolk for garnishing, and chop up the rest.

Take a half-pint of hot white sauce, and add the chopped eggs and the grated cheese. Mix cold boiled rice with a little butter, make it into small rolls and fry them, and make a round crouton of bread for each piece of cucumber to stand on. Arrange the cucumber on the croutons, fill the centre of the pieces with the egg sauce, garnish with the yolk of egg, and the rice rolls arranged alternately with the croutons.

Serve with the rest of the sauce.

FRIED CUCUMBER

¶ After peeling a cucumber, cut it into thick slices and let the slices stand in cold water for half an hour. Drain them well, sprinkle them with salt and pepper, dip them in yolk of egg and breadcrumbs, and fry. Serve with bread sauce, and garnish with slices of lemon.

CUCUMBER SOUFFLÉ

¶ Cucumber, breadcrumbs, Béchamel sauce, lemon juice, onion juice, two eggs.

Cook a cucumber, reduce it to a pulp, and put one teacupful of this pulp with half a teacupful of breadcrumbs, half a cupful of thick white Béchamel sauce, a tablespoonful of lemon juice, a few drops of onion juice, and the yolks of two eggs well beaten. Mix all together off the fire, add the well-beaten whites of the eggs.

Butter small china custard-moulds, fill them with the mixture, and steam till firm in a bain-marie, or cook them in the oven.

ENDIVE

PURÉE OF ENDIVE

℃ Boil it as if for spinach, and when tender take it out of the hot water and put it under the cold-water tap, letting the water run on to it for some time. Then chop it up and put it through a sieve.

Make a white roux of flour and butter, and put the purée in it and stir all together. Let it all simmer for fifteen minutes, add a little cream.

LEEKS

PURÉE OF LEEKS

℃ Six leeks ; flour, one ounce of butter, one tablespoonful of cream or milk; nutmeg, salt and pepper.

After boiling the leeks carefully drain them, mince and pound them. Put the purée on the fire with the butter, a little flour and seasoning (very little nutmeg). Add the cream or milk, and stew gently for five minutes.

Serve with croutons of fried bread.

The yolks of two eggs can be stirred in at the last moment if liked, but this is not necessary.

BRAISED LEEKS

℄ Leeks, brown stock, butter, sugar, salt.

Parboil the leeks first, then drain and braise them in stock, to which is added butter and a little sugar. Baste them well, and serve hot.

LEEKS À L'AGNESI

℄ Leeks, butter, one egg, Parmesan cheese, a few spoonfuls of good white stock.

Cut up the leeks into pieces two inches long, and boil them in boiling water with salt ; then put them into cold water. Then boil the leeks with melted butter, a few spoonfuls of good white stock, and a dessertspoonful of grated Parmesan, also the beaten yolk of an egg. When well mixed put the leeks with the sauce in a fireproof dish into the oven, and brown them.

They can be cooked in the same way without the cheese and egg, and they are then called " Leeks alla Salza bianca."

LENTILS

RED LENTIL SOUP

℄ Lentils, stock, celery leaves, seasoning.

Make a purée of red lentils ; soak them first, then boil them, and pass them through a sieve.

Make a good stock of any scraps or bones of game you may have : a pint of stock to half a pint of purée. Stir the purée into the stock till it boils, then let it simmer gently for one hour.

Boil some celery leaves, and garnish with them.

Serve with croutons of fried bread.

LENTIL SOUP

❡ Lentils, carrots, turnips, onions, butter, stock, parsley, herbs, mushrooms.

Put the lentils into a saucepan with the chopped onions, carrots and turnips, all of which have been slightly fried in butter first. Remove the lentils when cooked ; drain, and put them into a casserole with two ounces of butter, a little onion, and some stock, two cloves, a table-spoonful of chopped parsley ; one chive, a little basil, and a quarter of a pound of mushrooms.

Thicken the stock with a brown roux, and let the whole simmer till cooked. Crush them into a purée, adding the carrot and turnip and a little more stock.

Serve with fried sippets of bread.

SAVOURY LENTILS

❡ One pint of lentils, two ounces of butter, two tablespoonfuls of cream.

The lentils should be well soaked for a whole day or night ; put them into boiling water and boil them for an hour. Drain them, boil them up again till they are tender. Put them through a sieve into a saucepan with the butter and a spoonful of onion juice. Stir for fifteen minutes ; then serve, adding the cream at the last moment.

SAVOURY LENTILS WITH RICE

℘ One pint of lentils, half a pint of rice, butter, pepper, salt, two onions.

Soak the lentils for twelve hours, then place them in hot water and boil them rapidly. Then allow them to simmer for about one hour, and drain. Put them back into boiling water and boil them till quite soft. Pass them through a sieve, and place them in a saucepan with butter, onion juice, pepper and salt as desired. Then take half a pint of rice and place it in a pot of boiling water. Cook well, and dry it before a fire for about fifteen minutes.

Place some butter in a frying pan, to which add about five chopped onions, which must be allowed to brown. Then put in the lentils and rice, and put it on the fire for fifteen minutes, stirring all the time.

Serve hot with pepper and salt as desired.

LENTILS AU BÉCHAMEL

℘ One quart of lentils, half a pint of white sauce, two ounces of butter, one small onion, one teaspoonful of parsley ; salt and pepper.

Soak the lentils well. Chop the onion and fry it in one ounce of butter, then add the lentils, well drained. Season with pepper and salt, cover with hot water, and simmer, covered for two hours.

Make a half-pint of white sauce (see p. 7). When the lentils are soft take off the saucepan lid to let the water boil away. Let the lentils get dry, then add an ounce of butter, the parsley, and white sauce. Season and stir over the fire. Serve very hot.

POTPOURRI OF LENTILS

¶ One pint lentils, two anchovies, one shallot, stock, butter, olive oil.

Place one pint of lentils in an earthenware pot of not quite boiling water ; as it boils the lentils will rise to the surface, when they should be skimmed off.

Next place two cut up anchovies in oil and butter ; add a shallot and fry till brown. Then put them in the lentils and add the stock. Serve hot.

DÀL BHÀT
(*Curried Lentils*).

¶ One pint of lentils, a tablespoonful of coriander seeds, and ground tumeric, two ounces of butter, two or three onions.

Soak the lentils well in cold water, chop up the onions and fry them in butter ; then put to this a tablespoonful of the seed and powder. Drain the lentils and boil them in a saucepan with some stock or milk, and the onions. Keep the lentils the consistency of rather thin porridge by adding more milk or stock if necessary. Serve with plain boiled rice like curry.

LETTUCES
LETTUCE SOUP

℺ Two large cos lettuces or four small ones, pepper, salt, water, one egg, milk.

Boil the lettuce till tender in boiling water and salt. Pass them through a sieve and add a little milk to the pulp, and seasoning. Re-heat ; take off the fire, and stir in the beaten yolk of one egg.

STEWED LETTUCE

℺ This is a good way of dealing with old lettuces.

Boil them in salted water ; transfer them to cold water and slice them. Put them in a saucepan with a little cream and an ounce of butter ; cook and serve hot.

LETTUCE A L'ESPAGNOLE

℺ Lettuces, rashers of fat bacon, stock, onion, parsley, bay leaf, clove, salt, mignonette pepper.

Slice the lettuces in half, blanch them in boiling water, then drain them well. Put them in a casserole, sprinkling them with salt, and on them lay slices of fat bacon, an onion, parsley, a bay leaf, and cloves. Moisten them in stock, season with salt and mignonette pepper, and bake. The casserole should be covered with greased paper.

Prepare a slice of hot buttered toast for each half-lettuce.

Make a sauce with a white roux of butter and flour, and white stock ; season and flavour with a bunch of mixed herbs.

When the lettuces are baked, drain, remove the bacon, and serve them on the hot buttered toast, with the sauce poured over them.

Lettuces cooked in this way are very good served in clear soup. They do not then, of course, require the sauce.

THE ONION

The use of the onion as food can be traced back further than any other modern vegetable. It came from the East, from India and from Egypt. It was regarded as a symbol of Eternity or Infinity from its formation, each sphere enclosing another, and in the religion of ancient Egypt it was invoked as a god. An oath could be taken on or by an onion as a sacred root.

As a practical contribution to its handling, if an onion is held in a bowl of water while it is cut or peeled, the volatile oil will not stain the fingers or bring tears to the eyes ; and it is useful to know that cold water will remove onion stains from knives more effectively and quickly than hot water.

If an onion is to be added to flavour a dish of meat already cooked, such as curry, mince or

rissoles, the onion should be boiled before it is
cooked with the dish, or it will be still hard when
the rest of the dish is ready to be served.

CREAM OF ONION SOUP

❡ Two teacups of onion purée, one head of
celery, two ounces of butter, half a pint of milk,
two tablespoonfuls of chopped parsley.

Cream sufficient onions to make two teacupfuls of onion purée. Melt in a double saucepan
two ounces of butter with two ounces of flour ;
mix thoroughly, and add half a pint of cold milk,
and cook, stirring all the time till it boils and
thickens.

Cook a large head of celery in boiling water,
and when cooked pass it through a sieve. Add
the same amount of the water in which the celery
was cooked as celery pulp, and add it, with the
onion purée, to the soup ; also add two tablespoonfuls of chopped parsley, and if too thick
dilute with more milk.

Serve with fried croutons of bread.

BROWN ONION SOUP

❡ Two large onions, butter, bread, one and a
half pints of water or milk.

Slice the onions thinly, fry them lightly in
butter, then put them into a saucepan with the
water or milk, and boil for twenty minutes.

Pour into a tureen on to slices of bread.

PURÉE OF ONIONS

℃. Cook the onions in milk or water till tender ; pass them through a sieve. Season with salt and pepper and a little nutmeg, and cover them with a Béchamel sauce.

GLAZED ONIONS

℃. Six large onions, a little sugar, two ounces of butter, brown stock.

Boil the onions for about twenty minutes, then put them into cold water. Skin them and take out their centres. Stand them in a covered stew-pan with the butter, and with a teaspoonful of sugar in the centre of each. Cook them slowly. From time to time add a little stock. Season with salt and pepper.

Let it reduce, and baste the onions with it.

BRAISED ONIONS

℃. Put large peeled onions in a fireproof dish, with butter, and bake them three hours, basting them well with the butter. Put the onions on a hot dish to serve, put a little boiling water in the dish they cooked in, and stir into it with a wooden spoon the solid brown juice, making thick gravy.

Pour this over the onions to serve.

STUFFED ONIONS

℃. Six good-sized onions, quarter of a pound of bacon, ham or tongue, bread crumbs, two ounces of butter, one ounce of flour, one pint of milk, a few tablespoonfuls of cream, a little chopped parsley.

74

Boil the onions for an hour. Prepare the stuffing by chopping the bacon finely, adding grated breadcrumbs, salt and pepper and a little cream. Mix it into a paste. Drain the onions, cutting out their centres with a vegetable cutter or small knife. Fill them with the paste, put them in a baking tin in the oven, with a little butter on them and breadcrumbs over them.

Make a sauce of butter and flour stirred together ; add the milk gradually, stirring well. Season with salt and pepper and grated nutmeg, and chopped parsley. Cook it ; add a spoonful or two of cream before pouring over the onions to serve them.

Another recipe for
STUFFED ONIONS

¶ Onions, vegetable stock, breadcrumbs, one egg, chopped mushrooms, spice, pepper, salt, butter.

Parboil the onions, drain and put them into cold water. Remove the inside from the root end until two layers remain. Chop the extracted onion and fry it in butter ; add to it the mushrooms, fry together, and then put in the breadcrumbs ; add the parsley, spice, and seasoning ; bind it with the egg. Fill the onions with the mixture, sprinkle them with breadcrumbs, and place them in a well-greased marmite pot and let them fry slightly with the lid on.

75

Nearly cover them with the vegetable stock, replace the lid, and bring them to the boil. Place the marmite in the oven and cook the onions till tender (for about an hour). Take off the lid to reduce the liquid, and baste the onions.

Thicken the gravy if necessary, and serve in the same dish sprinkled with parsley.

SPICED ONIONS

❦ Six small onions, two anchovies; parsley, quarter of a pint of claret, quarter of a pint of stock; flour and butter, half a teaspoonful of capers; pepper, cloves, bayleaf, and salt.

Make a brown roux of the flour and butter, and add the wine and stock to it. Let it simmer for a few minutes, and then add the onions, which must have been cooked in boiling water for twenty minutes. Put in the parsley, cloves, and the bayleaf, and let the whole cook slowly. Take out the onions and put them on the dish in which they will be served.

Strain the sauce and reheat it, with the capers and the anchovies chopped fine. Bring it to the boil, and pour over the onions.

GATEAUX AUX OIGNONS
An Alsatian Recipe.

❦ Pastry, onions, eggs, two tablespoonfuls of cream.

Line a dish with pastry, keeping a piece the same size for the top. Chop up some young onions and fry them in butter. Remove them from the fire, and add to the onions three well-beaten eggs and three tablespoonfuls of cream. Mix them, and pour on to the pastry.

Cover them with a pastry top, and bake it.

ONIONS AU GRATIN

❡ First boil three or four large onions till tender, then drain them very carefully and cut them in quarters. Well butter a fireproof dish, put in the onions, seasoned with pepper and salt.

Pour over them a simple Béchamel, and mix with the sauce a good layer of breadcrumbs.

Bake for about an hour.

PEAS

Grimod de la Reynière, the author of " L'Almanach des Gourmands," in a lyrical passage in praise of green pea-soup, says that a perfect dish of " petit pois " is enough to establish the reputation of a great cook. This is the recipe he gives for :

PETITS POIS À LA FRANÇAISE

❡ Choose your peas carefully, shell, wash and drain them ; put them in a casserole with good butter, a little salt, the hearts of two or three small lettuces, a bunch of parsley, and shallots, into which put a little piece of the herb savory or mint and two cloves. Cook these over a slow fire, stirring them from time to time, but not adding any water. When they are nearly cooked, taste them and put in the casserole half a slice of bread and butter dipped in flour.

When the peas are cooked serve them.

Colonel Kenney Herbert, in his book, " Vegetarian and Simple Diet," says the best way of cooking peas is to " jug " them ; that is, cook them in a closed vessel in their own juice. This is a recipe :

JUGGED PEAS
Even old peas can be made tender if cooked in this way

℣. Shell your green peas and put them into a jar or bottle with a screw lid or anything with a closely-fitting top. Put in with the peas a table-spoonful of butter, a saltspoonful of salt, a tea-spoonful of powdered sugar ; a dozen mint leaves, and a very little black pepper. Cover the vessel tightly and put in a saucepan of boiling water to reach half-way up the jar. Put the saucepan on the fire and boil quickly for half an hour.

If the peas are old they may take rather more than half an hour to cook.

Take out the mint leaves before serving. Lettuce leaves and young onions may be used for flavouring instead of mint if preferred. These should be tied together and removed when the peas are dished up.

78

GREEN PEA-SOUP

℃, One quart of peas, one onion, two ounces of butter ; mint.

Shell the peas, break up the pods, and put them in a saucepan with water in which other vegetables have been cooked. Let them simmer for some hours. If the soup is for dinner, put them on the stove early in the morning. Strain it, and into the liquid put the shelled peas, the onion, the butter, and some sprigs of mint. Boil till the peas are soft. Pass through a sieve.

A teaspoonful of spinach juice added at the last moment will improve the colour, and a few table-spoonfuls of cream may be added before serving.

Another Recipe for
GREEN PEA-SOUP

℃, Half a pint of shelled peas and the shells, half a pint of milk ; mint, pepper and salt.

Boil the shells, which must be quite fresh and young, in water till tender, then pass them through a sieve and season with salt and pepper. Put the pulp on the fire and add the milk to it, then add the peas themselves, which have been already boiled with mint. Let the whole simmer for a few minutes, and serve with a slice of fried bread.

Another Recipe for
GREEN PEA-SOUP

℃, Half a peck of young peas, half a lettuce, six ounces of onions, one ounce of sugar, a hand-ful of spinach ; parsley.

79

Shell the peas, cut up the pods and put them in a saucepan with the shredded lettuce, the chopped onion, sugar, and a bunch of parsley, with enough cold water to cover them. Simmer till the pods are soft. Pour off the liquor into another saucepan, and pass the pods through a sieve, taking out the bunch of parsley. Now boil the peas themselves with the spinach leaves in the saucepan containing the liquor the pods have been cooked in.

When the peas are soft, pour off the liquor into a basin, pass the peas through a sieve and add them to the purée the pods have already made. Mix the purée into the liquid in the bowl by making a roux of an ounce of flour and an ounce of butter in a pan over a slow fire, adding to it alternately some of the purée and some of the liquor until both are blended. Boil, and serve with little croutons of fried bread.

A spoonful of cream may be added to the soup at the last minute if a very rich purée is wanted.

Keep a few of the peas to be put whole into the soup.

SOUFFLÉ AU POIS

❧ Half a peck of peas, two eggs, two ounces of butter, one ounce of flour, half a pint of milk; salt, pepper, and a little onion juice.

Shell the peas, break up the pods, boil them. Pour off the water they have cooked in, and in this boil the peas. When they are soft pass them through a sieve, keeping a few peas for the sauce. Beat up two eggs, and stir them into the purée of peas with an ounce of melted butter.

Season with salt to taste, a pinch of pepper, a few grains of cayenne, and a few drops of onion juice.

Butter ramakin moulds and fill them with the purée. Stand them in hot water, cover them with greased paper, and bake them till set. Serve with white sauce made of the milk, flour, and butter, seasoned to taste, and add the peas.

GREEN PEA PURÉE

This is a good way of cooking green peas that are no longer young. Carrots may be cooked in this way, also broad beans.

¶ One pint of peas, one ounce of butter, a twig of fresh mint, salt, a little sugar, a tablespoonful of thick cream.

Boil the shelled peas, or " jug " them, with a twig of fresh mint, then drain and pass them through a sieve. Put this in a pan with an ounce of butter, the cream, a little salt and sugar.

POTATOES

Potatoes are so recent an addition to the garden of civilization that they have no legendary history, though a plant whose fruit is a bitter poison and whose roots beget wholesome "apples in the earth " is mysterious enough to deserve a mythological romance. But although it has not one yet, it will have one in time ; for when the Irish have exterminated one another, some future archæologist will deduce from the existence of the beautiful Irish silver potato rings a theory that the potato had some occult significance in Celtic culture, and was therefore the origin of some of those more puzzling peculiarities of the principles of Irish politics which will be perplexing our archæologist's brother historians.

To turn from prophecy to practice, there are certain elementary rules to be observed in cooking potatoes. First of all, potatoes to be cooked together should be all about the same size.

There are so many varieties of potatoes, and they differ so much from each other in quality, especially the main crop winter potatoes, that these differences must be taken into account before they are cooked.

Only waxy potatoes, " Kidney " or Dutch potatoes, are suitable for potato salad, for instance, while floury ones are best for potato soup or for mashing (pommes de terre en chemise). Some potatoes are much nicer steamed than boiled, and in any case, the ideal way to boil potatoes is to cook them in their skins and remove the skins before serving them.

Potatoes " en robe de chambre," or baked in their skins, are very good, but the skins must be pricked well with a fork first or they will be indigestible.

Only very good potatoes fry well. Some potatoes should be boiled before they are fried, and new potatoes *must* be boiled first.

Potatoes and Jerusalem artichokes are the only vegetables put into cold water to boil, instead of into hot water.

CREAM OF POTATO SOUP

¶ Three-quarters of a pound of potatoes, one quart of milk, one and a half ounces of butter, one ounce of flour, a small onion, one heaped teaspoonful of salt, a good pinch of celery salt ; parsley and pepper.

Boil the potatoes, remove their skins, and pass them through a sieve. Boil the milk with the onion in it, then take out the onion and stir the milk gradually into the potatoes. Take half the butter, melt it, work the flour into it, add salt and pepper and a few grains of cayenne ; when smooth stir into the soup. Bring it to the boil, sprinkle with a little finely chopped parsley, and add the rest of the butter just before serving.

POTAGE PARMENTIER

¶ Three good-sized potatoes, two onions, two ounces of butter, one quart of water or stock in which rice or vegetables have been boiled, salt and pepper.

Chop the onions and fry them in the butter, then pour in the boiling stock or water, and boil for an hour. Add the potatoes, peeled and sliced; boil for thirty minutes. Put small square slices of bread in the tureen and pour the soup on to them.

A Richer Recipe is :

Chop onions, celery, carrots and leeks and fry them in butter. Pour in the boiling stock, and add some whole-peeled potatoes. Cook it for an hour, then pass it through a sieve and put it back on the fire ; skim it while it simmers. Beat up the yolks of two eggs with a little cream and butter ; mix this with a little of the hot soup and strain into the tureen, then pour in the soup.

POMMES DE TERRE AU BEURRE NOIR

¶ Boil the potatoes, then peel them ; cut them in pieces and arrange them on a dish ; put fried parsley round the potatoes, and pour over them black butter sauce.

POTATOES À LA MAÎTRE D'HÔTEL

¶ Boil new potatoes, cut them into slices and put them into a saucepan with a little white sauce, chopped parsley, a squeeze of lemon juice ; pepper, salt, and two ounces of butter. Shake the pan until it is all well mixed, and serve hot.

A somewhat similar Recipe for old potatoes is :

POTATOES À LA CRÈME

❡ Boil the potatoes and cut them in slices. Make a white sauce in a saucepan with butter, a spoonful of flour, pepper, salt, a little grated nutmeg, and chopped onions ; add half a pint of cream (or milk), put on the fire and stir till it boils, then add the cooked potatoes and serve very hot.

POTATOES LYONNAISE

❡ Half a pound or more of new or waxy potatoes, one ounce of butter, one onion, salt, pepper, parsley.

Slice cold boiled potatoes. Scald an onion, then chop it small and fry it in butter till it is light brown. Have some clarified butter, add a little oil to it, and in this sauté the potato slices ; mix the onions and potatoes together, sprinkle with finely-chopped parsley, and serve straight from the pan very hot.

POMMES DE TERRE EN MATELOT

❡ Boil potatoes, peel them and cut them into slices. Put them in a saucepan with butter, salt, pepper, parsley, and chopped onion, also a little flour. Add a little good stock and a glass of wine.

POMMES DE TERRE A L'ÉTUVÉE

❡ Six large potatoes, two ounces of butter, one tablespoonful of flour ; salt and pepper, chives, parsley, one clove, bayleaf, thyme, stock or water, glass of claret.

Steam six large potatoes, peel and cut them in slices. When cold put them in a casserole with the butter, flour, salt and pepper, the chives and parsley chopped together, and one clove, a bayleaf, and thyme tied into a bouquet. Toss over a moderate fire for five minutes ; add a tumblerful of stock or water, and half a tumblerful of claret. Cover the pan, and let the potatoes simmer for thirty minutes.

Take out the seasoning, serve in the casserole.

FRANKLIN'S POTATOES
Excellent served with roast chicken.

❡ Two pounds of partly cooked potato, one pint of bread sauce ; breadcrumbs, salt and pepper.

Slice the half-cooked waxy potatoes. Make some bread sauce (page 9), and dilute it with a little more milk.

Put a layer of bread sauce in a soufflé dish and then a layer of potatoes. Sprinkle with salt and pepper, and finish with a good sprinkling of breadcrumbs.

Bake for thirty minutes in a slow oven.

POMMES DE TERRE ANNA
This way of cooking potatoes in butter was invented in Paris at the Café Anglais. It requires a fireproof dish with a closely fitting lid.

❡ Peel and cut raw potatoes into thin slices— all of the same thinness, otherwise they will not cook evenly. Put them into cold water for about a quarter of an hour. Butter the dish they are to be cooked in, and then arrange in it the slices of potato (which must be dried when they come out of the cold water). The slices of potatoes must be arranged in layers and tightly packed, and melted butter or little pieces of butter put generously over each layer. The dish must be entirely filled with potato slices, and butter spread over the top. The lid must be made airtight with a paste made of flour and water. Bake it in a slow oven for forty-five minutes. Then take out the dish, cut the potato cake in it across into four pieces, turn them upside down, put the cover on again and bake for another ten minutes.

Serve on a very hot plate, pouring the melted butter in the dish over the cake.

AN AMERICAN POTATO DISH

❡ Potatoes, flour, butter, salt, Hungarian paprika (or ground black pepper), milk.

Wash and peel five or six potatoes ; cut them into very thin slices. Grease a pudding dish, put a layer of the slices in and sift flour over it, then put little bits of butter on the flour ; repeat the layers of potato slices, sifted flour and pieces of butter till the dish is full. Season each layer with salt and Hungarian paprika ; if this cannot be obtained use ground black pepper. Then pour milk in the dish till it is full, and bake very slowly in the oven for two hours. Serve in the dish.

POTATOES ALL' UOVO

℃. Potatoes, eggs, butter, milk, breadcrumbs, salt.

Boil the potatoes and mash them, while hot, with butter, hot milk (if possible a little cream), salt to taste, and a well-beaten egg. Hard boil two, three or more eggs, according to the quantity of potatoes and the size of the dish.

Into a well-buttered fireproof dish put a layer of mashed potato, then a layer of slices of hard-boiled eggs ; pepper and salt. Then put another layer of potato and another of egg, till the dish is filled. Cover with mashed potatoes, sprinkled with breadcrumbs and morsels of butter. Bake quickly till the top is brown, and serve in the dish it has been baked in.

POMMES DE TERRE EN RAGOUT

℃. Medium-sized potatoes, one onion, herbs, two cloves, about three-quarters of a pint of stock, a little flour, and butter.

Peel a dishful of potatoes. Make a roux of the flour and butter in a fireproof of casserole ; put into it a bunch of herbs, and a small onion with two cloves stuck into it. Put the potatoes in, and add enough stock, seasoned with pepper and salt, to cover them. Put into a moderate oven and cook till the potatoes have soaked up the liquor. (Baste them if necessary.) Then serve hot.

POMMES DE TERRE AU LARD

℃ Bacon, butter, flour, good stock, pepper and salt, thyme, a bayleaf, an onion or two, potatoes.

Cut some bacon into cubes or small pieces, and fry them in a little butter. Stir in a table-spoonful of flour, a little good stock, flavour with pepper and salt, thyme, a bayleaf, and one or two onions. Boil for a few minutes before adding slices of potato that have been washed and peeled. Cover the pan and cook for about forty minutes. Remove the herbs before serving.

Onions and herbs may be omitted. A glass of claret may be used, with a smaller quantity of stock, and greatly improves the dish.

POTATO SOUFFLÉ

℃ Quarter of a pound of potatoes, two eggs, chopped parsley.

Bake the potatoes, skin them and put them through a sieve. Separate the yolks and whites of the eggs and beat them, adding to the potatoes first the yolks and then the whites. Add minced parsley, pepper and salt to season, and bake about fifteen minutes.

Serve straight from the oven.

POMMES DE TERRE AUX CHAMPIGNONS

℃ One pound of potatoes, quarter of a pound of mushrooms, one shallot, one chive, half an ounce of butter, one teaspoonful of flour, a little stock, salt, black pepper, the yolk of an egg.

Boil the potatoes, peel and cut them into thick slices. Put them in a saucepan with the mushrooms chopped up, a chopped chive, chopped shallot, and a piece of butter. Put it on the fire. When the butter is melted, stir in the flour, add salt and pepper, and moisten it with stock. Cook it slowly, let the sauce reduce, and thicken with the yolk of an egg beaten with a spoonful of vinegar.

POTATO GNOCCHI

℄ Eight or nine potatoes, three tablespoonfuls of flour, three eggs, one ounce of grated cheese, butter, salt.

Boil the potatoes for ten minutes, then skin them ; finish cooking them in the oven. Mash them up with some of the grated cheese, the flour, a little salt, and the well-beaten eggs. Knead them into a smooth paste. Make the paste into little rolls, flour them, and boil them with salt in boiling water for five or six minutes. Serve with the rest of the grated cheese strewn over them, and some fried melted butter poured over them.

POTATO SALAD

℄ Cook eight or nine average-sized kidney potatoes in their skins, then remove the skins. Cut them into slices about a quarter of an inch thick. Put them into a glass bowl with a few ladles of hot broth or stock, and leave them to absorb it for a few hours.

Make a salad dressing as follows :

One tablespoonful of vinegar and half a table-spoonful of tarragon vinegar, five tablespoons of oil, one of minced parsley, a dessertspoonful of finely chopped onion, cayenne, and salt to taste.

Or if preferred, the salad can be covered with a thin mayonnaise.

Surround it with young lettuces which have been sprinkled with oil and vinegar.

LEMON CREAM PIE

℃. One cup of sugar, one cup of water, one raw potato grated, juice and grated rind of one lemon. Mix all the ingredients together and bake in pastry top and bottom.

PETITES TIMBALES DE POMMES DE TERRE À LA HENRI HOCQUARD

This Recipe was brought home from the Soudan by the head cook on the French man-of-war " Justine."

℃. Make a purée of potatoes as in recipe on page 83, only use a little cream instead of the butter, and the whites of two eggs beaten to a stiff froth ; mix this all together. Butter little moulds and fill them only three-quarters full with the mixture, for the white of egg will make it rise. Cook in a slow oven, turn out and pour over the timbales the following sauce :

Melt red currant and white currant jelly together, adding a liqueur glassful of maraschino.

PURÉE DES POMMES DE TERRE À L'ALBERT NOEL

Albert Noël was one of the famous French chefs.

❡ Peel and wash some good potatoes, put them in a saucepan with a pint of milk and a pinch of salt ; cover up the saucepan and boil till the potatoes mash easily with a fork ; pass them through a sieve and add a piece of butter and sugar to taste. Put into a dish and bake.

Pound three good-sized macaroons into very fine crumbs, sprinkle the potato purée with them, and put into a quick oven for five minutes.

SALSIFY

SALSIFY FRITTERS

❡ Boil the salsify till it is tender. Beat up an egg with a tablespoonful of flour. Pulp the salsify with a wooden spoon, stir into it the beaten egg when it is of the consistency of thin batter or thick cream. Drop a large spoonful at a time into boiling fat, and fry.

SALSIFY SALAD

❡ Slice the salsify and cook it in salted water with a little vinegar in the water, half an onion, a bay leaf, and a sprig of parsley. Drain, and steep it in oil and vinegar.

Serve on lettuce leaves covered with mayonnaise. Decorate with chopped parsley and orange.

SEAKALE

SEAKALE AU BÉCHAMEL

℀ Cut the white ribs in length and breadth the size of a finger. Boil till tender. Pass the green parts of the leaves through a sieve, and prepare as for spinach.

Dish the seakale in the centre of the dish, with the purée of green leaves round it. Pour a Béchamel sauce over it.

SORREL

Sorrel should be cooked like spinach, only mixed with a little lettuce to make it less bitter.

Strip the leaves from the stalks, chop and pound the leaves finely, and make them into a purée with a little butter; add salt and pepper.

POTAGE BONNE FEMME

℀ Quarter of a pound of sorrel leaves, quarter of a pound of onions, two ounces of lettuce leaves, three ounces of butter, one egg, a pint of milk, a little flour, salt, sugar, slices of bread.

Chop up the onion and fry it in the butter for five minutes, but do not brown it. Shred the lettuce leaves and sorrel leaves, and add them to the onion with an ounce of chervil, a good pinch of salt, and an equal amount of white sugar. Stir all together on the fire for five minutes, and then add the flour (one ounce). Let this cook for another five minutes, and then gradually pour in three-quarters of a pint of milk and an equal quantity of water. Bring this gently to the boil and let it simmer for a quarter of an hour.

Beat up an egg well, put into it an ounce of butter ; pour a little of the hot soup into the cup with the egg to melt the butter.

Have ready three or four slices of dried bread to put in the soup tureen ; pour the soup on to the bread, and then stir in the egg mixture.

PURÉE OF SORREL

❡ Two pounds of sorrel leaves, yolks of two eggs, one ounce of butter, one ounce of flour, a tablespoonful of milk, a quarter of a pint of stock, half a teaspoonful of sugar.

Boil the sorrel leaves with a pinch of salt and pepper for about twelve minutes, using plenty of boiling water. Then drain well and chop the leaves very finely.

Beat up the yolks of two eggs with a tablespoonful of milk in a cup.

Make a smooth paste of the butter and flour over a slow fire, adding the stock and sugar. Stir the sorrel into this sauce.

When the sorrel and the sauce are well blended, stir in the prepared yolks of eggs. Stir over the fire for five minutes, and serve hot.

SPINACH

Spinach must be well washed, boiled for two or three minutes in boiling water with a handful of salt, then strained in the colander, put under the cold-water tap, squeezed dry, and then chopped up finely or passed through a coarse sieve.

For five or six pounds of spinach allow a quarter of a pound of butter. Melt the butter.

SPINACH SOUP

℮ One pound of spinach, one pint of white stock, one pint of water, half a pint of milk, half an ounce of butter, half an ounce of flour, pepper and salt.

Cook the spinach in boiling water, with a piece of sugar and bicarbonate of soda, for half an hour. Drain it, rub it through a sieve. Pour in the stock, boil it ; mix the butter and flour to a smooth paste and thicken it, add the milk last, with pepper and salt to taste.

Serve with croutons of toast.

AN ITALIAN WAY OF COOKING SPINACH

℮ Spinach, sultanas, raisins, anchovy, butter, fried bread.

Cook two lbs. of spinach, drain it, chop it very fine, and put it into a casserole with a teaspoonful of anchovy butter, and three ounces of mixed sultanas and seeded raisins.

Make it very hot, and serve with fried croutons of bread.

SPINACH SOUFFLÉ

℆ Spinach, yolks of two eggs and whites of four, two ounces of butter, two ounces of flour, half a pint of milk.

Make two tablespoonfuls of spinach purée by boiling the leaves and putting them through a sieve or pounding them. Mix the flour smoothly with a quarter of a pint of milk. Boil a quarter of a pint of milk and the butter together, and thicken by pouring in the flour and milk ; stir till it is smooth and boil it. Add the spinach purée, stir in the beaten yolks of two eggs and the whites of four eggs whipped to a stiff froth.

Bake in a soufflé dish for thirty minutes.

SPINACH AND MUSHROOM PUDDING

℆ Spinach, lemon, butter, eggs, mushrooms.

Wash the spinach ; cook it in salted water for a few minutes ; drain it well, pound it and rub it through a sieve. Place it in an earthenware pot with some butter and a few drops of lemon juice, and boil it for a short time ; when cool, the beaten yolks of three eggs may be added.

Place it in a buttered shape, leaving a space in the centre, and cook it in a bain-marie for one hour. Put it on a dish and fill the space with cut-up mushrooms which have been cooked in butter over a quick fire, with flavourings to taste.

ÉPINARDS AU SUCRE

❧ One pound of spinach, salt, sugar, grated lemon rind, two macaroons, ratafia biscuits.

Boil a pound of spinach, season it with a little salt and sugar, a little grated lemon rind, and two crushed macaroons. Garnish with ratafias.

TOMATOES

TOMATO SOUP

❧ One pound of tomatoes, one ounce of onion, one pint of milk, one ounce of butter, two teaspoonfuls of flour, salt, pepper, a teaspoonful of bicarbonate of soda.

Boil the tomatoes till they are soft and pass them through a sieve. Add the bicarbonate of soda to the purée. Boil the milk for fifteen minutes with the onion. Put the butter in a saucepan and stir in the flour ; when smooth pour in the milk and remove the onion ; add salt and pepper to season. Boil it up and add the tomatoes ; heat, but do not boil it again.

97

SAVOURY TOMATOES

℃. Three large tomatoes, one tablespoonful of cream, one tablespoonful of cheese, two tablespoonfuls of breadcrumbs, bread.

Cut the tomatoes in half, and prepare a round of toasted bread for each half. Scoop out the insides of the tomatoes and mix them with the breadcrumbs, cheese and cream, and half a teaspoonful of sugar. Fill the halves with this mixture, cover them with buttered paper, and bake till the paper is brown.

Butter the rounds of hot toast, and serve the tomatoes on these hot.

TOMATOES À L'INDIENNE

℃. Chutney, flour, milk, one egg, one pound of tomatoes, curry powder, butter.

Cut up one large tomato into thick slices ; dust them with salt, pepper, and curry powder, and dip them in liquid batter. Bake for ten minutes.

Fry some rounds of bread in butter, spread them with chutney, and place the baked tomatoes on them. Sprinkle with chopped parsley, and serve very hot.

DEVILLED TOMATOES

℃. Three good-sized tomatoes, two and a half ounces of butter, a little flour, one egg and one hard-boiled yolk, one teaspoonful of dry mustard,

two tablespoonfuls of malt vinegar, salt, cayenne,
half an ounce of sifted sugar.

Make a sauce, by adding the yolk of a hard-
boiled egg, the mustard, a pinch of salt, a few
grains of cayenne, and the sugar to two ounces
of creamed butter ; then add the whole egg
beaten up, and the vinegar ; cook this, stirring
till it thickens.

Slice the tomatoes (first scalding and skinning
them), season them with salt and pepper, cover
them with flour, and fry them in half an ounce
of butter. Put them on a hot dish and pour the
hot sauce over them.

TOMATOES À LA BRUXELLES

¶. One large tomato for each person, as many
eggs as tomatoes, breadcrumbs, a little grated
cheese, pepper and salt.

The tomatoes must not be too ripe, but firm.
Slice a piece off with the stalk ; scoop out the
inside with a teaspoon. Into each tomato break
an egg. Pass the tomato pulp through a sieve,
mix it with breadcrumbs and cheese, salt and
pepper, till it is a thick paste. Sprinkle salt and
pepper on each egg, and cover each tomato with
the paste. Bake them in the oven till the eggs are
set—not more than three or four minutes.

TOMATOES DES ILES D'HYÈRES

¶. Tomatoes, butter, chopped onion, salt,
pepper, spices, olive oil, stock, rice.

Choose large round tomatoes. Cut them in half horizontally, take out the seeds, and put half of the rounds in a deep dish.

Wash some rice carefully and mix it with butter and a little chopped onion ; season with salt, pepper, and other spices, and fill the hollow tomatoes with this mixture. Sprinkle the stuffed tomatoes with olive oil, cover them with the other halves of the tomatoes which have been set aside. Moisten them with stock, and bake in a slow oven for thirty-five minutes. The rice will be perfectly cooked.

Another recipe for
DEVILLED TOMATOES

ℂ, One pound of tomatoes, slices of lean ham or bacon, mustard, one ounce of butter, flour, milk, pepper, salt, and cayenne.

After slicing the tomatoes in half, make a paste of mustard, salt, pepper, cayenne, butter, and flour. Spread each half tomato with this and fry them.

Grill the slices of ham and serve each tomato on a slice of ham.

TOMATO SALAD

ℂ, Only tomatoes that are perfectly ripe should be put into a salad. If it is desired to peel them, put them for a minute into scalding water ; they will then skin quite easily.

For a salad, tomatoes should be cut into rounds horizontally, in order not to waste the pulp and juice. Arrange them in the salad bowls and add a few chopped chives or some of the green part of spring onions. Season them with black pepper, salt, and a little basil.

Make a dressing of salad oil and tarragon vinegar—six parts of oil to one of vinegar. Decorate, if possible, with shreds of capsicum.

Slices of stale bread should be served with this salad—a slice on each salad plate and the salad put over it ; this is a great improvement.

TOMATO AND HORSERADISH SALAD

⁋ Tomatoes, lettuce, horseradish, whipped cream, vinegar, salt, and cayenne pepper.

Skin the tomatoes by plunging them in boiling water for a minute and then peeling. Cut them in half and arrange them in a salad bowl with lettuce leaves, and cover with horseradish sauce made with four tablespoonfuls of whipped cream, a tablespoonful of vinegar, three tablespoonfuls of horseradish, salt and cayenne.

TURNIPS

Turnips, unless they are very young and small, should be cut in half or in quarters. They must be peeled and blanched in boiling salt water for five minutes. Then they should be simmered in either milk, milk and water, or weak stock, till they are tender. Whatever liquid they are cooked in will provide the foundation of the sauce to serve with them.

A delicious method of cooking turnips is to take the pieces of turnip when they are nearly cooked, fry them in salted butter, and serve them very hot, with a little chopped parsley sprinkled over them.

TURNIP SOUP

℆ Three pounds of turnips, milk, two tablespoonfuls of cream, butter, sago, salt and pepper.

After boiling the turnips, mash them and add a little milk, pepper and salt. Rub through a sieve and add a lump of butter. Heat the milk with sufficient sago to thicken it, and when it is cooked add the purée of turnips, and cook for five minutes.

Stir in the cream before serving.

PURÉE OF TURNIPS

℆ Turnips, salt and pepper, butter, flour, a quarter of a pint of cream or milk, one egg.

Boil the turnips until they are soft enough to pass through a sieve, Mash them into a pulp, and season with salt and pepper.

Put a piece of butter wrapped in flour into a saucepan, mix them well, and add, stirring all the time, a quarter of a pint of cream or milk. Let it boil till it thickens, and beat in, off the fire, a well-beaten egg.

Add this sauce to the purée and serve.

RAGOUT OF TURNIPS

℄ Chop a small onion and fry it in butter. Do the same with five or six small turnips. Cover them with stock and cook until all are tender. Thicken the gravy with flour browned in butter, and serve very hot.

NAVETS GLACÉS

℄ Trim and boil the turnips in salted water. When they are nearly cooked, drain them and fry them in a little butter. Sift a little white sugar over them and stir in, when they begin to brown, a little stock seasoned with pepper and salt. Baste them with the stock, adding as much more as is needed to glaze them.

BAKED TURNIPS

℄ Six small turnips, two ounces of Parmesan cheese, one ounce of breadcrumbs, half an ounce of butter ; nutmeg, pepper, salt, and cayenne, one cup of milk or gravy.

Thinly slice the turnips and arrange them in a pudding dish in alternate layers of turnip, then grated cheese, pepper and salt, and a dust of nutmeg. Add the milk or gravy last of all. When the dish is full, sprinkle breadcrumbs over the top and little bits of butter, and bake.

PURÉE OF TURNIP TOPS

℃. Boil the turnip tops in a bain-marie or double saucepan until cooked. When done, squeeze them between two plates and pound them. Then make the purée into a ball and put it into cold water till just before it is to be used, when it should be put back in the pan with a little butter, pepper and salt, and quickly heated through.

A little cream improves it.

VEGETABLE MARROWS

Vegetable marrows should not be watery when they are cooked, and they are apt to be if they are merely boiled, especially if they are cut into pieces and boiled.

It should be peeled and steamed or baked whole till it is tender and nearly cooked ; then it should be cut in half, the seeds removed, cut again into conveniently sized pieces, and these put into a buttered frying pan to finish cooking. By this method they retain their full flavour and lose their superfluous moisture. The slices can be sprinkled with chopped parsley and served plainly or with a sauce.

Young vegetable marrows are extremely nice if they are cooked whole when they are only five or six inches long. There is no need to cut them in half to take out the seeds, for at that age there will be no seeds to extract, but as they do not come into the market so small, this advice is only for those who have their own marrow vines.

FRIED VEGETABLE MARROW

℃. Cut a vegetable marrow into little pieces about two inches long, and not thicker than a pencil. Flour these well all over by shaking them in a floured cloth. Have ready a deep pan full of boiling fat, and fry the vegetable marrow in a frying basket. Serve very hot with small slices of lemon.

VEGETABLE MARROW WITH TOMATOES

℃. One marrow, two large tomatoes, one onion, one ounce of butter, pepper and salt, half a pint of milk or water.

Slice the tomatoes and onion and fry them in butter. Cut the marrow into neat pieces, removing all seeds. Add them to the tomatoes with salt and pepper. Pour in the milk and boil gently till the marrow is cooked. Take great care that the milk does not burn.

VEGETABLE MARROW CAKES

℃. One large vegetable marrow, one large onion, one egg, slice of bread, two tablespoonfuls of grated Parmesan.

Cut the vegetable marrow and onion into small pieces and boil them till soft. Drain them well and put them through a sieve. Soak a slice of bread in the water the vegetables have boiled in, squeeze it dry and add it to the pulp. Stir into it the grated cheese and the beaten egg. Mix it all well together, then form it into little cakes and fry them in butter.

VEGETABLE MARROW STUFFED WITH SAGE AND ONIONS

❧ One vegetable marrow, one breakfastcup of soaked bread, one egg, two large onions, one ounce of butter, pepper and salt, one dessert-spoonful of minced sage.

Cut the marrow in half lengthways and take out the seeds. Parboil the onions, chop them and mix them with the bread, sage, egg, butter, salt and pepper.

Put the stuffing into the marrow, put the halves together, brush butter over it and bake for thirty minutes.

PICKLED VEGETABLE MARROW

❧ Choose a large marrow, cut it into small square pieces. Then put into an earthenware jar with a lid, a layer of salt and a layer of marrow alternately.

The next day pour from it any liquid there may be, and to each pound of marrow add half a pint of vinegar. Then add one ounce of mustard, half a pound of loaf sugar, one ounce of ground ginger, six chopped chillies, one shallot, two cloves, and one ounce of turmeric.

Boil the mixture for half an hour and cool.

WALNUTS

WALNUT PIE

℃. Quarter of a pound of shelled walnuts, mashed potatoes, brown stock, mushroom ketchup, pepper and salt.

Butter a piedish, put in a layer of potato, pepper and salt. Chop the walnuts finely and cover the potatoes with them. Pour in half a pint of sauce made of good brown stock and mushroom ketchup, cover with potato. Bake.

WALNUT KETCHUP

℃. Fifty green walnuts, one pint malt vinegar, one and a half ounces of salt, six shallots, two ounces of anchovies, a little nutmeg, ginger, horseradish, mace, pepper, a glass of claret. Choose very young walnuts. Crush them a little, cover them with the salt and vinegar, and leave them to soak for a full week, stirring them once a day. Then strain the vinegar into a double saucepan, add the claret, the minced shallots, the anchovies, two teaspoonfuls altogether of mixed nutmeg, ginger, horseradish, mace and pepper, all finely grated. Let it simmer slowly for three-quarters of an hour, and let it get cold.

Strain it into bottles, cork them and seal the corks to make them air-tight. Keep in a dry, cool place.

GARBURE BÉARNAISE

A garbure is a soup which is much made in the South of France, and which is to be eaten with a fork.

Metaphorically, a soup with " garbs " or " sheaves " in it and requiring the use of a fork came to be called a garbure.

℃. Make a vegetable soup of onions, haricot beans, cabbage, potatoes, carrots and turnips ; season it well.

Put into a fireproof dish some slices of French roll, and pour over them some of the vegetable soup. Sprinkle them with chopped ham and Parmesan cheese ; brown them, and serve with the vegetable soup, in which the pieces of vegetable remain.

The soup and garbure are handed together in separate dishes.

VEGETABLE STEW WITH BARLEY

℃. Fry some onions, carrots, turnips, celery, tomato, and potatoes which have been cut up small, in butter. Put them all into a double saucepan with a handful of pearl barley and a bouquet of herbs. Stew gently till the barley is cooked. Serve with sippets of bread.

VEGETABLE PIE

℆ Spanish onions, tomatoes, tapioca, cold potatoes.

Boil some Spanish onions in a small saucepan only half full of water. Let them get cold ; then cut them in slices. Slice an equal quantity of tomatoes and put them all in a pie dish with some tapioca, which must have been soaked, pepper and salt.

Pour in enough of the water the onions boiled in to moisten it, cover it with a crust of slices of cold potato, put little bits of butter on the potatoes, and bake in the oven.

III
CHESTNUTS

" The chestnut is for the man who takes its shell off."

An Italian Proverb.

CHAPTER III

CHESTNUTS

CHESTNUTS are not appreciated in England as they should be, but they are well worth more consideration than they get.

The Italian custom of offering a bowl of boiling chestnuts and a flask of wine as an impromptu meal for a stray visitor might very well be adopted for the benefit of the friend who drops in after dinner or the guest who stays late and needs refreshment as well as speeding after midnight.

The difficulty of skinning chestnuts is easily overcome. Make an incision in the skin, put the chestnuts in the oven for ten minutes, then the skin will come off quite easily.

CHESTNUT SOUP

¶ Fifty chestnuts, one onion, four lumps of sugar, one quart of brown stock, two ounces of butter.

Slightly roast and peel fifty chestnuts. Put them into a saucepan with two ounces of butter (leaving six or seven whole), a chopped onion, pepper and salt, and four lumps of sugar, and let them simmer for forty-five minutes. Remove the chestnuts and mash them through a sieve.

Put the pulp again on the fire into another pan, and add to it a quart of good stock, and the whole chestnuts which have been put on one side. Make it very hot, and serve with fried sippets of bread.

CREAM OF CHESTNUT SOUP

℄. Three-quarters of a pound of chestnuts, one small onion, one stick of celery, a sprig of parsley, one and a half pints of white stock, three-quarters of a pint of milk, pepper and salt, two table-spoons of cream.

Cook and peel the chestnuts and pass them through a sieve. Put the purée into a saucepan, add the stock and the seasoning ; simmer for one and a half hours without boiling, then add the milk. Put through a sieve, re-heat, and add some chopped parsley and the cream just before serving.

Another Recipe for
CREAM OF CHESTNUT SOUP

℄. Two ounces of butter, one ounce of flour, three-quarters of a pound of chestnuts, one glass of sherry; parsley, half a pint of milk.

Melt the butter and stir the flour into it. When smooth, add half a pint of milk, and cook until thick.

Cook and skin the chestnuts in the usual way. Pass them through a sieve and add them to the sauce with the minced parsley and the sherry.

RAGOÛT DE MARRONS

℄ Two pounds of chestnuts, one ounce of butter, enough stock to cover them, salt, pepper, a sprig of thyme, a lump of sugar.

Skin and peel the chestnuts, put them in a saucepan just large enough to hold them, with a pinch of salt, a lump of loaf sugar, and a sprig of thyme, one ounce of butter, and add enough seasoned stock to cover them. Put the lid on the saucepan, bring it to the boil and let it simmer gently for an hour. The chestnuts should remain whole and absorb all the liquid. Serve hot.

PURÉE OF CHESTNUTS

℄ Fifty chestnuts, white stock, quarter of a pint of cream or milk, butter.

Make an incision in the skin of fifty large chestnuts, and then bake them for about ten minutes. Take them out and peel them, then boil them until tender, drain them, and put them into a saucepan with enough white stock to cover them, and boil slowly till they are quite soft. Pass them through a sieve, add a quarter of a pint of cream or milk, a lump of butter, half a cupful of the stock in which they were boiled, and salt and pepper to taste. Heat thoroughly and serve.

MARRONS À LA DIABLE

℄ Peel and roast in the oven as many chestnuts as are required. When cooked, season them with pepper, salt and paprika, and serve in little cases.

MARRONS BRAISÉ À LA MADÈRE

℄ One pound of chestnuts, one wineglass of marsala or sherry, half a pint of stock, one ounce of butter, salt and pepper to taste.

After the chestnuts have been roasted and skinned they must be fried in the butter, and when they are brown the stock, wine and seasoning must be added. The mixture should then be passed through a sieve and re-heated.

A little cream added just before the purée is taken off the fire is a great improvement.

TOMATOES STUFFED WITH CHESTNUTS

℄ Two ounces of butter, one ounce of flour, two eggs, half a pint of milk, twelve chestnuts, six large tomatoes, one shallot, one teacup of bread-crumbs, pepper and salt, bayleaf and nutmeg.

Roast and peel the chestnuts. Cook the shallot in a little butter, and after removing it cook the chestnuts in the same way. Drain and mash them through a sieve. Then put a quarter of a pint of milk into a casserole, with half an ounce of butter, a bayleaf and a little nutmeg. Stir in the crumbs when it boils, and let it simmer for ten minutes. Take out the bayleaf, remove the pan from the fire, and stir in the yolks of two eggs. Add the chestnut purée to this and fill the tomato skins with this mixture. Then cook the tomatoes in the rest of the butter and cook over a slow fire for fifteen minutes. Lift them out carefully and keep them hot.

Now into the butter left in the pan stir gradually the flour and then the tomato pulp, and lastly the rest of the milk. Bring to the boil, stirring all the time, and let them simmer for ten minutes.

Sprinkle chopped parsley over the tomatoes, make them very hot and pour the sauce round them.

CHESTNUT SALAD

℄ Slice two teacupfuls of boiled chestnuts, season with grated orange peel, and serve on lettuce leaves covered with a mayonnaise sauce made without mustard, and to which whipped cream has been added.

MARRONS À LA DUCHESSE

℄ Peel, boil and cook thirty chestnuts in stock till they are tender. When cooked drain them.

Make a brown sauce and add to it a teacupful of chopped tongue.

Put the chestnuts into an entrée dish and pour the sauce over them.

Serve very hot with croutons of fried bread.

NESSELRODE PUDDING

Nesselrode Pudding was invented by Count Nesselrode's cook, Mony, and the famous cook, Carême, was so jealous of its success that there was a fierce quarrel over it. It is a pudding worth quarrelling about.

℄ Twenty chestnuts, one and a half pints of syrup, a stick of vanilla, yolks of two eggs, two ounces of sugar, half a pint of cream, one wine-glassful of maraschino, one ounce of raisins, one ounce of currants.

Wash and peel the chestnuts, and let them simmer in a pan with the syrup and vanilla till cooked. Then drain them and pass them through a sieve.

Put the yolks of two eggs into another pan, with two ounces of sugar and half a pint of boiled cream, and stir till it thickens. The mixture must not be allowed to boil. Add to this the chestnut purée, also a wineglass of maraschino.

Stone one ounce of raisins, add to them one ounce of currants, cover them with syrup and water and cook. Drain and let them cool.

Now partly freeze the chestnut purée, working it with a wooden spatula. Whip a quarter of a pint of cream, add the cream to it, and go on working till all is frozen. Then add the currants and raisins, and put the pudding into an ice mould and let it remain on ice for two hours.

THE SAUCE. Put a quarter of a pint of cream in a pan with the yolks of two eggs and one ounce of sugar. Proceed as before, stirring till it thickens without letting it boil. Take it off the fire and stir for another three minutes ; add a wineglass of maraschino. Put it on ice till cold.

Turn out the mould on to a napkin on a dish, and serve the sauce in a separate dish.

COMPÔTE DE MARRONS

℄ Thirty chestnuts, one pound of apples ; sugar.
Roast the chestnuts in the oven till they are

cooked, then remove their skins and flatten them. (They must be cooked till they are soft.) Arrange them neatly in a fipeproof soup plate.

Make a purée of apples stewed with sugar, and spread this purée over the chestnuts, pouring in the juice. Cover the dish and let it simmer gently, adding more of the apple syrup from time to time.

To serve, put a dish over them and turn the cake or " cheese " out neatly, pouring a little more syrup over it.

Another Recipe for
COMPÔTE DE MARRONS

℅ Peel thirty good chestnuts, and after cooking them remove the inner skins.

Make a syrup of a teacupful of water, half a teacupful of sugar, and a wineglass of sherry, also the rind of half a lemon. Put the chestnuts into it and cook slowly for twenty minutes.

Strain the syrup over the chestnuts when they are cooked, and serve hot or cold, with sponge cakes handed separately.

Another Recipe for
COMPÔTE DE MARRONS

℅ Take some good chestnuts and roast them. When they are soft peel them and roll them out flat. Arrange them neatly in a dish ; there must be enough to cover this quickly. Spread apricot or plum syrup on the chestnut paste, or any other syrup liked ; apples stewed with sugar will do. Cover the dish and let it boil gently, from time to time adding a little more syrup as it boils away.

It must be served hot. When ready put a plate over the dish in which it is cooking, turn it out as you would a mould, and pour a little more syrup over it.

MOUSSE AUX MARRONS

℃ Boil twenty-four chestnuts, peel them and pound them ; put them in a saucepan with half a pint of water, three and a half ounces of sugar, and vanilla to flavour. Boil this paste, working it until it is very smooth, then stir into it half a pint of cream whipped up with a beaten white of an egg. Fill a mould with this cream, let it stand on ice for three hours. Turn out to serve.

MARRONS À LA VALENTINE

℃ Peel and cook till tender in milk and water thirty chestnuts. Drain them and put them on a sieve.

Stew half a pound of prunes very slowly in a syrup of sugar and water. When nearly cooked, add the chestnuts, and if necessary more syrup. Allow it to cool, and when nearly cold add two tablespoonfuls of maraschino.

Prepare previously some cream of rice—two tablespoonfuls of Carolina rice boiled in a pint of milk in a double saucepan for four hours, and allowed to get cold.

Pour the compôte of chestnuts and prunes when cold into a silver dish, and make a wall round them of the creamed rice. Decorate it with crystallized violets and pistachio nuts.

HOT CHESTNUTS AND PRUNES

℄ Peel, blanch and boil till tender a pint of chestnuts. In another saucepan stew one pound of prunes (which have been soaked overnight) with enough water to cover them. Drain the prunes, reserving the juice. Mix the prunes and the chestnuts, adding a little powdered cinnamon, sugar and lemon juice. Moisten with the prune juice, add a wineglassful of sherry, and serve hot in a silver dish.

MARRONS GLACÉES IN HALF AN HOUR

℄ Peel and boil some chestnuts. Put them on a napkin and press two together. Do the same with the rest. Dip each pair into clarified sugar and boil for a few minutes. Coat them thickly with sugar, brown them in the oven, and squeeze a very little lemon juice over them.

To be eaten cold.

MARRONS AU CAFÉ IN GLASSES

℄ Make a purée of chestnuts and flavour it with vanilla. Nearly fill champagne glasses with this purée and pour over it cream of coffee made as follows :

Heat three-quarters of a pint of milk with a quarter of a pint of very strong black coffee and eight lumps of sugar, and add a handful of coffee berries. As soon as it boils take it off the fire and let it stand till cold, covered over. Then strain it and stir into it two well-beaten eggs.

Put it back on the fire in a double saucepan to thicken, but remove it before it boils or it will curdle.

CHESTNUT SOUFFLÉ

℄ One pound of chestnuts, three eggs, one gill of milk, half an ounce of butter.

Boil the chestnuts, skin them and pass through a coarse sieve. Stir in the milk, the melted butter, separate the yolks from the whites of the eggs and beat them each well. Add to the chestnut purée first the yolks, then the whites. Pour into a buttered soufflé dish and bake quickly. This can be used as a sweet or a savoury soufflé, and must be seasoned accordingly.

COMPÔTE OF ORANGES AND CHESTNUTS

℄ Eight or nine oranges, one and a half pounds of chestnuts, three-quarters of a pound of castor sugar, one and a half pounds of cooking sugar, half a vanilla pod.

Skin the oranges, carefully removing all white pith. Cut them into round slices, and put them in a glass dish in the form of a well, leaving the middle clear. Sprinkle one pound of castor sugar over the layers of orange, and last of all some grated orange peel.

Partly roast and peel about thirty chestnuts, and cook them till tender in hot water.

Boil one and a half pounds of sugar in three teacups of water till it pearls, and put the chestnuts in it with a vanilla pod. Bruise them well and cook them in the syrup. Put the chestnuts in the middle of the dish, reduce the syrup till it is thick, and pour it over them.

MONT BLANC

ℂ One pound of chestnuts, a quarter of a pound of chocolate, a quarter of a pound of sugar, a little milk, a vanilla pod, a little cream.

Roast and skin the chestnuts, stew them with the sugar and chocolate and enough milk to moisten them until they are soft enough to rub through a wire sieve into a mould. Turn out when cold, sprinkle with grated chocolate, and pour it over cream sweetened and whipped not too stiffly. The chestnuts should be arranged in a high mound and should be entirely covered by the cream so that the effect is quite white.

CHESTNUT AMBER

ℂ Half a pound of chestnuts, half a pint of milk, two eggs, one ounce of butter, one ounce

123

of white sugar, lemon, vanilla, two ounces of breadcrumbs, puff paste.

Bake the chestnuts and skin them. Put a little water in a pan and boil the chestnuts in it till they are soft enough to rub through a sieve. Peel the rind of a lemon very thin and heat it in the milk for twenty minutes with a vanilla pod, and strain it on to the crumbs. Mix the butter and sugar into a smooth paste, add to it the beaten yolks of the eggs, the juice of the lemon, also the chestnut purée and the breadcrumbs, stirring well.

Have ready a piedish lined with puff paste, put the mixture in and bake in a moderately hot oven for half an hour. When the pastry is cooked, put the whites of the eggs beaten stiffly with a little sugar on the top of the dish, and put back into the oven to set and slightly colour the meringue.

MARRONS À LA BIGARADE

℄ Chestnuts, milk, sugar, cream, orange compôte, maraschino.

Roast and peel fifty chestnuts, then put them to simmer in milk and water till they are floury. Drain them. Put into a saucepan twelve ounces of sugar and boil it till it pearls on the surface. Put in the chestnuts, and bruise them well, add vanilla flavouring, and mix them well together. Rub them through a sieve.

Whip very stiff half a pint of cream, sweeten it with sugar and a little vanilla, and pile it up into a cone ; carefully strew the cream with the vermicellied chestnut purée, keeping the cone shape, and serve with a compôte of oranges flavoured with maraschino.

The compôte of oranges is served in another dish.

CHESTNUT CAKE

℃. Take two pounds of fine chestnuts, and boil them in water till they are soft, then skin them and pass them through a wire sieve.

Take one pound of sugar and make a thick syrup flavoured with vanilla. Pour it into the chestnut flour, stirring it well. Save a little of the syrup. Stir the chestnut mixture till it forms a thick paste, then put it on the dish it is to be served on, and shape it into the form of a crown. Decorate it with preserved fruit and sliced almonds, and two hours before it is to be eaten glacé it with the remains of the syrup.

This chestnut cake should taste very much like marrons glacées.

I V
MUSHROOMS

" I have five cooking pots for you, all containing admirable foods—egg-apples and stuffed marrows; filled vine leaves seasoned with lemon; cakes of bruised corn and mincemeat; sliced fillet of mutton cooked in tomatoed rice; a stew of little onions and mushrooms; further, I have ten roast fowls and a roast sheep; two great dishes, one of Kenafa and the other of pastry made with sweet cheese and honey; fruits of every kind—melons, cucumbers, limes, and fresh dates."

CHAPTER IV

MUSHROOMS

IF red mullet are the "woodcock of the sea" on account of their delicate taste, mushrooms might be called the oysters of the fields, for no other food has quite the rare flavour of these elfin-like mysteries that grow by the light of the moon, or, to be more accurate, in darkness.

In cooking mushrooms, a silver spoon should always be used, not for any occult reason connected with fairies, but because if the mushrooms are not mushrooms the silver will turn black. Another simple test of their wholesomeness is salt. Sprinkle the fresh fungi with salt on their pink accordian-pleated side ; if they are mushrooms their pinkness will turn black, if they are poisonous this flesh will turn yellow.

Mushrooms should always be eaten hot, and if all that are cooked are not eaten it is safer to throw them away, wiser not to save them to be warmed up for another meal, as mushrooms sometimes develop injurious qualities when they are stale.

CREAM OF MUSHROOM SOUP

⁌ Half a pound of mushrooms, two pints of stock, two ounces of butter, one ounce of flour, one cupful of cream and milk mixed, half a wineglassful of Sauterne; salt, pepper, and a little onion.

129

Chop up the mushrooms and a slice of onion. Put this into the white stock and simmer for twenty minutes ; pass through a sieve. Put it back on the fire ; thicken with a roux made of the butter and flour, season with pepper and salt, and stir in the cream. Add the wine at the last moment.

PURÉE OF MUSHROOMS

℃. Chop finely a good handful of fresh, clean mushrooms and put them in a stewpan with an ounce of butter, the juice of half a lemon, pepper and salt. Stir this over the fire for five minutes, and then add the crumb of a French roll soaked in milk, and a little cream ; stir all together over the fire and boil for ten minutes, and then rub the purée through a sieve and serve.

MUSHROOMS UNDER GLASS

℃. Mushrooms, toast, butter, salt, pepper, a little cream.

The bell-like glass covers sold for the purpose of covering dishes from the time they are put in the oven till they are on the dinner table or sideboard are very useful, as none of the flavour is lost (see p. xv).

Cut rounds of toasted bread and put on the buttered dish ; on the pieces of toast arrange the mushrooms, season with salt and pepper. Put morsels of butter on each mushroom, and moisten with a little warm cream. Cover with the glass and bake in the oven for twenty minutes. Do not lift the cover until the mushrooms are actually to be served.

MUSHROOMS WITH OYSTERS

℀ One dozen oysters, one dozen large mushrooms ; butter, salt and pepper.

Peel the mushrooms, removing their stalks, and fry them lightly in a little butter, then arrange them face downwards on a buttered fireproof dish. On each mushroom put an oyster, season with pepper and salt, and a morsel of butter on each oyster. Bake in a hot oven until the oysters are cooked. If a sauce is wanted it should be Béchamel sauce.

CREAMED MUSHROOMS

℀ One pound of mushrooms, three ounces of butter, quarter of a pint of milk, a dessertspoonful of flour ; salt, pepper, half a lemon.

Put two ounces of butter and the juice of half a lemon in a saucepan ; when the butter is melted add the mushrooms, cook them for three minutes.

Make a sauce in a smaller saucepan with one ounce of butter, and a dessertspoonful of flour worked smoothly together ; warm the milk and stir it in gradually, adding pepper and salt to flavour. Stir the sauce for about six minutes. Have a hot dish ready for the mushrooms, and serve them very hot with the sauce poured over them.

MUSHROOM PUDDING

❦ One pound of mushrooms, half a pound of flour, two ounces of breadcrumbs, three ounces of butter.

Make a paste of the flour, breadcrumbs and butter, with enough water to moisten it. Roll it out and line a greased pudding basin with it. Peel the mushrooms, season them and fill the mould with them, adding one ounce of butter and a quarter of a pint of water. Put on a cover of the paste, cover with a greased paper, and steam for two hours.

POTATO PUDDING WITH MUSHROOMS

❦ Eight potatoes, two ounces of butter, quarter of a pound of cream, four eggs, mushrooms.

Peel the potatoes and boil them, taking care not to overcook them. Strain off the water and mash them, adding two ounces of butter and the cream a little at a time till they form a smooth paste. Then add four yolks of eggs well beaten, and mix well. Place the mixture in a buttered dish, placing mushrooms in the centre in a cavity which must be covered with pastry. Bake, and serve while hot.

MUSHROOMS AU GRATIN

❦ Half a pound of mushrooms, one egg, dried thyme, a piece of bacon.

Chop up six of the mushrooms and put them

into a saucepan with salt and pepper, a little mixed thyme and a piece of bacon. Fry these slightly and add one well beaten egg. Stir until it is all cooked. Peel the rest of the mushrooms and take off their stalks. Fill them with the mixture, cover them with breadcrumbs, and put pieces of butter on the top. Put on a greased dish and brown them in the oven.

Make a good brown sauce of gravy and onion thickened with flour and butter.

Place the mushrooms on a silver dish and pour the sauce over them.

MUSHROOM OMELET

℅ Quarter of a pound of mushrooms, four eggs, butter, a spoonful of sherry.

Slice the mushrooms and lightly fry them in butter, to which has been added a spoonful of sherry.

Make an omelet in the usual way, and while it is in the pan, before folding it, put in the mushrooms in the middle of the omelet. Fold the omelet over them and serve hot.

Pour the sherry sauce the mushrooms have been cooked in into the dish with the omelet.

CHAMPIGNONS AUX FINE HERBES

℅ Half a pound of mushrooms, half a pint of stock or water, one ounce of butter, two eggs, juice of half a lemon, two level tablespoons of flour ; pepper and salt, half a teaspoonful of minced parsley.

Put the mushrooms (after peeling them) into a saucepan with the butter for a few minutes ; then add two tablespoons of flour ; pepper and salt, and parsley. Stir all together and after adding the stock, stew for thirty minutes.

Fry some slices of bread in boiling oil or butter ; drain them and place the mushrooms on them.

Pour the sauce through a strainer ; beat the yolks of the eggs, add to them the lemon juice, and stir this into the sauce. Heat the sauce, but be careful not to let it boil. Pour it over the mushrooms.

CHAMPIGNONS À L'ÉCRIVISSE

❡ The meat of one crab, quarter of a pound of mushrooms, two ounces of butter, two level tablespoonfuls of flour, one teaspoonful of finely chopped parsley, one teacupful of white stock, the yolks of two eggs, two tablespoonfuls of sherry, paprika and salt.

Make a sauce of butter, flour and stock ; add the yolks of two eggs, salt and paprika, the crab meat and the mushrooms. Boil it for three minutes before adding the parsley and sherry, then set aside to cool. Fill the crab shells with the mixture (washing the crab shells first), and sprinkle with stale breadcrumbs mixed with melted butter.

Draw three creases with the back of a knife across the mixture in the crab shells, and then three shorter ones at right angles.

Bake till the breadcrumbs are brown.

V
FISH

" This Bouillabaisse a noble dish is,
    A sort of soup, or broth, or brew,
    Or hotch-potch of all sorts of fishes
    That Greenwich never could outdo ;
    Green herbs, red peppers, mussels, saffern,
    Soles, onions, garlic, roach and dace ;
    All these you eat at Terré's tavern
    In that one dish of Bouillabaisse."

CHAPTER V

FISH

ALL the oldest cookery books are full of recipes for cooking fresh-water fish, because before modern inventions revolutionized transport it was difficult for those who lived inland to get sea fish fresh, and the country was well stocked with stew ponds from the days when the Church's law of abstinence prevailed.

Salmon, of course, was plentiful in all big rivers ; in fact, the Thames was so full of salmon before its waters were polluted by our enlightened civilized ways, that when boys were apprenticed in London it was stipulated in their indentures that their masters were not to feed them on salmon more than so many days a week. Salmon was the cheapest thing to feed boys on, in those days.

But are salmon fresh-water fish ? and are eels ? and how do they acclimatize themselves to fresh water and salt water in turn ? If a salmon or an eel could speak they would have far more interesting accounts to give of themselves than any four-footed animal. Life at the bottom of a muddy pond must be dull, yet who would not like to be able to chat with the enormous carp in the pond at Versailles ? the one famous carp who is older than the French Revolution, and

139

who comes to the surface of the water only when there is political trouble in Paris.

But as this is a cookery book and not a work on natural history it is time to return to the point and explain that with the exception of pink trout, fresh-water fish are not as good to eat as sea fish.

A Marseilles Recipe for
BOUILLABAISE

❧ Two large onions, olive oil, any kind of fish, a bayleaf, half a lemon, two tomatoes, glass of white wine, peppercorns, four cloves of garlic, one tablespoonful of chopped parsley, a taste of saffron, slices of bread.

Slice two large onions and put them into a deep aluminium saucepan with four spoonfuls of olive oil ; fry them a pale brown. Wash all the fish (any kinds of fish will do), though those usually used—because caught in the Mediterranean—are whitings, turbot, lobster, red mullet, gurnet, crayfish ; the more different kinds the better.

Add the fish well washed and cut into small pieces, and just cover them with warm water ; add salt to taste, a bayleaf, half a lemon without rind or pips, two tomatoes cut in dice with the seeds removed, a glass of white wine, a few peppercorns, and four cloves of garlic. Let it all boil slowly for twelve minutes. Then it should be reduced to about one-third of its original quantity. Add a tablespoonful of chopped parsley and a taste of saffron, and boil it for another minute.

Put into a tureen which has been heated twenty-four slices of French rolls or bread cut half an inch thick, and pour the contents of the saucepan over it, a little at first to soak the bread.

A Provençal Recipe for
BOUILLABAISSE

¶ Gather together as many different kinds of fish as possible ; the best kinds for this dish are—langouste, red gurnet, conger-eel, whiting, crab, etc. Shell them and take out the flesh ; cut them up and put them on two plates—on one the firm fish like langouste, and on the other the soft, such as whiting.

Put into a saucepan three chopped onions, four cloves of garlic crushed, three peeled tomatoes seeded and chopped, a sprig of thyme and one of fennel, parsley, a bayleaf, and a piece of orange peel.

Put into this all the firm fish and cover them with half a glass of oil ; a little more than cover them with boiling water, season them with salt, pepper and saffron, and cook very quickly ; the saucepan should be half covered with the flames of the fire or gas.

After five minutes' boiling add the other fish, and continue the cooking at the same speed for another five minutes ; take it off the fire. Put some pieces of French roll at the bottom of the tureen, and pour some of the liquid over them. Pour the fish on another dish, and serve both.

The quick boiling is essential, otherwise the oil will not amalgamate.

COD

COD À L'HOLLANDAISE

¶ A piece of cod, lemon, onion, thyme, a bayleaf, potatoes, Hollandaise sauce (see page 16).

Boil the cod in cold water with some slices of lemon, salt, a sliced onion, a sprig of thyme and a bayleaf. In the same water cook enough potatoes to surround the cod when it is dished up.

Make some Hollandaise sauce. Serve the cod with potatoes round it and sauce over it.

CRAB

HOT CRAB

¶ One crab, two ounces of butter, three ounces of breadcrumbs, two tablespoonfuls of vinegar, one tablespoonful of oil ; pepper, salt, nutmeg.

Put the meat from a boiled crab into a basin and stir the nutmeg, oil, vinegar and seasoning into it. Add the butter and the breadcrumbs.

Return it to the shell, strew it with breadcrumbs, and brown it in the oven.

142

CHAMPIGNONS À L'ÉCRIVISSE

℃. Crabs, a few mushrooms, one ounce of butter, one ounce of flour, yolks of two eggs, nearly half a pint of white stock, two table-spoonfuls of sherry, parsley, pepper and salt.

There should be enough crab meat to fill a breakfast cup. Make a sauce with the butter, flour, and white stock, add salt and pepper to season. Stir in the beaten yolks of the eggs ; then add the chopped mushrooms (about half a teacupful). Cook the mixture for three minutes, then add parsley, and set it aside to cool.

Trim and wash the crab shells, fill them with the mixture and cover them with breadcrumbs and morsels of butter. Mark the crumbs with the back of a knife, drawing it across them in parallel lines, and bake them till brown.

BAKED JOHN DORY
This fish derives its name from the French jaune d'orée

℃. Remove the flesh from the bone in two large unbroken pieces. Make a broth from the head and bones (see p. 145). Beat up an egg and brush the inside of the fillets with it, pepper and salt them, and sprinkle them with finely chopped chives, chervil and parsley.

Butter a fireproof dish, strew it with some of the chopped chives, chervil and parsley, put the fish together again and put it in the dish with three tablespoonfuls of white wine and double the quantity of the broth that you have made from the head and bones. Bake it in a fairly slow oven.

Make the rest of the broth into a white sauce, flavouring it with anchovy and lemon juice.

When the John Dory is almost ready, pour the juice from the dish into the sauce. Have ready some pieces of stewed cucumber or stewed tomato, garnish the fish with these, pour the sauce over it. Put the dish back in the oven for a few minutes, and serve it with croutons.

COLD RED GURNET

℄. Three large gurnets, one and a half ounces of butter, two lemons, yolks of two eggs, a bunch of herbs, two carrots, two good-sized onions, two ounces of flour.

Boil the fish for half an hour in water with plenty of salt, the carrots and onions cut in slices, a bunch of mixed herbs. When the fish is cooked, drain it and cut into pieces about three or four inches in length, removing from them all skin and bones. Arrange these pieces neatly on the dish in which they are to be served. Do not have too large a dish, as it will look nicer if the pieces of fish are arranged high in the form of a pyramid.

Then pour over it the following sauce :

Melt a piece of butter the size of an egg in a

small saucepan, add two tablespoonfuls of flour, stirring it into a smooth paste, and add to it some of the water the fish has boiled in, being careful not to put into the sauce any pieces of vegetable or anything solid. When you have enough sauce, squeeze in the juice of two lemons ; remove it from the fire and stir in the beaten yolks of two eggs. The sauce must be hot, but not hot enough to curdle the eggs. Add more pepper and salt if necessary. Pour the sauce over the fish, and put in a cool place. Serve it garnished with lemon.

A good way of cooking
HADDOCK

℄. Choose a good-sized fresh haddock. Remove the flesh from each side of the bone in two large fillets. With the bones, head and tail make a broth, by covering them with cold water in a saucepan with a saltspoonful of salt ; bring slowly to the boil, and add three ounces of onion, one of celery, a bunch of parsley and herbs, and mignonette pepper. Let it simmer until a good fish broth has been obtained. Skim and strain this off into a sauté pan with an upright rim ; add a glass of chablis, graves or sauterne, and bring it to the boil. Put the fish in, let it boil up again, and then let it simmer (not boil) for eight minutes.

Take out the fillets, put them on a hot dish and keep them hot while the broth in which the fish has cooked is thickened in a saucepan containing a roux prepared beforehand. Stir into it in small pieces half a gill of freshly made shrimp purée, and when it is well amalgamated and skimmed pour it over the fish. Garnish with small potatoes, or pieces of stewed cucumber.

HALIBUT

HALIBUT À LA BÉCHAMEL

℄ Eight fillets of halibut (about one and a half pounds), three tablespoonfuls of butter, three-quarters of a pint Béchamel sauce, a dessertspoonful of lemon juice, a teaspoonful of onion juice; salt and pepper; eggs, lemon, parsley.

Prepare the Béchamel sauce (see page 7). Melt the butter in a bowl with pepper, salt, lemon and onion juice, and stand it in a pan of boiling water to keep it melted while you dip each fillet of fish in it. Roll up and skewer each buttered fillet, flour them and put them on a fireproof dish in a hot oven for twelve minutes.

Take out the skewers when they are cooked, pour round them the hot Béchamel sauce, and decorate them with the yolks of hard-boiled egg grated, strips of the whites, little three-cornered slices of lemon, and small pieces of fried parsley.

HALIBUT À LA WELSH RABBIT

℄ Fillets of halibut, Welsh rabbit (see page 26). Put the fillets of halibut into a dish with pepper,

146

salt, a squeeze of lemon juice, and melted butter brushed over them. Bake them.

Put them on the dish they are to be served in, and pour over them a Welsh rabbit.

HERRINGS

STUFFED HERRINGS À LA PRESIDENTE

¶. A herring for each person ; parsley, breadcrumbs, butter, one egg.

Choose large fresh herrings with soft roes. Split the herrings, take out the roes and chop up the roes with parsley and soft breadcrumbs ; season them with a little pepper, and mix well.

Melt a little butter in a saucepan, break an egg into it and stir it ; then add the chopped roe mixture. Stir it, and don't let the egg set until the ingredients are well mixed.

Take out the herring bones ; fill the fish with the stuffing and bake them in a pie dish with a little butter for about twenty-five minutes.

Put the herring on a hot plate, add a little milk to the liquor in the dish they have cooked in ; stir it over the fire for a minute, pour the sauce over the herrings and serve them very hot.

HERRINGS À LA BOHEMIENNE

¶. Take as many herrings as are required. Split them open, remove the bones, and lay them out flat. Season them with pepper and salt, and put a small piece of butter on them. Place them on a gridiron and grill, then turning them over.

Prepare a brown sauce with a little butter and flour, Worcester sauce and Harvey's sauce.

Fold back the herrings, pour the sauce over them and serve them with red currant jelly.

LOBSTER

LOBSTER À LA BORDELAISE

❦ Lobster, white wine, onion, parsley, thyme, garlic, bayleaf.

Shell a lobster and divide it into eight pieces. Let it boil in a wineglassful of white wine with the herbs. Drain well and put each piece of lobster in a clean pan.

Make a roux of butter and flour, and fry two small onions chopped up in it ; moisten it with some of the liquor in which the lobster was boiled ; stir it, and add two wineglassfuls of tomato sauce and a pinch of cayenne pepper.

Pour this over the lobster, heat it and serve.

LOBSTER À LA BÉCHAMEL

❦ A lobster weighing two pounds, or two smaller ones, three-quarters of a pint of milk, one and a half ounces of butter, one and a half ounces of flour, yolk of an egg , breadcrumbs, salt, nutmeg, half a bayleaf, a teaspoonful of lemon juice. one of minced parsley ; cayenne.

Take all the lobster meat and chop it in small pieces. Make a Béchamel sauce with the milk, butter, flour (see page 7), flavour it with a bay-leaf boiled in the milk. Remove the bayleaf, stir in the yolk of an egg beaten up with lemon juice, parsley, salt, a little grated nutmeg and cayenne. Put the lobster meat into the sauce, fill the lobster shell with the mixture, cover it with breadcrumbs and morsels of butter, and bake it till the crumbs are brown.

STUFFED LOBSTER

℣. One large lobster or two small ones, yolks of two eggs, a dessertspoonful of minced parsley, four tablespoonfuls of breadcrumbs, a little milk, one ounce of butter, one ounce of flour ; salt, pepper, nutmeg, to season.

Remove the meat from the lobster ; there should be a breakfastcupful. Make a white sauce with milk, butter and flour, season it with chopped parsley, salt, pepper and a little grated nutmeg.

Chop up the lobster meat with the yolks of two hard-boiled eggs worked into a paste, and stir it into the sauce. Put the mixture in the shells of the lobster, cover it with crumbs and morsels of butter, and bake it till the crumbs brown.

DEVILLED LOBSTER

℣. One lobster, three tablespoonfuls of milk, half a teaspoonful of dry mustard, one ounce of butter, half a teaspoonful of curry powder, toast.

Put the butter into a saucepan with a little mace, the curry powder, cayenne, salt, and half a teaspoonful of dry mustard.

Cut the lobster up into small pieces, and add it. Stir it all together until hot, then add the milk and let it all simmer for five minutes.

Prepare some large slices of hot buttered toast, and serve the lobster on it.

GRILLED LOBSTER

❧ Open a lobster and break its claws. Sprinkle it when open with dry mustard, pepper and salt, and cover it with little pieces of butter.

Grill it, and as the skin comes away from the shell, slip in pieces of butter between the shell and the flesh. Sprinkle it from time to time with the juice and butter which comes from it. After twenty minutes sprinkle it with breadcrumbs ; place pieces of butter on the top, and brown it either in the oven or under the grill.

Serve with a maître d'hôtel sauce, to which is added a spoonful of mustard.

PEPPER POT

❧ One lobster or crab, prawns, oysters, anchovy, onion, stock, Worcester sauce, spinach.

Take a boiled lobster or crab, and remove the flesh from the shell. Add twelve prawns and twelve oysters, also a breakfastcupful of cooked spinach.

Make a cupful of gravy, using the shells of the fish ; fry an onion and place all the fish in a frying pan for half an hour and fry it very slowly in a pint of stock. Add pepper, salt, Worcester sauce and anchovy to taste.

MACKEREL

MACKEREL AUX FINES HERBES

℘ Mackerel, butter, shallot, parsley, orange, fennel, mint, sweet basil, thyme, spices.

Draw the mackerel without opening its belly, and make an incision in its back from the neck to the tail without flattening it.

Mince a handful of herbs, consisting of parsley, fennel, mint, sweet basil and thyme, and make them into a paste with butter, pepper, salt and mixed spice.' Rub this seasoned butter all over the flesh of the fish ; place it on a gridiron and grill it on both sides.

Make a sauce of gravy and shallot boiled with the juice of an orange.

Support the fish in the dish, the back uppermost, with quarters of orange, and pour the sauce in boiling hot.

GERMAN MACKEREL

℘ One mackerel, two tablespoonfuls of bread-crumbs, two ounces of butter, one onion minced, one teaspoonful of chopped parsley, lemon.

Make a mixture of the breadcrumbs, minced onion and parsley, lemon juice, salt and pepper, but do not cook it.

Stuff the mackerel with this after splitting and boning the fish.

Prepare a buttered paper ; wrap the mackerel in it after seasoning the fish and placing a small piece of butter on the top of it.

Bake for twenty or thirty minutes, and serve it out of the paper with bread sauce.

CREAM OF MACKEREL

❧ One mackerel, bread, pepper, salt and cayenne, one tablespoonful of anchovy essence ; butter.

Remove all the skin and bones from a boiled mackerel, and put it in a saucepan with a quarter of a pint of milk. Let it simmer, then take it off the fire and beat it till it becomes a cream.

Add a small piece of butter, season it with anchovy, pepper and salt. Re-heat it, and when very hot pour it into china ramakin cases and serve with a crouton of fried bread on the top.

The usual way of cooking
RED MULLET

❧ Red mullet, salt, pepper, and butter, lemon.

Take as many sheets of white paper as fish ; make them into cradles, oil them and bake them for a few minutes to harden them. Sprinkle the cradle with pepper and salt, and lay on it a piece of butter.

Deposit each red mullet—which on no account should have its liver removed—in the cradle, and put a piece of butter on the top of each fish. Arrange the paper cases in a flat baking dish, and bake them in the oven for twenty or thirty minutes.

Serve them in the cases, with pieces of lemon.

RED MULLETS AU VIN

℄ Butter a flat casserole and place the mullets in it, with a little butter, white wine, minced shallots, pepper and salt, and an additional piece of butter on each fish. Bake them and just before serving sprinkle lemon juice and minced parsley over them.

Serve them in the same dish.

FILLETED RED MULLET

℄ Four red mullets, four ounces of mushrooms, one tablespoonful of mushroom ketchup, two tablespoonfuls of white wine, one tablespoonful of minced parsley, two ounces of butter, one shallot, flour, milk, bread, salt and pepper.

Stew the mushrooms, the sliced shallot, and the parsley with one ounce of butter, pepper and salt, for thirty minutes.

Fry four slices of bread the size of the fillets of red mullet. Spread over them the mushroom paste.

Fry the fillets of mullet in butter over a quick fire, lay them on the bread, and pour over them a sauce made of the ketchup, white wine, a little milk, and water in which the livers and heads of the fish have been stewed, and flour.

MUSSELS

℃. This fish was called by Grimod de la Reynière the oysters of the poor, and there are very few shell fish which surpass them in flavour. This fish is one of the chief attractions of the Normandy Matelote.

Mussels must be perfectly fresh and taken straight from the rocks where they live. Scrape the shells and wash them ; put them in a saucepan of boiling water on the fire till they open.

Prepare a sauce by melting a piece of butter the size of an egg in a saucepan, stir into it a tablespoonful of flour ; when smooth add a little milk and some of the water the mussels have cooked in. Season it with salt, pepper and minced parsley, and add the mussels.

OYSTERS
OYSTERS PAPRIKA

℃. The oysters are baked and served with the following sauce :

Not quite a tablespoonful of melted butter, three-quarters of a teaspoonful of lemon juice, the same amount of sauterne, a pinch of finely minced parsley, and salt and paprika to taste. Before mixing the ingredients, rub the cup or bowl with a clove of garlic.

BAKED OYSTERS

ℂ, One dozen oysters, one and a half ounces of butter, one tablespoonful of lemon juice, salt, pepper, cayenne.

Make some neat small squares of toast, one for each oyster ; put an oyster on each piece of toast, with salt and pepper, and bake. Serve with the following sauce :

Cream the butter, adding the lemon juice, a pinch of cayenne, and a saltspoonful of salt.

A VENETIAN WAY OF COOKING OYSTERS

ℂ, One dozen oysters, breadcrumbs, butter, pepper, half a pound of macaroni, one gill of milk, lemon.

Cook the macaroni in boiling water for about fifteen minutes ; drain it. Butter a pie dish and put the macaroni at the bottom.

Cut the oysters in four and lay in the macaroni. Season with pepper, lemon juice, and pour the milk over them. Cover them with breadcrumbs, and place small pieces of butter on the top.

Bake, and serve very hot.

OYSTERS IN BACON

℄ Six oysters, six thin slices of bacon, bread.

Wrap each oyster in a thin slice of bacon, after bearding and dusting it with pepper and a squeeze of lemon juice.

Fry them, and serve them on fried bread.

HUITRES EN COQUILLE

℄ Oysters, butter, parsley, white wine, flour, breadcrumbs.

Blanch and beard the oysters, then put them in a pan with their own liquor, a little butter, some chopped parsley, and a glass of white wine—chablis is best. Do not on any account let them boil. Take out the oysters and put them into well-buttered scallop shells.

Reduce the sauce, and add to it a little flour and butter to thicken it. Pour the sauce over the oysters, sprinkle them well with breadcrumbs, place pieces of butter on the top, and brown them in the oven in a baking tin.

PLAICE

PLAICE AU VIN

℄ Fillets of plaice, three ounces of butter, a small onion, one ounce of potato flour, a little cooking sherry or other white wine, parsley.

Melt the butter in a shallow stewpan ; in it sprinkle a chopped onion ; then put in the fillets of fish, drying them on a cloth first. Pour in enough wine to cover them ; cook quickly for five minutes, then cover them with the lid and let them simmer quietly till they are cooked. Remove the fish on to a hot dish ; keep it hot while you thicken the sauce by stirring in potato flour. Pour it over the fillets, and garnish them with a little chopped parsley before serving hot.

STEWED PLAICE

℞ One plaice, one onion, pepper, salt and butter, one egg, pinch of ground ginger, mace, lemon.

Fillet the plaice, and sprinkle the fillets with lemon juice, salt and cayenne. Stew bones and trimmings of the fish with salt, pepper, a pinch of ginger and mace, and stock.

Slice and fry the onion in butter, and put it into a clean pan ; add the fish. Strain the liquor over the fish and let it all simmer gently for thirty minutes. When cooked, take out the fillets and add the well-beaten eggs to the liquor when it is cool. Let it simmer until it thickens, but do not let it boil, and pour over the plaice, which should be dished on a thick slice of toast.

PRAWNS

FRICASSEE OF PRAWNS

℞ Prawns, flour, tomatoes, onion, butter, garlic, shrimps.

Shell a pint of prawns and four dozen shrimps.

Make a roux and fry an onion in it. Stew the prawns and shrimps in a casserole with a clove of garlic, pepper and salt, one pound of tomatoes, and a pint of boiling water for an hour.

CURRIED PRAWNS

℃. Twenty-four prawns, curry sauce, three eggs.
Prepare a curry sauce (see page 12). Hardboil the eggs and cut them into slices. Let the prawns cook gently in the curry sauce for thirty minutes, then add the slices of egg, and serve with a border of boiled rice.

SALMON

PAIN DE SAUMON À LA RUSSE

℃. One pound of salmon, yolks of two eggs, nearly half a pint of milk, three-quarters of an ounce of butter, half an ounce of sugar, four tablespoonfuls of vinegar, two leaves of gelatine, a dessertspoonful of flour, a dessertspoonful of salt, a teaspoonful of mustard; cayenne.

Boil the salmon and flake it. Mix the flour, the dry mustard, the sugar, and a pinch of cayenne; add the melted butter, the beaten yolks, and the milk. Cook in a double saucepan until it thickens, stir in the vinegar, and the gelatine previously soaked in cold water. Strain it on to the salmon. Mix well, and fill a mould.
Serve cold with horseradish sauce.

SALMON WITH GREEN SAUCE

℄ Boil the salmon in water with a sliced carrot, an onion, a bunch of herbs, salt and pepper, and serve it with green mayonnaise sauce.

SCALLOPS

℄ One dozen scallops, rice, curry sauce.

In another pan stew the scallops gently till partly cooked, then cook them in a curry sauce very slowly for one hour.

Pour the mixture back into the shells, and put a border of cooked rice round them.

SHRIMPS

SHRIMP ROLLS

℄ Shrimps, watercress, butter, cayenne, bread.

Lay some shrimps in the centre of thin slices of bread and butter. Roll the slices up into tight rolls, and serve with lettuce and watercress.

SHRIMPS À LA CZARINE

℄ One pint of picked shrimps, three-quarters of a pint of milk, nutmeg, a roux of butter and flour, anchovy essence, salt, cayenne, mace.

Make a white roux of butter and flour, and add to it the milk and seasoning. Add a few drops of anchovy, and cook for a few minutes.

Put the shrimps into this sauce, and make them very hot. Serve with sippets of fried bread.

SHRIMP CROUSTADES

℀ Shrimps, onion, parsley, flour, butter, pepper, salt, mace, bread.

Shell a pint of shrimps. Boil the shells in half a pint of water with a little onion and parsley; strain it. With this liquor, and flour and butter, make a white sauce flavoured with mace.

Fry the shrimps in butter and add these to the sauce, which must be reduced till it is like very thick cream.

Have some small round fresh dinner rolls with a soft crust. Cut a piece off the top of each and remove all the crumb. Fry the cases and the pieces of crust removed in very hot butter. Fill the cases with the shrimp mixture, replace the top as a lid. Bake in the oven, and serve hot.

SKATE

BAKED SKATE

℀ Skate, peppercorns, vinegar, minced herbs, mixed spice, parsley, beer (if liked), salt.

Make the skate into fillets and dust each fillet with salt, mixed spice, pepper, and finely chopped parsley. Put the fillets in a fireproof dish, dust over them chopped mixed herbs, and pour in vinegar in which has been put some whole peppercorns, or equal quantities of vinegar and beer. Cover the dish with greased paper, and bake it for an hour and a quarter.

SKATE AU BEURRE NOIR

℃. Fillets of skate, parsley, an onion, salt, vinegar, butter.

Boil the fish in water with a sliced onion, salt, and a little vinegar. When it is cooked, drain it well. Fry some parsley in boiling butter till it is crisp.

Serve the fish with the fried parsley, and a sauce of black butter (see page 8), to which a dash of vinegar has been added.

SKATE AU VIN BLANC

℃. Skate, a glass of white wine, one ounce of butter, parsley, two shallots, a chive, two or three mushrooms, three leaves of basil; salt, peppercorns, grated breadcrumbs.

Cook the fish in the usual way, and serve it with the following sauce : Melt the butter in the wine, and add the other ingredients chopped very finely and passed through a sieve. Let the sauce simmer for fifteen minutes over a slow fire, and serve it poured over the skate.

RAIE MARINÉE FRITE

℃. Fillets of skate, vinegar, salt, pepper, parsley, chives, a clove of garlic, cloves, an onion.

Divide the fish into small pieces and let it soak for two or three hours in a little water with vinegar in it, also add a chopped onion, a clove of garlic, pepper, salt, cloves, and chopped chives. When it is time to cook the fillets, drain them well, wipe them dry, flour and fry them. Serve them with parsley fried crisply.

SMELTS

The Scotch call this exquisite fish " Sparlings," which is derived from its French name, " Eperlans." It is considered in France the most delicate of all fish. Brillat Savarin called it the beccafico of the sea, as turbot is called the pheasant, and red mullet the woodcock.

When fresh, smelts have a scent like cucumber, though Beauvilliers found that they smelt of violets. Here are two ways of cooking them :

BAKED SMELTS

℄ Put some butter into a fireproof dish, a glass of white wine, a few drops of anchovy sauce, and the juice of half a lemon.

Arrange the fish prettily in this dish, sprinkle them with salt, mace and cayenne, and cover them with breadcrumbs. Put dabs of butter on the breadcrumbs, and bake them till brown.

FRIED SMELTS

℄ Dip the fish in flour, then egg and breadcrumb them, and fry them in suet.

Serve them in a napkin, garnished with fried parsley.

This is the most usual way of cooking them.

SOLES

SOLE AU VIN BLANC

¶ Sole, onion, sweet herbs, a clove, peppercorns, salt, butter, white wine, the yolk of half an egg.

Carefully trim the sole and put it in a flat earthenware casserole, surrounded with slices of onion, a bunch of sweet herbs, a clove, four peppercorns, and a little salt. Put some small dabs of butter over it, and cover it with white wine. Cover with a lid and cook it slowly for ten minutes, or until done. Remove the fish and prepare a sauce from the liquor in which it was cooked by removing the onions and the herbs, and by shaking into it the yolk of half an egg to thicken the gravy. Strain it over the fish.

SOLE AUX FINES HERBES

¶ Sole, butter, parsley, chives, breadcrumbs.

Well grease a fireproof dish, and spread over the bottom a layer of breadcrumbs and chopped parsley, and a pinch of chives. Then put in the sole and cover it with another layer of breadcrumbs, parsley and chives, pepper and salt. Sprinkle a few raspings over the top, and add small pieces of butter. Cover it with a buttered paper, and bake it. Serve it in the same dish.

SOLE OTERO

¶ One small sole, half a pint of shrimps, four large potatoes, butter, pepper, salt.

Choose four large potatoes or as many as are required ; they should be chosen to lie well on their sides. Bake them in the oven. When cooked, cut a neat oval in the topmost side of each potato, and scoop out the inside without damaging the skins. Mash up the potato so removed with butter, pepper and salt.

Cook a small sole, remove the bones, and divide into small pieces. Mix it with half a pint of picked shrimps, and cover the fish with a sauce Mornay. Add the mashed potato, and with this mixture refill the cases ; replace the end and re-heat. (Sauce Mornay, see page 20).

Serve them in a silver dish on a napkin.

TROUT

TROUT À LA BÉARNAISE

℆ Trout, butter, chives, minced parsley, oil, thyme, pepper and salt.

Fill the trout with a paste of butter and herbs. Brush the fish over with oil or butter, sprinkle it with pepper and salt, and grill it.

Serve with Béarnaise sauce (page 6) over it. The sauce can be served in a separate dish.

TRUITES AU BLEU

℆ Half a pint of white wine, half a pint of water, an onion, a carrot, parsley, herbs, a bay-leaf, celery, tarragon, leek, pepper, salt, trout.

Put into a fish kettle the wine and water, cut up an onion, a carrot, and a little parsley, a bouquet of herbs, a bayleaf, thyme, celery, tarragon, a leek, pepper and salt, and in this court bouillon boil the trout.

Serve with a Mousseline or Hollandaise sauce.

TURBOT

TURBOT À LA TARTARE

℈ Turbot, breadcrumbs, butter, pepper, salt, tartare sauce, chives, an egg, thyme.

Put the turbot in a fireproof dish ; heat some butter and pour it over, then sprinkle some chopped parsley, thyme, and chives over it, and season it with black pepper and salt. Leave it for one hour. Then brush it over with egg, sprinkle it with breadcrumbs and bake.

Serve it with a tartare sauce poured over it.

WHITING

WHITING CREAMS

℈ One whiting, half a pint of milk, two eggs, four ounces of butter, three ounces of onion, parsley, salt, pepper, a little cream.

Fillet a large whiting ; put the head, tail, skin and bone into a saucepan with half a pint of cold milk, a pinch of pepper and half a teaspoonful of salt. Bring it to the boil slowly, then add the chopped onion, a teaspoonful of chopped celery, a large piece of parsley, and a teaspoonful of herbs. Cook it gently for thirty minutes, then strain it into a stewpan and cook the fish in it till it is soft enough to make a purée.

Take out the fish when it is cooked, pass it through a sieve with a lump of butter the size of an egg, an ounce of flour made into a paste, with an ounce of butter. Beat up two whole eggs and mix this with the fish purée ; flavour it with salt and pepper, add a little cream, and steam it for twenty-five minutes in small buttered moulds.

Thicken the broth with a roux of flour and butter, and add a good squeeze of lemon juice. Turn out the moulds, pour the sauce over them, and serve hot.

A DELICATE WAY OF COOKING WHITINGS

℃. Whitings, flour, butter, parsley, spring onions, stock, cream.

Rub some small whitings in flour till it adheres to them ; then put a good piece of butter into a frying pan and lay the fish in. Fry them very slowly without letting them get coloured or dry.

Mince some parsley and green onions very finely, and mix them with a little good stock and two tablespoonfuls of cream. Mix well and pour it over the fish just before they are quite cooked. Move them about, but do not break them.

TO COOK FRESH-WATER FISH

❧ Fish, butter, onion, anchovies, breadcrumbs, brown gravy.

Put some pieces of butter at the bottom of a flat fireproof dish, and lay the fish, after boning it, in it.

Fry half an onion and a few washed anchovies in butter, and pour over the fish. Strew them with dry breadcrumbs grated from the crust of a loaf, put in a little brown gravy. Bake, and baste it constantly till cooked, and serve it in the same dish.

AN EXCELLENT FISH SALAD

❧ One teacupful of cooked macaroni, one teacupful of flaked cooked fish, three ounces of grated horseradish, a quarter of a pint of cream, half a teaspoonful of made mustard, a tablespoonful of tarragon vinegar, salt and pepper, chopped tarragon, and lettuces.

Cut the macaroni into equal lengths, and mix it with the fish. Whip the cream, and add to it the horseradish and seasoning. Stir in the vinegar.

Surround the fish with crisp lettuce hearts, washed and well drained ; sprinkle it with finely chopped tarragon, and pour over all the sauce.

A GOOD FISH SOUFFLÉ

❧ Partly boil the fish in salted water (turbot, halibut or sole should be used for a soufflé).

Remove from it all skin and bone, and mince it finely. Season the purée with salt and pepper, mix with it a little cream and the well-beaten white of two eggs.

Butter a soufflé dish, fill it with the mixture, and tie a band of greased paper round the top above the rim of the dish.

Steam it or bake it for about half an hour.

LAVINIA'S SOUCHET

⁋ One sole, one pint of water, one medium-sized onion, one carrot, one small turnip (if the carrot is not a very good sweet one, add a small lump of sugar), pepper and salt.

Take all the bones of the sole and simmer them in the water with the vegetables and salt and pepper for one hour. Then strain the liquid, return it to the saucepan and put in the sole itself, cut in pieces. Boil it for five minutes.

Put some chopped parsley at the bottom of the tureen and a few little pieces of the previously boiled carrot and turnip.

BROWN FISH

⁋ Either mackerels or herrings, brown stock or gravy, a quarter of a pound of butter (or less for a small amount of fish), two tablespoonfuls of flour, a piece of lemon peel, a teaspoonful of mixed spice, a wineglassful of claret, or a dessert-spoonful of mushroom ketchup.

Trim the fish, removing its bones, fillet it, and boil it in water with salt and pepper for forty-five minutes. Then strain off the liquor and colour it with browning.

Fry the butter brown, stir into it the flour ; when it is smooth, add this to the liquor with the spice, salt and pepper, and a piece of lemon rind. Boil it and then put in the fillets of fish. Let them simmer for twenty minutes, adding brown gravy if it is too dry.

When it is cooked and ready to serve, remove the lemon peel and pour in the wine (or the ketchup). Serve hot.

A MOOLOO OF FISH

⁌ One cocoanut, green chillies, an onion, garlic, butter, vinegar, any fish.

Take one pound of filleted fish, fry it lightly and leave it to cool. Make a small opening in a cocoanut, scrape the interior and half fill it with hot water. Leave it till cool, and strain the water into a basin, then put in a little more hot water and rub it well into the cocoanut, and again strain it off.

Cut up two or three onions, three green chillies, and add to it half a clove of garlic. Fry them all in butter, and add the cocoanut water. Pour all the contents of the frying pan over the fish, add a little vinegar, some sliced green ginger, pepper and salt.

Let it simmer for a few minutes, and serve.

FISH CUSTARD

❡ Haddock, whiting or any other small quantity of fish, one pint of milk, one egg.

Take the skin, bones, head and tail of the fish and boil them in the milk with pepper and salt. Half boil the fish itself. Strain in the milk the trimmings of the fish have boiled in and add the beaten egg. Pour the custard into a mould and put the fish in flaked. Steam the mould in hot water for forty-five minutes, then turn it out, garnish it with strips of lemon peel and cucumber.

This is a good way of using up cold fish.

VI
EGGS

" Choose eggs oblong,
    Remember, they'll be found
    Of sweeter taste and whiter than the round."
                                    HORACE.

" I am much of his (Horace's) opinion, and
could only wish that the world was thoroughly
informed of two other truths concerning eggs—
one is how incomparably better roasted eggs
are than boiled ; the other—never to eat any
butter with egg in the shell."
                                    WILLIAM KING.

" The vulgar boil, the learned roast an egg."
                                    POPE.

CHAPTER VI

EGGS

FROM very ancient times an egg has been the symbol of creation, a symbol common to the most ancient civilizations—the Chinese, Chaldeans, Persians, Hindus, Egyptians, and Jews. The origin of the " Easter egg " is as old as the tradition that the world was created at Easter-time or in the spring—so old that the origin is lost beyond the memory of the childhood of the world. The actual custom of giving eggs as gifts at Easter can be traced from Europe to Persia, though the practice prevailed in Ancient Egypt and India and among the Jews. The Magian or Persian interpretation was an allusion to the " egg of the world," for the possession of which Ormuzd, the angel of Good, and Ahriman, the power of Evil, were to fight until the end of time and the consummation of all things. The Egyptian legend was very similar —Osiris enclosed in an egg two white pyramids, symbols of the good he wishes to confer upon mankind, but his wicked brother Typhon secretly hid in the egg twelve black pyramids, emblems of the evil he wished to wreak on mankind. Therefore, said the Egyptians, in this world good and evil are irrevocably mingled. Typhon, the personification of evil and destruction, lived in the sea, according to the Egyptians, hence their reluctance to venture upon the water and the explanation of the fact that they never colonized.

It is curious that in what were supposed to have been pre-scientific eras, an egg should have been chosen for the emblem of the universe, for this planetary universe is very much the shape of an egg, though if that was known then the knowledge was lost and had to be re-discovered. And the alternative symbol of the egg as the source of all life seems to show that the ancient sages knew as much about evolution as the scientists of to-day, which is very little, for the eternal riddle—"which came first, the egg or the chicken," remains unanswered.

ŒUFS AU BEURRE NOIR

℄ Two ounces of butter, four eggs, vinegar.

Put into a frying pan two ounces of butter, and heat it till it is brown ; it must not burn.

Break four eggs into a dish, and just before serving add a few drops of vinegar which has been boiled.

Serve them with the black butter poured over them.

FRIED EGGS WITH SAFFRON SAUCE

℄ Cook half a breakfast cupful of Patna rice in a large saucepan of boiling water as for curry, and put it on one side.

Prepare a Béchamel sauce, to which a pinch of red saffron has been added in the early stages.

Fry as many eggs as are required. Put the rice in a silver dish, pour over it the saffron sauce, and lay the fried eggs on the top.

ŒUFS MOLLETS À LA ROBERT

℃ One egg for each person, onion sauce, a wineglassful of white wine.

Make an onion sauce (see page 22), adding a wineglassful of white wine to the ingredients.

Boil the eggs long enough to set the whites firmly enough for the shells to be removed without breaking the egg, yet with the yolks soft. Drop the whole eggs into the hot onion sauce, and serve them very hot, with or without a wall of mashed potato round the dish.

DEVILLED EGGS

℃ Eggs, two tablespoonfuls of Worcester sauce, one dessertspoonful of French mustard, one ounce of butter, thick brown gravy, salt and cayenne pepper.

Boil the eggs for eight minutes ; peel them, cut them in half, and remove the yolks. Make a paste of the yolks, cayenne and salt. Cut a tiny piece off the bottom of each half white to make it stand up, and fill each one with the paste. Pour over them a sauce made of the gravy, French mustard, and Worcester sauce. Serve very hot and sprinkle them with chopped parsley.

ŒUFS ROTIS EN LA BROCHE

❡ Eggs, herbs, butter, saffron, ginger, sugar.

Take as many eggs as you wish to cook. Take off the end of each shell and pour out the egg. Set aside the shells.

Take sage, mint, sweet marjoram, and other herbs ; chop them finely, and then fry them in butter with the beaten eggs. Put the cooked eggs on a board and chop them finely, adding a little saffron, ginger and sugar. Fill the shells of the eggs with this stuffing, and put them in the oven for a few minutes.

ŒUFS À LA BONNE SUISSE

❡ Gruyère cheese, butter, bread, white wine, parsley, shallots, black pepper, nutmeg.

Put half a pound of grated Gruyère cheese in a casserole with two slices of buttered bread, a glassful of white wine, parsley, chopped shallots, black pepper and nutmeg. Boil this till the cheese is melted ; add six eggs, the whites of which have been well whipped ; cook them as long as scrambled eggs, garnish them with sippets of bread fried in butter, and serve hot.

ŒUFS AU RIZ

❡ Three sardines, three anchovies, one and a half ounces of butter, four eggs, quarter of a pound of boiled rice, salt and cayenne.

Beat up the eggs with the seasoning. Melt the butter and throw into it the rice ; season it with salt and pepper. Stir it over the fire, and add the beaten eggs, the anchovies and sardines, which have been boned and chopped small. Stir it all the time, make it very hot, and serve it either on fried bread or in small ramakin cases, decorated with sippets of fried bread.

EGGS À LA MAÎTRE D'HÔTEL

℄ Eggs, butter, parsley, bread, lemon, salt and pepper.

Boil three or four eggs hard ; cut them in half horizontally, and cut a little slice off each end of the white, so that the eggs will stand up. Do not touch the yolks.

Fry round pieces of bread in butter, one piece for each half-egg, and arrange the half-eggs on the croutons on the dish in which they are to be served, buttering the dish. Make some maître d'hôtel butter ; that is to say, take the juice of a lemon, a dessertspoonful of finely chopped parsley, a little pepper and salt, and work it all into two ounces of butter. The butter should be firm and cold. When it is mixed, roll it into little balls with butter pats. Put the dish with the eggs into the oven till they are hot, pour a little melted butter over them, and add at the last moment a little pat of maître d'hôtel butter, serving quickly before the butter has quite melted.

BACHELOR EGGS

℄ Bachelor eggs are poached eggs served with fried ham on muffins. Split and toast the muffins.

Fry a round piece of ham for each half-muffin, and on each round place a poached egg.

This dish can be served with Sauce Hollandaise.

FROTH EGGS

℄ Eggs, butter, parsley, pepper and salt.

Beat up the white of each egg separately, and when stiff put it into a china ramakin. Make a hole in the middle and slip the yolk in whole. Sprinkle it with salt, pepper, and minced parsley, and put a small piece of butter on the top. Do this with the others, and bake them all until they are just set.

BIRDS' NESTS

℄ Six eggs, butter, one cup of sour milk, slices of bread, half a teaspoonful of minced parsley, half a teaspoonful of chopped onion.

Cut six slices of bread an inch thick ; take a paste cutter and cut each slice in rounds. With a smaller cutter take a round out of the rounds already cut, leaving a ring.

Put some butter in a frying pan and fry the rings of bread pale brown. Butter a pudding dish and put the rings in it after they are fried. Drop the uncooked yolk of an egg into the middle of each ring. Pour a little milk on each one, and season it. Bake them, and serve them as soon as they are set.

CURRIED EGGS

℄ Three eggs, half a pint of milk, one ounce of butter, half an ounce of flour, quarter of a teaspoonful of curry powder, quarter of a tea-spoonful of salt, pepper.

Hard boil the eggs. Melt the butter and stir in the flour, curry powder, etc., and gradually stir in the milk, which must be hot.

Cut the eggs in half lengthways, and then again, and heat them in the sauce. Serve them very hot.

EGG TARTLETS

⟨ Eggs, tomato sauce, vinegar, chopped parsley, pastry cases.

Nearly fill a deep pan with boiling water, salted and flavoured with vinegar—half a teacupful to three pints. Break as many eggs as are required into this from a height ; this will make them the shape of balls. Keep the water boiling gently for three minutes. Remove them very carefully with a slice, drain them on a cloth, trim them, and place each egg into a pastry case. Pour a little tomato sauce over each one, and sprinkle it with chopped parsley. Serve them very hot in a silver entrèe dish.

A Soubise sauce can be used instead of tomato sauce, if onions are preferred, or the cases can be filled with devilled shrimps and served with rice.

SCALLOPED EGGS

⟨ Three eggs, half a pint of milk, three or four ounces of cold meat (ham, veal, chicken, or fish), one ounce of butter, one ounce of flour, pepper, salt, breadcrumbs.

Hard boil the eggs and chop them small. Mince the cold meat or fish ; season with salt and pepper. Make a white sauce with the milk, butter and flour. Butter a baking dish and line it with fried breadcrumbs. Put in a layer of chopped eggs, pour some of the sauce over the egg, then put a layer of the minced meat, then another layer of chopped egg, more sauce, and then the rest of the meat. Cook them with more breadcrumbs, heat thoroughly in the oven, and serve.

EGG TIMBALES

℔ Three eggs, one ounce of butter, one ounce of flour, three-eights of a pint of milk, chopped parsley, salt and pepper, celery salt, cayenne.

Break the eggs and seperate the yolks from the whites. Make a roux of the butter and flour, and stir in the milk. Into this beat the yolks of the eggs until the sauce is thick ; add salt and pepper to taste, with a pinch of celery salt and cayenne.

Beat the whites of the eggs until they are quite stiff ; put the stiff froth into the sauce with a spoon. Have some buttered ramakins, arrange them in a baking tin in hot water. Fill them with the mixture and bake them in a slow oven.

Serve with hot tomato sauce.

ROOFS

This is a Lincolnshire dish. The country people made it with the tops of cottage loaves.

℔ Two baps (see p. xv), two hard-boiled eggs,

one dessertspoonful of anchovy essence ; butter and pepper.

Split the rolls and take out the soft dough inside. Spread both pieces inside liberally with butter.

Shell and chop the eggs finely ; mix them with the anchovy and seasoning, and spread them on both pieces. Put the halves together and bake them till they are very hot and crisp.

CONVENT EGGS

ℂ Three eggs, four onions, one pint of milk ; butter, salt and pepper.

Boil the onions until half cooked ; drain and cut them in slices. Make a sauce of the milk with a little flour, butter, pepper and salt.

Fry the slices of onion in a little butter, and then add them to the sauce and let them simmer for fifteen minutes.

Hard boil the eggs, slice them, and put them into the sauce with the onions. Let them simmer for a little, and then serve.

SAVOURY CUSTARDS

ℂ Put into a basin six spoonfuls of stock, with the yolks of six eggs and the whites of two. Mix all together and season with pepper and salt.

Butter some small moulds, pour in the eggs and cook them in a bain-marie till set. They could be baked if necessary. Turn them out very carefully and serve them with a green sauce.

A delicious breakfast dish

CHASSE

❦ Onion, butter, lard, tomatoes, ham, potatoes, cheese, red pepper, eggs.

Cut up an onion and fry it in butter and lard, then add six tomatoes and a slice of ham, both cut up. When well browned, put in some water and three potatoes cut in dice. Cook it until the potatoes are done. Before serving mix in grated cheese, well flavoured with red pepper.

Pour the sauce on to a very hot dish, and place poached eggs on the top.

SAVOURY PANCAKES

❦ Three eggs, six tablespoonfuls of flour, onion and parsley, milk.

Make a batter of the three eggs and a little milk beaten together with the flour. Stir in a tablespoonful of minced onion and parsley, and season it with pepper and salt. Leave the batter for a few hours, and then make it into pancakes, a small saucerful at a time.

SAVOURY YORKSHIRE PUDDING

❦ Two eggs, four heaped tablespoonfuls of flour, one pint of milk, one large onion, salt.

Separate the whites and yolks of the eggs, and whip the whites stiffly. Beat the yolks into the milk with salt ; add the flour, stirring it in till it is a smooth batter. Mix in the whites.

Have the greased tins ready ; heat them, pour in the batter, and bake them in a quick oven for twenty minutes.

EGG CANAPÉS

℄ Eggs, onion, mushrooms, butter, flour, white wine, salt, pepper, stock, bread.

Hard boil as many eggs as are required. Lightly fry a cut-up onion and three chopped mushrooms in two ounces of butter ; when slightly brown add a little flour, a quarter of a glassful of white wine, salt and pepper, and enough stock to moisten it. Let it simmer for thirty minutes to reduce.

Peel the eggs ; remove the yolks whole ; cut the whites into rounds and add them to the sauce. Now pour the sauce, which should be rather thick, into a silver dish, and place the whole yolks on the top on croutons of fried bread.

SNOWBALL EGGS

℄ Six eggs, two pints of milk, sugar to taste, vanilla.

Separate the yolks from the whites of the eggs and beat them separately. Whisk the whites to a very stiff froth with a pinch of salt. When they are beaten well, add about three table-spoonfuls of sugar, and beat them again.

Boil the milk in a double saucepan with sugar to sweeten it and vanilla to flavour. When the milk boils, take a tablespoonful of the frothed

white of egg and drop it into the mil
remain for three minutes, then take it
put it on the dish it is to be served on _
the white of egg in the same way, by s
(Three or four can be boiling at the sa
    Arrange the snowballs in a pyrami
dish.
    Into the saucepan with the milk stir
of the eggs. Stir the mixture all the tim
not let it boil. When it is thick, stand i
cool, and pour it over the snowballed e
it is cold.

Have the greased tins ready ; heat them, pour in the batter, and bake them in a quick oven for twenty minutes.

EGG CANAPÉS

℃ Eggs, onion, mushrooms, butter, flour, white wine, salt, pepper, stock, bread.

Hard boil as many eggs as are required. Lightly fry a cut-up onion and three chopped mushrooms in two ounces of butter ; when slightly brown add a little flour, a quarter of a glassful of white wine, salt and pepper, and enough stock to moisten it. Let it simmer for thirty minutes to reduce.

Peel the eggs ; remove the yolks whole ; cut the whites into rounds and add them to the sauce. Now pour the sauce, which should be rather thick, into a silver dish, and place the whole yolks on the top on croutons of fried bread.

SNOWBALL EGGS

℃ Six eggs, two pints of milk, sugar to taste, vanilla.

Separate the yolks from the whites of the eggs and beat them separately. Whisk the whites to a very stiff froth with a pinch of salt. When they are beaten well, add about three table-spoonfuls of sugar, and beat them again.

Boil the milk in a double saucepan with sugar to sweeten it and vanilla to flavour. When the milk boils, take a tablespoonful of the frothed white of egg and drop it into the milk. Let it remain for three minutes, then take it out and put it on the dish it is to be served on. Cook all the white of egg in the same way, by spoonfuls. (Three or four can be boiling at the same time.)

Arrange the snowballs in a pyramid on the dish.

Into the saucepan with the milk stir the yolks of the eggs. Stir the mixture all the time and do not let it boil. When it is thick, stand it aside to cool, and pour it over the snowballed eggs when it is cold.

VII
MEAT

" We cannot entertain you as the lordly inns on the roads do, and we have small change of victuals. But . . . there are some few collops of red deer's flesh, and a ham just down from the chimney, and some dried salmon from Lynmouth Weir, and cold roast pig, and some oysters. And if none of these be to your liking, we could roast two woodcocks in half an hour, and Annie would make the toast for them. . . .

" Tom Faggus—he stopped to sup that night with us, and took a little of everything : a few oysters first, and then dried salmon, and then ham and eggs done in small curled rashers, and then a few collops of venison toasted, and next to that a little cold roast pig, and a woodcock on toast to finish with, before the Schiedam and hot water. He seemed to be in fair appetite and praised Annie's cooking mightily."

CHAPTER VII

MEAT

No recipes are given for plainly roasting or boiling, though perhaps this is the place to remind people that every joint of mutton is improved by being roasted with a clove of garlic inserted into it.

The secret, of course, of successful roasting or baking is to cook the meat slowly and baste it well.

Kidneys must either be cooked quickly or for a very long time, otherwise they become tough.

Hashed mutton, more honoured as a music-hall joke than as a dish, can be excellent food. The reputation of the once famous Long's of Bond Street was built up entirely on their hashed mutton.

It was made of fresh meat and cooked and seasoned in a way they kept secret. The recipes given here for this dish are all old and devised by chefs as skilled as the cook who presided in Long's kitchen.

A great deal of the dullness of English meat dishes would be removed if we adopted the Continental and Eastern habit of serving with them purées and compôtes of fruit.

ÉPAULE DE MOUTON À LA SOUBISE

℄ A small shoulder of mutton, a quarter of a pound of breadcrumbs, one ounce of chopped suet, two ounces of ham or bacon, one egg, one teaspoonful of chopped parsley, half a teaspoonful of chopped lemon peel.

Bone the shoulder, and make a stuffing of the breadcrumbs, ham, suet, parsley, lemon peel, adding pepper and salt, and bind it with the yolk of one egg. Fill the space in the shoulder where the bone was with the stuffing ; roll up the mutton and tie it very tightly. Roast in the oven very slowly, basting in the usual way, and serve with onion sauce.

BRAISED SHOULDER OF MUTTON

℣ One shoulder of mutton (weighing about four pounds), ten or twelve onions, half a pound of rice, one ounce of butter.

Bone the shoulder (which should be a lean one), pepper and salt it inside, and roll it and skewer it or tie it firmly in the shape of a large sausage. Keep the bone. Put the butter in a stewpan, and when it begins to brown put in the meat. Turn the meat until it browns all over. Then put in about ten good-sized onions skinned; let them get brown, then put the bones in the pan, add pepper and salt, *no water*, and put the lid on. See that it fits tightly, and stew the mutton slowly for two hours.

Throw the rice into a saucepan of boiling salted water and cook it for twenty minutes ; then strain it. When the mutton has stewed for two hours, take out the bones and put in the rice ; stir it well into the gravy that the mutton has made, and let it simmer with the mutton for fifteen minutes. Then serve the mutton on a hot dish with the rice and gravy round it.

NECK OF MUTTON À L'ALLEMANDE

℄ Trim a neck of mutton for braizing, and with a sharp knife lay bare the fleshy part by removing the covering of fat and sinew.

Cover the bare part with bacon, and put it into a pan with carrots, turnips, onions, parsley, cloves, mace, and a few peppercorns. Moisten it with sufficient stock to cover the mutton, and let it simmer very slowly in the oven, basting constantly.

Serve with a Cumberland sauce poured over it and a dish of stewed prunes (see page 12).

ROAST AND STUFFED
LEG OF MUTTON

℄ Leg of mutton, butter, onions, breadcrumbs, sage, egg, and apple.

Make a forcemeat of two ounces of onion, four ounces of breadcrumbs, one apple chopped fine, one ounce of green sage, add salt and pepper, and one egg beaten up. Bone a leg of mutton, cut off all the fat, and stuff it with the forcemeat ; insert a half a clove of garlic, and roast in the usual way—very slowly, basting often.

EPIGRAMMES DE MOUTON À LA SMYRNE

❡ Epigrams of mutton or lamb consist of alternate cutlets, one kind cut from the neck and fried as they are in butter, the other kind cut from the breast, braized, boned, and breadcrumbed before they are fried, and fitted with a bone end to look like ordinary cutlets.

Prepare a dish of cutlets in this way, and pour over them a white piquante sauce made of white stock instead of brown, to which a tablespoonful of chopped and stoned raisins have been added, and hand in a separate dish some pickled onions.

SWEET PEPPER STEW

This is a genuine Hungarian recipe for Hungary's equivalent of Irish stew. The paprika, or sweet pepper, with which it is flavoured, is the flavour which permeates every dish in Budapest. It has even given its name to an English novel.

❡ Mutton, flour, paprika, potatoes, bacon, tomatoes, stock, wine, carraway seeds, onions, salt and pepper.

Cut up and fry an onion in butter, and add the mutton cut into small pieces, some pieces of bacon, and potatoes peeled and cut in slices. Fry all a pale brown. Put the potatoes, meat and onions into a casserole and cook slowly. Season it with paprika, salt and pepper, and add a quarter of a pint of red wine and a quarter of a pint of water or stock, and a few carraway seeds put into a muslin bag.

AN EXCELLENT HASH OF FRESH MUTTON

❧ Partly roast one pound or more of collops of mutton, and cut it into rather thick slices. Sprinkle them with flour and season them with cayenne pepper and salt.

Put into a casserole a chopped shallot, a dessertspoonful of Worcester sauce, a dessertspoonful of Harvey's sauce, a glass of port wine, and a large tablespoonful of red currant jelly.

Add the prepared mutton, and let it simmer in this sauce for ten minutes.

TWO EXCELLENT WAYS OF DOING UP COLD MUTTON

❧ Lettuce, cucumber, peas, onion, beetroot, butter, and cold mutton.

Put into a casserole a good lump of butter. Slice a cucumber and add it, also two small beetroots or one big one, one onion, and one lettuce. Just cover this with water and put it on a slow fire ; then add a cupful of cooked peas and the meat cut in slices and sprinkled with flour, pepper and salt. Cook for about ten minutes and serve in the casserole.

STEW OF COOKED MUTTON

❧ Cold mutton, two wineglassfuls of claret, one shallot, one teaspoonful of minced parsley, one large tablespoonful of red currant jelly, one dessertspoonful of chutney ; spiced pepper, one and a half ounces of glaze.

Put the glaze in an enamel saucepan, chop the shallot fine, and when the glaze is melted add it, and also the wine, parsley, red currant jelly, and chutney. Pour this into a marmite, and add the slices of mutton, which should be cut very thin. Heat thoroughly and serve in the same dish.

CASSEROLE OF MEAT AND RICE

⁋ One pound of cold mutton, or veal or chicken, one cupful of rice, one egg, stock, salt, pepper, celery salt, onion, and lemon juice.

Boil enough rice in water to line a greased mould. Line the mould with the rice cooked and drained. Remove fat from the cold meat, chop it finely and season it with pepper and salt, a little cayenne, celery salt, lemon juice and onion juice. Mix it with a beaten egg and four table-spoonfuls of breadcrumbs. Fill up the mould and moisten it with hot stock. If no stock is available, use some of the water the rice has boiled in. Cover the meat with rice. Put greased paper over the mould and steam for three-quarters of an hour. Turn out carefully and serve with tomato sauce round it.

OATMEAL PIE

⁋ Cut up the remains of a cold joint. Mix half a pound of fine oatmeal with half a teaspoonful

of powdered dried herbs, a dessertspoonful of
flour ; pepper and salt. Dip each slice of meat in
this and place it in the bottom of a piedish, then
put in a layer of cut-up uncooked potato and a
little onion, another layer of meat, etc.

Make the crust as follows :

Boil a quarter of a pound of dripping in about
half a pint of water, pour the oatmeal, seasoned
with pepper and salt, into the dripping. Make a
crust very quickly without using a rolling pin,
quickly make a cover of it for the pie, and bake
for about thirty minutes.

A VERY GOOD DRY CURRY

❡. One pound of meat, one clove of garlic, one
dessertspoon of curry powder, one dessertspoonful of chutney or tamarind preserve, one pound
of onions, two ounces of butter, one dessertspoonful of curry paste, salt, squeeze of lemon
juice.

Brown the onions in the butter, and then dry
them. Mash the garlic to a pulp and put it in
a double saucepan—in which the whole curry
should be cooked to prevent catching. Then mix
the curry powder and paste and the chutney
into a thin paste with the lemon juice. Mash the
dried onions into this and let all simmer together gently till mixed. Then add the meat cut
in small cubes and let it simmer very gently for
three hours. By this time all the liquid should
be absorbed.   Serve surrounded by rice.

BEEF

FILETS DE BŒUF À LA CARLSBAD

❧ Remove the undercut from a sirloin of beef. Cut it into slices about a quarter of an inch thick. Season and fry them lightly in butter. Serve in a silver dish. Pour over them a horseradish sauce and decorate with red currant jelly.

Hand separately a dish of compôte of cherries.

AN EXCELLENT HASH OF COLD BEEF

❧ Cut an onion up into small pieces and mix it with a dessertspoonful of minced herbs. Put a piece of butter into a pan, and when it is melted add the onion and herbs. Cook them till they are a pale brown, then stir in a level tablespoonful of flour and make it into a smooth paste. Season the mixture with cayenne pepper, salt, and nutmeg, and add a pint of good gravy.

Boil this very slowly for ten minutes, then pass it through a strainer, and add half a wineglassful of mushroom catsup ; then add the slices of cooked beef and let them get heated right through. Serve with sippets of toast.

MINCED BEEF WITH CHESTNUTS AND RAISINS

❧ One pound of beef, chestnuts, sultanas, red wine or gravy, a purée of lentils or peas.

Make a purée of lentils or peas (see p. 81).

Mince the beef and an equal amount of chestnuts which have been previously skinned. Mix
the beef and the chestnuts together with a little
chopped parsley, flavouring it either with a few
cloves or a little grated nutmeg. Moisten the
mince with red wine or gravy. Put it in the oven
for ten minutes, and then mix in some sultanas.
When it is cooked serve hot with the purée round
it.

This is a useful dish for the winter ; it is very
nourishing and sustaining ; can be kept hot for
hours without spoiling, and is therefore suitable
for shooting parties or winter expeditions.

BEEF STEWED WITH TOMATOES AND OLIVES

℄ Four pounds of beef, without bone, half a
pound of olives, two ounces of butter, four or
five good-sized tomatoes, salt, pepper, parsley
and a small onion.

Put nearly two ounces of butter in a stewpan,
and when it is melted and steaming put in the
beef. Turn it till it is brown on both sides ; then
pepper and salt it well, and cover the pan. Leave
it to simmer for three and a half to four hours.

Cut the tomatoes in half horizontally. Lay
them skin sides down, and sprinkle the cut
surface with pepper, salt, chopped parsley, and
a little chopped onion. Put a morsel of butter on
each half, and bake for twenty minutes.

Before the beef is quite cooked, stone the olives and put them in to stew with the meat.

Serve the meat cut in slices neatly arranged on a hot dish with its own sauce poured over it and the baked tomatoes in a circle round it, with spoonfuls of olives between each half tomato.

BIFTEKS NIÇOIS

℃. Buy one pound of minced beefsteak. Fry a chopped onion in butter, and add to it the beef and sufficient stock to moisten it. Remove it from the fire, season it with pepper and salt, and stir in a few tablespoons of cream. Form it into rounds and fry them.

Dish on croutons of fried bread, and drop a spoonful of horseradish sauce on each one.

PINK HASH

℃. Take a glass jar of smoked beef and shred it finely. Boil it in cold water and drain.

Make a roux of flour and butter ; add to it the beef and a quarter of a pint of cream, and cook for three quarters of an hour.

Serve with fried sippets of bread.

VEAL
BLANQUETTE DE VEAU

℃. One and a half pounds of veal cutlet, quarter of a pound of mushrooms, a bunch of mixed herbs, one clove of garlic, a little flour and stock, one ounce of butter.

Fry the veal in butter. Make a sauce with the mushrooms cut in shreds, the mixed herbs, garlic, a piece of butter the size of a walnut, salt and pepper, and sift in a little flour. Put all these ingredients in a saucepan with a little stock, and let it reduce.

Into this sauce put the veal, add a squeeze of lemon juice, and if liked the yolk of an egg or a little cream.

Another Recipe for

BLANQUETTE OF VEAL OR LAMB

℃. One pound of cold meat, two ounces of butter, two ounces of flour, half a pint of milk, half a pint of white stock, salt, pepper, mace, mushroom ketchup.

Cut the cold meat into strips, removing superfluous fat. Boil the milk with two leaves of mace in it ; heat the stock. Make a roux of the flour and butter, adding the milk and stock gradually, stirring well. Add the salt, pepper, and mushroom ketchup. Pour the sauce over the slices of meat and heat all together. When hot, garnish it with sippets of toast, a sprinkling of chopped parsley. Serve with a border of mashed potatoes or green peas.

RAGOUT DE VEAU

℃. Two pounds of veal, quarter of a pound of fat bacon, quarter of a pint of sour cream, quarter of a pint of milk, two large onions, one ounce of butter, bayleaf, parsley, thyme, pepper, and salt.

Divide the veal into cutlets ; cut the bacon into thin rashers and the onions into rings.

Put the butter in a pan or casserole that has a well-fitting lid. Stir the butter till it is melted ; lay the rashers of bacon side by side so that they cover the bottom of the pan, and on the bacon put the onion rings and the herbs tied together. Leave the pan uncovered on the fire while you sprinkle both sides of the fillets of veal with pepper and salt. When the bacon, etc., in the pan is hot, lay in the veal. Put on the lid and let it stew gently for one hour and a half.

Take out the veal and bacon and arrange them on the hot dish they will be served on. Remove the bunch of herbs, and into the pan pour the milk with a spoonful of vinegar and the sour cream. Put it on the fire and stir it all the time till the cream and milk and the thick gravy in the pan are mixed into a brown sauce.

Pour it over the veal and serve very hot with rice boiled as for a curry.

COTELETTES DE VEAU À LA MARECHALE

❦ Take some veal cutlets and trim them. Prepare some fine breadcrumbs and mix with them an equal amount of grated Parmesan cheese.

Brush the cutlets with yolk of an egg, roll them in the breadcrumbs, and fry a golden brown.

Serve them with a purée of sorrel or spinach, and pour a hot orange sauce over the cutlets.

VEAL À LA BRETONNE

℀ Cook enough turnips to make a dish of purée. Pass them through a sieve when tender, and season with pepper and salt. Mix with it two tablespoonfuls of cream or milk.

Trim some cutlets, brush them with yolk of egg, season them with pepper and salt and roll them in fine breadcrumbs. Fry golden brown.

Serve them in a silver dish, placing the turnip purée in the middle and the cutlets round it.

VEAL À LA BOULANGER

℀ Prepare some well-trimmed veal cutlets. Boil one pound of apples with a little water and sugar, and a few pieces of thin lemon rind, and pass them through a sieve to make a purée.

Season the cutlets with pepper and salt. Grill them, and before serving cover the top of each with a paste made of butter, chopped parsley, pepper and salt. Press well into the meat ; this is done by making incisions in it.

Dish them in a silver entrée dish, with the purée of apple in the centre and the cutlets put round it.   Hand tomato sauce separately.

PORK
PORK À LA MANCELLE

℀ Trim the fat from some cutlets taken from the loin, dredge them with flour and season with pepper and salt. Put a piece of butter in a casserole and slightly fry the cutlets in this ; add two onions chopped up, a little parsley, a carrot, a turnip, and a little stock. Let them all simmer very slowly for about two hours.

Peel and cook about thirty chestnuts, pass them through a sieve and make into a purée ; add a little butter, pepper and salt.

Take out the cutlets, add a little flour to the gravy and a little stock to make a good brown sauce. Strain and pour it over the cutlets, which should be dished round the purée of chestnuts.

PORK À LA MARSEILLAISE

℆ Divide the cutlets from a loin of pork ; coat them with the yolk of an egg, powder with breadcrumbs and fry a golden brown in butter.

Cook two pounds of onions till tender in stock ; pass them through a sieve ; season with pepper and salt.

Serve in a mound in the centre of a silver entrée dish, with the cutlets round.

FRIED PORK WITH COMPÔTE OF QUINCES

℆ Take as many cutlets as are required. Brush them with the yolk of an egg, season them with pepper and salt and roll in breadcrumbs. Fry a golden brown and serve with a compôte of quinces handed separately.

CUTLETS OF PORK À LA MARÉCHALE

℄ Trim some cutlets from a loin of pork, season with pepper and salt, and put a small piece of butter on each. Put under the grill, and just before they are cooked make a paste of a little butter, pepper, salt, and chopped parsley. Before serving the cutlets make an incision in them and spread them with the paste.

Make an orange sauce and serve the cutlets very hot, with the sauce handed separately.

TONGUE

STEWED OX TONGUE

℄ Stew a tongue in enough water to cook it for three hours, or until it is tender.

Into the stock it will make in the pan put a bayleaf, pepper and salt to season, some slices of tomato, and a teaspoonful of Worcester sauce. Make a sauce by reducing the stock ; add a few little mushrooms ; serve round the hot tongue.

TONGUE WITH ALMOND AND RAISIN SAUCE
An Italian dish

℄ Slices of tongue, raisins, almonds, candied peel, chocolate, vinegar, tomato, sugar, butter.

Fry some slices of onion in a saucepan, and add to them as many slices of tongue as are required, frying them very lightly. To this add a little tomato purée mixed with stock and let all simmer very gently.

Put into a basin a tablespoonful of sugar with a dessertspoonful of vinegar, a few chopped almonds and stoned raisins and very little grated chocolate, also a few strips of candied peel. Mix together and pour over the tongue in the casserole. Cook for five or ten minutes, and serve.

BRAISED TONGUE WITH CHERRY SAUCE

¶ Take some slices of cooked tongue and heat them in a brown gravy, to which has been added a carrot, an onion, two cloves, and a few peppercorns. Make it very hot, strain it, pour it over the tongue, and serve with hot cherry sauce.

HAM

MOUSSELINE DE JAMBON

¶ Cooked ham, cream, and eggs.

Mince and pound half a pound of cooked ham, add to it a quarter of a pint of thick cream, a quarter of a pint of milk, and the yolks of two well-beaten eggs.

Whip the whites separately and add them to the mixture ; season with pepper and a little chopped parsley, and steam in a bain-marie for forty-five minutes. Serve with a compôte of pineapple or a spinach mould.

HAM COOKED WITH RED WINE AND ALMONDS

℄ Ham, red wine, orange, macaroons.

Cut as many slices of ham as are required. Put into a casserole two pounded macaroons, two tablespoonfuls of red wine, and two peppercorns cut in half. Put the slices of ham in this and cook them slowly.

Before serving, add the juice of half an orange.

SWEETBREADS

℄ Sweetbreads must be soaked in cold water and then blanched before being cooked. To blanch sweetbreads, put them in cold water in a stewpan, bring the water slowly to the boil, and when it has boiled for a minute take out the sweetbread and put it into cold water.

To braise sweetbreads in the best way, cover the bottom of a stewpan with bacon rind ; into the pan slice an onion and a carrot, and put a bunch of fresh herbs (parsley, thyme, and a bayleaf). On these ingredients put the sweetbreads, covered with a piece of buttered paper, the size and shape of the pan. Put the lid on the pan and stand it on gentle heat for a few minutes, then pour in a wineglass of white wine. When this begins to reduce, add salt, pepper, and enough stock almost to cover the sweetbread. The covered stewpan must now be put into a hot oven for three-quarters of an hour.

When the sweetbreads are cooked, put them on a hot dish (without the vegetables or bacon rind). Strain the liquor it has cooked in, add more salt and pepper if necessary, and lemon juice. Pour the sauce over the sweetbreads.

SWEETBREADS À LA D'ARMAGNAC

℄ Sweetbread, onions, parsley, spice, chives, bacon, mushrooms.

Line a casserole with pieces of bacon, then put in some slices of onion, a few whole chives, some chopped parsley, a pinch of salt, pepper, and a few mushrooms.

Blanch the sweetbreads and put them into the casserole, covering them with the slices of bacon, etc. Put on the cover and cook in a moderate oven. When cooked remove the bacon and baste the sweetbreads with the gravy, sprinkle them with breadcrumbs, and cook again till golden brown. Serve very hot with a mushroom sauce.

Pieces of veal cooked with the sweetbreads improve the flavour.

FRIED SWEETBREADS WITH CREAM SAUCE

℄ Sweetbread, butter, flour, breadcrumbs, lemon.

Slice the sweetbread and slightly fry in butter. Then dip it in egg and breadcrumbs and fry till cooked a pale brown.

Serve with a white Béchamel sauce.

SWEETBREADS DIPPED IN BATTER AND FRIED

℄. Sweetbread, flour, eggs, butter, onions, parsley, chives, bayleaf, cloves, lemon.

Blanch and slice the sweetbread. Put into a casserole a sliced onion, one or two chives, salt, pepper, a bayleaf, two cloves, the juice of one lemon, and let the slices of sweetbread steep in this mixture for two or three hours.

Make a batter of two tablespoonfuls of flour, a little water to make into a paste, one well-beaten egg and a piece of butter. The paste must be of the right consistency, not too thick.

Remove the slices of sweetbread, dip them in the batter, and fry them a golden brown in butter.

Drain them and serve with fried parsley.

KIDNEYS

SHEEPS' KIDNEYS À L'ÉPICURIENNE

℄. Draw a knife nearly through each kidney from the outer or rounded part, without dividing it. Smear them with butter and grill them. Serve them on toast with the hollow part uppermost, and fill the hollows with Tartare sauce.

Pour Gubbin's sauce over them. (Page 15.)

FRIED KIDNEYS WITH BROWN SAUCE

℄. Kidneys, butter, onions, bacon.

Quarter the kidneys and fry them in butter till brown, then cut up two onions and fry them also. Drain off the butter and pour over the onions half a pint of thick gravy, well seasoned. Remove the fat when it boils, and add it to the kidneys, and let it all simmer for fifteen minutes.

Prepare some mashed potato and fry some rashers of bacon.

Dish the kidneys in the centre, with a border of mashed potato and garnish with the fried bacon.

ROGNONS DE MOUTON SAUTÉ À L'OSEILLE

℀. Kidneys, pepper, salt, cayenne, butter, sorrel, nutmeg.

Slice as many kidneys as are required, and season with pepper, salt and cayenne ; paprika can be added if desired. Fry them in butter.

Prepare a purée of sorrel by passing it through a sieve, adding pepper, salt, and a little nutmeg. Serve the sorrel in the middle of the dish and pour the kidneys round. Serve very hot.

ROGNONS AU MORILLE

℀. Veal kidney, butter, salt, mignonette pepper, mushrooms, shallot, half a wineglassful of sherry or madeira, chopped herbs, parsley, potato.

Take a good veal kidney, cut it lengthways, remove the fat and gristle, and chop it finely. Put into a pan with some butter, and fry it quickly with the salt and pepper.

In another pan fry some mushrooms with a tiny

piece of shallot, and add to them half a wineglass-ful of sherry or madeira, some chopped herbs, and parsley.

Fry the kidney and mushrooms together for a few minutes, and serve very hot in an earthen-ware casserole, with potato straws handed sepa-rately.

STEWED KIDNEYS

ℂ Half a pound of beef or mutton kidneys, pint of stock, one small onion, two ounces of butter, bunch of herbs, flour, pepper and salt.

Fry the kidneys (which should be sliced) in the butter, then add sufficient flour to thicken. When a good brown, put the kidneys and gravy into a marmite, add the stock, herbs, and the sliced onion. Cover and stew for three hours.

OXTAIL

ℂ Oxtail, bacon, onions, carrots, turnips, bay-leaf, clove of garlic, thyme, and basil.

Blanch an oxtail and cut it up, then put it into an earthenware casserole with the onions, car-rots, turnips, a bunch of herbs, a clove of garlic, a bayleaf, thyme, basil, and two cloves. Just cover the whole with stock or water, put pieces of bacon on the top, cover with the lid, and put in a very slow oven for four or five hours, watch-ing often to see that it does not get too dry.

Serve in its own casserole with a purée of lentils or haricot beans.

STEWED OXTAIL

℃. One oxtail, one large onion, one pound of tomatoes, bunch of herbs, two cloves, one dessertspoonful of lemon juice, butter and flour.

Cut up the oxtail and put into a casserole ; just cover with water, and let it boil. Remove the scum, and add the onion in slices, and all the seasoning. Put on the lid and stew gently for two hours, then add the tomatoes, and let it simmer for another thirty minutes.

Strain off the gravy and add the butter and flour made into a roux to thicken ; squeeze a dessertspoonful of lemon juice into it, and pour back into the casserole.

Boil the whole for another fifteen minutes, and serve in the casserole.

BRAINS

BRAINS PIQUANTE

℃. Brains, a little ham, slices of beetroot, onion, one gill of stock, two tablespoonfuls of white wine, salt, pepper, parsley.

Scald the brains in boiling water, then boil them, with two slices of chopped ham, slices of beetroot and onion, a bayleaf, a little parsley, salt, pepper, in the stock and wine for thirty minutes.

Serve the brains with sauce piquante.

VIII
COLD SUPPER DISHES

"'I do not think what you have tasted so far of my cooking deserves so high a eulogy, else what will you have left to say about those dishes on your left—those heavenly roast chickens stuffed with pistachios, almonds, rice, raisins, pepper, cinnamon, and paste of lamb? Their aroma, my friend, their aroma!' 'Allah be good to us,' said my brother; 'never was such an aroma! The birds are the soul of all savour and their stuffing a poem.'"

CHAPTER VIII

COLD SUPPER DISHES

THIS chapter has been compiled to help the hostess who wants to be able to prepare Sunday evening supper the day before. On long, light summer evenings a cold late supper can be the pleasantest meal in the week, but it ought to be restful for the hostess as well as for her guests, and if the mind of the cook won't rise above " the remains of the joint and a trifle," the task of providing a more imaginative meal involves the effort of chasing elusive ideas through many cookery books.

Salads, of course, must be made at the last moment, except fruit salads, which are improved by being prepared the day before.

Creams and jellies have a chapter to themselves and are not included in this one.

MAYONNAISE OF COD

℀ Cod, mayonnaise sauce, gelatine.

Cook some cod and break it into squares ; coat them with thick green mayonnaise sauce, which can be made still thicker with the addition of a little gelatine (two sheets to half a pint).

Dissolve the gelatine in a little water and add it very slowly to the oil which will be used for the mayonnaise.

When the sauce has set, arrange the fish in a square silver entrée dish ; decorate it with truffles, chopped yolk of egg, and surround it with a green salad.

COLD CRAB SOUFFLÉ

℘ One large crab, four leaves of gelatine, mayonnaise sauce, lettuce, tomato, aspic jelly.

Boil the crab, take all the meat except that from one claw. Mix it in a bowl with pepper and salt to flavour, moisten it with equal quantities of mayonnaise sauce and aspic jelly, and add the dissolved gelatine.

Serve it on a salad of lettuce and tomato slices.

COLD LOBSTER SOUFFLÉ

℘ One lobster, not less than one pound in weight, four leaves of gelatine, quarter of a pint of cream, one lettuce, one hard-boiled egg, one tomato, a little mayonnaise sauce, two tablespoonfuls of milk, half an ounce of butter.

Extract all the lobster meat from the shell. Whip the cream well. Break up the shell, pound it, and let it simmer with the milk and butter, then let it get cold.

Keep a little of the lobster meat for decoration, and mince the rest of the meat finely ; mix it with the whipped cream, flavour it with pepper and salt, and add to it, cold, the liquor the shell has made. The liquor must be strained with the cream through muslin. Dissolve the gelatine and stir it into the lobster cream.

Make a salad of the lettuce leaves, slices of

hard-boiled egg and tomato (which should be skinned), and mayonnaise sauce.

Arrange the lobster cream on the salad, and decorate it with the pieces of lobster meat, and serve.

HADDOCK À LA MAXIMILIAN

℃. Scrape all the flesh from a good-sized smoked haddock after it is cooked, and dish it in a mound.

Prepare a thick Tartare sauce ; pour it over the haddock purée, and leave to get cold.

Make a salad of cold tomatoes cut in slices, chopped tarragon, and hard-boiled egg, and make a wall of this salad round the purée.

COLD GREY MULLETS

℃. Grey mullets, one gill white wine, six leaves of gelatine, two oranges, two lemons, onion, a bayleaf, salt and pepper.

Boil the fish in enough water to cover them, with the onion, and bayleaf, the wine and gelatine. When cooked, put the fish into the dish it is to be served in, slice the oranges and lemons, removing the pips but not the skins. Cover the fish with slices of the oranges and lemons ; pour over it the juice the fish was boiled in, and serve it cold.

COLD RED MULLETS

℃. Red mullets, flour, oil, small onion, clove of garlic, one gill of vinegar, a bayleaf, a little tarragon, sprig of fennel and rosemary, salt.

Flour the fish and fry them in oil. Put them on a dish.

In the oil fry some chopped onion and garlic, and when they are brown sift in a tablespoonful of flour. Stir in the vinegar, add the herbs, cook it till it is thick, then pour it over the fish. Serve cold. With this sauce over it the fish will keep for two or three days.

FILLETED HADDOCK WITH MAYONNAISE

℩ Fillet a fresh haddock, rub it over with lemon juice, and cook it for fifteen minutes in a moderate oven rolled in buttered paper. Take it out and let it get cold.

Make a very thick mayonnaise sauce. Arrange the fillets on a dish, pour the mayonnaise over it, arrange rows of capers on the top of the fish, and decorate it with lettuce and cucumber.

SARDINE SALAD

℩ Sardines, lettuce, cress, chervil, capers, two hard-boiled eggs, oil, lemon juice.

Divide the sardines into pieces, removing the backbones and tails. Put them into a salad bowl with lettuce leaves, cress, chervil, and a few chopped-up capers. Slice the hard-boiled eggs into rings, pound the yolks with salt, pepper, a little cayenne and a pinch of mustard.

Make a salad dressing of salad oil and lemon juice in the proportion of three spoonfuls of oil to two of lemon. Mix the salad well, and garnish the dish with slices of lemon and pickled nasturtium seeds.

SOLE SANDWICHES

℃ Fillet a sole and cook it between two plates in the oven, with a little butter, milk, pepper and salt. Let it get cold.

Cut some thin slices of brown bread and butter, lay a thin fillet between, sprinkle the fish with powdered parsley, and serve the sandwiches piled up on a dish with cold watercress as decoration.

EGG CREAMS IN POTS

℃ Eggs, half an ounce of gelatine, a quarter of a pint of cream, two ounces of grated cheese, salt, pepper, and cayenne.

Hard boil the eggs, allowing one egg for two people. Shell them and chop them finely. Heat the milk, dissolve the gelatine in a little of it, and add it to the rest ; add the cheese, pepper and salt. Stir it all over the fire, remove it, and when it is cool mix in the cream whipped stiffly.

Place a little heap of the egg in the pipkin, and surround it with the mixture, sprinkle it with chopped parsley and serve it very cold.

A salad should be handed with them.

GROUSE SALAD

℃ Shallots, chopped tarragon and chervil, castor sugar, eggs, pepper, salt, cayenne, salad oil, chilli vinegar, a quarter of a pint of cream.

Mince two shallots finely and mix them with seven teaspoonfuls of chopped tarragon and chervil, five dessertspoonfuls of castor sugar, the yolks of two eggs, five saltspoonfuls of mixed pepper and salt, and a pinch of cayenne. Mix all this well with twelve tablespoonfuls of salad oil and six dessertspoonfuls of chilli vinegar. And finally a quarter of a pint of whipped cream.

Make a border of hard-boiled eggs, put the pieces of grouse in the middle; decorate them with beetroot and pieces of anchovy, and pour the sauce over the grouse.

ŒUFS MOLLETS WITH GREEN SAUCE

℄. Boil as many eggs as are required until the yolks have just set (not more than five minutes). Peel them and serve them whole covered with a green sauce—either hot or cold. (See page 14.)

SPINACH AND EGG SALAD

℄. Young spinach leaves, a few spring onions, hard-boiled eggs, oil, vinegar, salt and pepper.

Wash and dry the young spinach leaves; mix them with a little chopped spring onions. Make a salad dressing of a little vinegar, plenty of oil, salt and pepper to taste. Mix it well, and put it in a salad bowl with slices of hard-boiled eggs.

TIMBALE OF SPINACH

℄. Cook the spinach in a bain-marie in its own juice, without the addition of any water. Drain and chop it, and pass it through a colander. Add a squeeze of lemon juice and a very little finely chopped onion and celery.

Press it into a mould, and serve it very cold, decorated with slices of hard-boiled egg.

COLD PURÉE OF SPINACH GARNISHED WITH GLACÉ CHERRIES

℘ Make a purée of spinach by draining and chopping it very finely without passing it through a sieve. Put it on ice, and serve it in a silver dish, decorated with glacé cherries.

Hand with it slices of cold tongue served on lettuce leaves on a long dish.

AGNEAU À LA MARIE

℘ Cut some slices from a cooked or uncooked leg of lamb. If uncooked, braise them very slowly with vegetables and stock till tender.

Prepare a thick curry sauce, and thickly coat the slices of lamb with it. Leave them to get cold and dish them round a mound of cold cooked rice. Decorate them with stuffed olives, and serve them with chutney.

COTELETTES D'AGNEAU À LA CHATELAINE

℘ Stew the best end of a neck of mutton whole with vegetables, seasoning and spice. When cooked, leave it to get cold, then separate the cutlets and trim them neatly, cutting away any superfluous fat.

Prepare a thick Soubise sauce, and thickly coat each cutlet with it. Dish them round a green salad, and serve them with a compôte of cherries or prunes. (Soubise sauce, page 23).

If preferred, cold devil sauce can be substituted for the onion sauce, in which case the sauce is served separately and the cutlets are coated with chopped parsley mixed with butter.

WESTPHALIA LOAVES

℄ Lean ham, potatoes, butter, salt, pepper, eggs.

Grate four ounces of lean ham, cook and mash one pound of potatoes, mix it with the ham, and add one ounce of butter, salt, pepper, and two eggs to bind all the ingredients. Mould it into loaves and fry them.

Serve them cold, decorated with parsley.

COLD ROLLED VEAL

℄ Five pounds of best end neck of veal (boned), one egg, one ounce of butter, a little bacon, one tablespoonful of parsley, cloves, bayleaves, a quarter of a pound of breadcrumbs, one onion, nutmeg, mace, lemon, thyme, pepper and salt.

Make the veal the same thickness by cutting nearly through the thick part of the veal horizontally as it lies on the table, and doubling the cut slice on to the thinner side.

Take about five ounces of the veal to make

the stuffing, chopping it finely (after freeing it from skin and gristle), with the parsley, thyme, a small slice of lean bacon, and a little piece of onion. Then pound it well with the butter, a little grated nutmeg, salt and pepper, and the breadcrumbs, and bind it with the beaten egg. When well mixed, spread the stuffing on the veal, and on the stuffing lay two or three rashers of bacon ; then roll the veal up tightly, fasten it securely, tying it round with tape and stitching it if necessary. Put it in a stewpan as small as will take it ; and nearly cover it with stock or, failing stock, water. Add to the pan any scraps of veal or bacon, parsley and thyme that are left over, the onion and cloves, bayleaves, and a piece of celery if possible. Let it simmer for two hours, and let it get nearly cold in the pan. Press it between two dishes.

Before serving cold, cut off the tapes and extract the thread that has sewn the rent. The stock will make an excellent soup.

TIMBALE OF VEAL

¶ One pound of veal, two tablespoonfuls of tomato sauce, one pint of stock, one teaspoonful of curry powder, two ounces of butter, one large onion, two ounces of rice.

Mince the veal and the onion, and fry it till it is a pale brown, in butter. Add the rest, and let it simmer till all the stock is absorbed. Mix it thoroughly and press it tightly into a mould.

Turn it out the next day, and serve it in a silver dish, decorated with tomato and watercress.

Weights should be put on the top of the mould to press the mixture down.

COLD PRESSED BEEF

℃. Six or eight pounds of brisket of beef, two carrots, two onions, two turnips, twenty peppercorns, two cloves.

Take from six to eight pounds of brisket of beef, which has been in brine for a few days. Put it in a large saucepan of warm water, with the carrots, onions and turnips all cut up small, twenty peppercorns and two cloves. Boil it very gently for seven or eight hours, or until the meat comes away from the bone. Slip out the bones when cooked, roll it in a cloth, and press it between two plates with heavy weights on the top.

Next day dissolve half an ounce of meat glaze in a tablespoonful of hot water, and brush this over the meat.

FILETS DE VOLAILLE À LA NESSELRODE

℃. Cut up a plump chicken and boil it in the French way with vegetables. When cooked, remove the pieces and strain them. Put them on one side.

Now prepare a poulette sauce, to which some of the liquor in which the chicken has been boiled has been added. Make it fairly thick.

Arrange the pieces of chicken in a circle on a large round dish, with a ring of slices of tongue in front of it, and a ring of hard-boiled eggs behind it. Leave the centre free. Pour the poulette sauce over the chicken.

Prepare a green salad, fill the centre with it and pour a thick green mayonnaise sauce over it. Serve it very cold.

CREAM OF RABBIT

℃. Rabbit, butter, a quarter of a pint of cream, pepper, salt, nutmeg, gelatine, cucumber, lettuce.

Cut up a rabbit and put it into a stewpan with two ounces of butter, cooking it for about twenty minutes without allowing it to get brown. Then take the meat off the bones and pound it in a mortar, and pass it through a sieve. Add to it a quarter of a pint of cream, pepper, salt, nutmeg, and a little dissolved gelatine. Put it into a mould and steam it for one hour. Turn it out when cold. Decorate it with cucumber and lettuce, and cover it with a rather thick Béchamel sauce.

COLD ROAST DUCK
with a Purée of Green Peas

℃. Cut up a cold roast duck, and arrange it round a pyramid of green peas made into a purée. Garnish it with parsley.

STUFFED PIGEONS
with cold Orange Sauce

℃. Pigeons, ham, veal, salt, pepper, pistachio nuts, carrot, turnip, onion, peppercorns, bay-leaf, parsley.

Bone four large pigeons, retaining the liver and bones for stock. Cut the birds in half, spread them on a board, and stuff them with the following mixture :

Pound the livers of the birds with two ounces of ham and three ounces of raw veal minced. Add salt, pepper, and ten pistachio nuts finely chopped.

When the stuffing has been thickly spread on the birds, roll them and tie them up with tape.

Put the bones and trimmings in a stewpan with a carrot, turnip, sliced onion, some peppercorns, a bayleaf, parsley, pepper and salt. Place the rolled pigeons on the top, and pour in one pint of water, taking care that it does not touch the birds. Put the lid on and let them simmer for forty-five minutes. Take out the pigeons and leave them to cool. Pour a cold orange sauce over them, and serve them on lettuce leaves.

BEETROOT SALAD
An old French Recipe

℃ Take a large cooked beetroot, cut it up into thick round slices. Hollow out a cup in the middle of each slice, and put them to steep in tarragon vinegar for a few hours.

Hard boil one egg, add to it one anchovy, one gherkin, a few capers and a little parsley. Chop them all up very finely. Mix them with oil and vinegar, and fill each hollow in the slice of beetroot with this mixture. Arrange them carefully in a silver dish with pieces of whole parsley.

CARROT SALAD

℃. Six large carrots, a little chopped cooked onion, celery, bayleaves, a little white wine.

Cut the carrots in slices, boil and drain them. When cold and dry, put them in a salad bowl with a little chopped parsley, a little chopped cooked onion, two bayleaves, and pour over them a little white wine.

SALADE À L'INDIENNE

℃. Prepare a salad of chopped lettuce, mustard and cress, and sliced tomatoes. Fill the centre of a round dish with it, and surround it with a ring of sliced hard-boiled egg.

Make a thick curry sauce and pour over. Leave it to get cold, and serve it with brown bread sandwiches of chutney. (Curry sauce, page 12.)

LALLAH'S CHUTNEY

℃. Eighteen large apples peeled and sliced, half a pound of preserved ginger, one and a half pounds of coarse brown sugar, quarter of a pound of sultanas, quarter of a pound of chillies, one ounce of mustard seed, quarter of a pound of salt, three shallots, two Spanish onions, three pints of vinegar.

Pour the cold vinegar over the salt and sugar. Boil all the ingredients together till tender—at least for two or three hours.

Bottle for use.

IX

DISHES FROM
THE ARABIAN NIGHTS

" Kim slid ten thousand miles into slumber—thirty-six hours of the sleep that soaked like rain after drought.

"Then she fed him, so the house spun to her clamour. She caused fowls to be slain, she sent for vegetables, and the sober, slow-thinking gardener, nigh as old as she, sweated for it ; she took spices, and milk, and onions, with little fish from the brooks ; anon, limes for sherbets, quails of the pit, then chicken livers upon a skewer with sliced ginger between.

"' I have seen something of the world,' she said over the crowded trays, ' and there are but two sorts of women in it—those who take the strength out of a man and those who put it back.' "

CHAPTER IX

THE ARABIAN NIGHTS

THE people of the Arabian Nights are gourmets ; the stories are full of expatiations of the luscious things they had to eat. Food is treated as a fit subject for poetic ecstasy. The tastes and food of the East, of Arabia, Persia, India, and China remain unchanged to this day. " All people who have natural healthy appetites love sweets ; all children, all women, all Eastern people, whose tastes are not corrupted by gluttony and strong drinks," said Thackeray.

The following recipes are for some of the real " Arabian Nights " dishes, as delectable to-day as hundreds of years ago. For anyone who wants to spend an " Arabian Night," here is a dinner complete from Hors d'œuvre to Savoury :

MUNKACZINA
An Eastern Hors d'Oeuvre
Brought from the East by Anatole France

¶ Take one or more oranges and cut them in slices crossways. Peel the slices and remove the pips and white in the middle of the round.

Arrange a bed of slices of orange at the bottom of the dish, and cover with finely chopped onion.

On the onion place a bed of stoned black olives, and sprinkle them with red pepper, salt and olive oil.

CHERBAH

An Arabian Soup very much eaten in the bazaars of Algeria and Tunis

❧ Cut into large pieces an equal number of tomatoes and onions ; fry them lightly in butter, with a large sprig of wild mint chopped coarsely, also two or three small red pimentos. Season with salt and pepper. When slightly browned, add two pints of hot water, a piece of mutton and four ounces of dried apricots, and cook it slowly.

Before serving take out the mutton and cut it into tiny pieces ; add some cooked vermicelli, and serve.

An Arabian way of cooking
RED MULLET

❧ Fry in oil some cut-up tomatoes, onions, spices, shallots, salt, pepper, garlic, and a little curry powder, and saffron. Add a little flour and water.

Grill the red mullets slowly in this sauce, and serve them very hot.

COLD CHICKEN STUFFED WITH PISTACHIO NUTS

❧ Make a stuffing of two ounces of minced cold veal freed from fat and gristle and skin, the same quantity of suet or butter, half an ounce of minced apple, half an ounce of powdered almonds, a little coriander seed, two ounces of pistachio nuts chopped finely, a little sugar and a pinch of salt, a little lemon peel, and half a drachm of mace or allspice.

Pound all these together, adding the pistachio nuts last, and mix with it the beaten yolk and white of one egg.

Stuff the chicken with this and boil it whole with vegetables in the French way.

Serve it cold with a thick poulette sauce, to which some of the liquor in which the fowl was boiled has been added, poured over it.

Decorate it with chopped pistachio nuts, and serve it with a dish of cold well-seasoned rice.

EASTERN KEBABS

¶ Fillets of mutton or veal, onions, apples, rashers of bacon, salt, curry powder, powdered ginger, rice.

For each small fillet of mutton or veal, which should measure about two inches each way, take a slice of apple, a slice of bacon, and a slice of onion. Arrange them on a dish and sprinkle them with curry powder, ground ginger and salt. Leave them for a couple of hours. Then skewer them together, the bacon, apple, meat, and onion alternately, so that each piece of meat and bacon is between onion and apple. Cover them with greased paper and bake them for an hour and a half.

Remove the skewers and serve them with rice like curry.

Victor Marguerite's Recipe
MOUSSAKA ARABIAN

⚓ Cut up aubergines lengthways, and leave them in a basin covered up. An hour later wash them and dry them, and fry them in butter till brown.

Fry also some small pieces of mutton with plenty of seasoning. Then in a round saucepan arrange layers of aubergine and of mutton; moisten it with stock and cook it in the oven.

Serve it with a tomato sauce and rice cooked as follows :

Put the rice into a large saucepan of salted boiling water, and boil it for fifteen minutes. Cook it very quickly, then take it out, drain it, and sauté it in butter; then put into another saucepan with the same amount of water as rice, and cook it till all the water is absorbed, very quickly, with the lid on.

IMARU BAYELDI

⚓ Choose five straight egg plants, cut off the stems and skin them from end to end, leaving about an inch of skin all round lengthways to hold them together.

Shred finely one pound of onions, sauté them in oil till a golden brown, and add three chopped-up tomatoes, a clove of garlic, and a handful of chopped parsley.

Put the aubergines in a pan, pour over them the fried vegetables, and cover them with stock or water. When cooked carefully remove the egg plants, place them on a dish, and with a spoon cut the body of the aubergine in half lengthways, leaving the strip of skin intact, and in between the two halves of the aubergine put the onion mixture.

Serve hot.

PISSALADINA

℃, Get from the baker a piece of uncooked bread ; pull it out and spread a plate with it. Fry in olive oil some chopped onions, but do not brown them. When cooked into a purée pour it on the paste, put black olives on the top, and decorate it with fillets of anchovy. Bake it and eat it hot.

BULGARIAN CREAM

℃, One quart of milk, a quarter of a pint of rose water, cream of almonds, five ounces of castor sugar, one ounce of gelatine.

First soak the gelatine in the milk, and stir it over the fire until it is melted ; add the sugar.

Take three saucers, and pour an equal amount of the mixture into each, sprinkling a little rose water over each. Let them set, remove the mixture carefully from the saucers, and place the contents of all three saucers in a round glass or china bowl one above the other, with a layer of cream of almonds between each mould.

Pour the rest of the rosewater over all.

Devonshire cream can be substituted for cream of almonds.

SESAME CAKES

℃ Three-quarters of a pound of flour, six eggs, quarter of a pound of lard, quarter of a pound of castor sugar, three tablespoonfuls of sesame seed ; cinnamon.

Cream the lard and sugar with a wooden spoon. Beat the yolks of the eggs, mixing in the crushed sesame seed, and add this to the sugar and lard. Mix it well, then stir in the flour. Arrange it in little mounds on greased paper in a baking tin, and bake them till they are faintly coloured.

ŒUFS À LA CONSTANTINOPOLITAINE

℃ Mix in equal proportions olive oil and Turkish coffee. Put into this mixture as many eggs as are required, in their shells, and cook them *very* slowly for twelve hours at least. After a long time the mixture penetrates the shells, makes the whites of the eggs amber colour, and the yolks the colour of saffron, and give to them a flavour of chestnuts. Serve.

X
RICE AND OTHER CEREALS

" Among other succulencies was a dish with garlic called ' rozbaja,' which has a great reputation and is exceedingly delicious if the rice, which is the basis of it, be cooked to a turn, and both the garlic and the aromatic seasoning be apportioned with nicety."

CHAPTER X

RICE AND OTHER CEREALS

PATNA rice is used for curries and savouries, and Carolina rice for sweet puddings. They are cooked quite differently. The plain boiled rice which is eaten with curry should always be cooked in boiling water on a quick fire and in a very large pan ; a little lemon juice should be added to the water, and a handful of salt. After ten minutes' boiling (it should not be boiled till it is sticky), strain it and put a little butter with it, and leave it to dry in a colander on the fire ; stir it occasionally with a fork.

Carolina rice should be cooked in a double saucepan—two tablespoonfuls to a pint of milk —very slowly until all the milk has been absorbed, or it should be put into a very slow oven. Both baking or boiling should take three or four hours.

The perfect milk pudding is put into the oven at night after the dinner is cooked, and should stay there all night and cook all the next morning till lunch time. It will then be brown all through and will taste like cream.

As it is extravagant to cook a milk pudding in this way on a gas stove, a hay box is an admirable substitute for a kitchen range.

The dislike of so many children for milk puddings—a prejudice which often remains with them through life—arises simply because the children have been given badly cooked puddings, lumpy tapioca and watery rice.

RICE À L'ITALIENNE

℠ Four ounces of rice, butter, pepper, salt, tomato, two ounces of Parmesan cheese.

Cook four ounces of rice in boiling water ; strain it well and stir into it one ounce of butter, and pepper and salt to taste. Moisten it with the pulp of ripe tomatoes. Stir it till the rice is all coloured with the tomato juice, and then add two ounces of grated Parmesan cheese. Stir it over the fire till the cheese is melted, and serve hot.

SAVOURY RICE

℠ Rice, butter, parsley, horseradish, chives, chervil, herbs, salt and pepper.

Put some rice in a fireproof dish with salt and water, and bake it as if it were a milk pudding. When it is half-cooked add chopped chives, chervil, herbs and parsley, and a little horse-radish. Stir it, cover it with a layer of bread-crumbs, and morsels of butter, and finish baking.

Another Recipe for
SAVOURY RICE

℠ Half a pound of rice, one pound of tomatoes, half a pound of potatoes, two ounces of ham, a quarter of a pound of onions, two chicken livers (or a sausage), a little butter.

Chop up the onion, ham and chicken livers or sausage ; fry them in butter. Cut the potatoes and tomatoes into small cubes. Boil the rice and drain it.

Half fill a fireproof casserole with brown stock, add the fried ingredients, also the raw potatoes and tomatoes, and let it simmer for ten minutes ; then stir in the cooked rice, cover the dish, and bake it for twenty minutes. Serve it hot in the dish it has been cooked in.

There must be sufficient stock, for the rice when finished must not be dry.

CROUSTADES DE RIZ

℃ Seven ounces of rice, white stock, one ounce of butter, one ounce of flour, half a pint of milk, salt, pepper, yolk of one egg, a little nutmeg.

Cook the rice in white stock. Make a white sauce with half a pint of milk, the butter and flour ; when the butter and flour are worked together into a smooth paste, add the milk by degrees. Thicken it by reducing it a little and adding the yolk of an egg well beaten. Flavour with a little grated nutmeg, salt and pepper. When the rice is a little cool, mix it with the sauce.

Have ready a buttered dish, spread the rice on this to a depth of three inches, cover it with a buttered paper, and a dish on the top of it to press it down firmly. When it is cold, cut it in round pieces, take out the centre from each piece ; brush these little cases with egg, breadcrumb them, and fry them in deep boiling fat.

RICE AND GREEN PEAS

℀ Cupful of boiled rice, cupful of young peas (boiled), one onion, parsley.

Chop the onion and parsley and fry them together. Have the rice and peas ready, each boiled separately and well drained. Stir the rice and peas into the pan with the onion, cook them and serve them hot.

RIZ Á LA MAÎTRE D'HÔTEL

℀ Four ounces of rice, three onions, one potato, quarter of a pound of butter, the white of one egg, one stick of celery, spoonful of mixed herbs, salt, pepper, one pint of water.

Boil the rice with the chopped onion, celery and potato in the water with salt and pepper until the rice has absorbed the water. Then stir in the butter, the herbs, and the white of egg beaten stiffly. Well butter a pudding basin and steam the mixture in it for two hours. Serve it hot with maître d'hôtel sauce.

RISOTTO À LA MILANAISE

℀ Six ounces of rice, one onion, two tomatoes, yolks of two eggs, one and a half ounces of Parmesan, pepper, salt, brown stock or gravy, butter.

Boil the rice ; chop the onion and fry it in butter. Boil the tomatoes till they are soft, peel them and beat them up with the yolks of two eggs, pepper and salt and the grated cheese. Mix this with the rice and put it in a saucepan on the fire till it is cooked. Add enough gravy to moisten it all, and serve it hot.

PILAUF

℄ One cupful of Patna rice, one cupful of stock, one cupful of tomato juice or pulp, pepper and salt.

Let the stock and tomato juice (flavoured with sufficient pepper and salt) boil, and then throw in the rice. Cook it with the lid off and shake the pan. When the rice has absorbed all the liquid, add a lump of butter and shake it till this is well melted. Serve hot.

Sour milk served in another dish is the correct accompaniment.

TIMBALE OF RICE

℄ A cupful of rice, one onion, a few nuts, the whites of two eggs, butter,

Boil the rice in white stock, and then add the onion and parsley chopped very small, the nuts and a little butter. Well whip the whites of the eggs and mix them in, and put the rice into a buttered mould. Steam it for an hour and a half. Turn it out to serve. Serve it hot with tomato sauce and a little grated horseradish.

MINESTRA ALLA CAPUCINA

℄ Wash, pound, and fry an anchovy in butter, with an onion cut in half, and four ounces of rice. Add salt and pepper to taste, and when the rice is a pale brown take out the onion and add the stock until the dish is of the thickness of rice pudding.

RICE IN RED WINE

℄ One and a half pounds of apples, quarter of a pint of red wine, a quarter of a pound of sugar, a quarter of a pound of rice.

Reduce the apples to a purée, and flavour them with lemon peel. Boil a quarter of a pound of Carolina rice in water, and then strain it.

Prepare a thick syrup by boiling a quarter of a pound of sugar with a half cupful of water. Put the rice into the syrup and mix it well ; add a quarter of a pint of claret.

Sprinkle a wetted mould with icing sugar, and put at the bottom a layer of apple purée, then a layer of rice, and so on till it is full. When it is set turn it out and pour over it a syrup of red wine and sugar. Put a ring of apple compôte round the shape.

RIZ MERINGUÉE

℄ Carolina rice, milk, lemon, cream, ratafia biscuits, brown sugar, eggs.

Put into a double saucepan a quart of milk, the grated rind of one lemon, and six ounces Carolina rice, and let it cook very slowly till the rice has absorbed the milk (about two hours), then take it off the fire and add a quarter of a pint of cream, and let it simmer again for a little. Remove it from the fire, and add to it six crushed ratafia biscuits and four ounces of brown sugar. Mix all well together, then whip the whites of three eggs very stiffly, and stir it quickly into the rice. Pour the mixture into a soufflé dish, and set it on a slow fire. Sprinkle sugar over it when it is nearly done, brown it with a salamander, and serve.

RICE À L'IMPERATRICE

⁋ A teacupful of rice, one and a half pints of milk, half a pound of sugar (or to taste), a vanilla pod, a little Kirsch, some preserved fruits, some cherries, an apricot, angelica, small cubes of pineapple, mixed peel, a greengage or other candied fruits.

Soak the rice in the milk with vanilla and sugar. Cook the rice, and while it is cooking soak the preserved fruits, cut into small pieces, in a little Kirsch. When the rice is cooked (it should be soft but not squashy), stir in the fruits and a liqueur glassful of Kirsch. Pour the mixture into a buttered mould and set it aside on ice to cool. Turn it out of the mould and serve it cold with a syrup made from red currant jelly.

The Eastern way of eating Rice
RICE CREAM POWDERED WITH SUGAR AND CINNAMON

⁋ Put two tablespoonfuls of rice into a pint of cold milk with six lumps of sugar and a vanilla pod. Cook it in a double saucepan very slowly (for three or four hours) till all the milk is absorbed. Then pour it into a dish, and when cold mix it with a little cold cream or milk.

Serve in a silver dish and sprinkle it with dark crushed sugar candy and a little cinnamon.

MACARONI

Macaroni must be cooked in boiling water with plenty of salt in it, and should not be boiled more than twenty minutes.

This is the best way of making macaroni cheese. The French call it

MACARONI À LA CRÉME

℀ Half a pound of macaroni, a quarter of a pound of Gruyère cheese, a piece of butter the size of an egg, a tablespoonful of flour, half a pint of milk; salt and pepper.

Break the macaroni into pieces about three inches long; boil them for twenty minutes in boiling water on a quick fire with a handful of salt in it. Then pour it through a colander and drain it. (The water it has boiled in will do for cooking fish or vegetables in.)

Put the macaroni back in the empty pan to keep it hot. Melt the butter in a small saucepan, stir in the flour, working it into a smooth paste with a wooden spoon; gradually stir in half a pint of boiling milk. Let it cook for ten minutes, being careful that no lumps form in it; then add the grated cheese, with pepper and salt to taste. When it has boiled up, put it over the macaroni, mix it well, and serve it very hot.

An Italian way of cooking
MACARONI

❡ Three-quarters of a pound of macaroni, one onion, six anchovies, one gill of white wine, one gill of fish stock or water, Parmesan cheese.

Half boil the macaroni. Chop the onion and anchovies very finely, also a little parsley. Put this in a pan with a little butter and fry it for about seven minutes. Put the macaroni in a saucepan with one gill of white wine and one gill of the liquor the fish has been cooked in ; add the onion and the anchovy mixture, and a little pepper, and let it simmer for twenty minutes. Serve hot with a little grated Parmesan cheese sifted over it.

MACARONI À LA CARDINALE

❡ Shell two or three dozen shrimps ; heat them in a white Béchamel sauce, with some cooked and chopped mushrooms. Keep this hot, and prepare some macaroni. Add it to the sauce, season it with pepper, salt, and paprika, and serve.

MINESTRONE À LA MILANESE

❡ Boil any vegetables that are handy in stock, and add pieces of bacon and some onions first fried in butter, chopped parsley, a clove of garlic, which has been bruised, and either rice or macaroni.

Put in first the vegetables requiring the most cooking, and do not make the broth too thin. Leave the garlic in for fifteen minutes only.

An Eighteenth-Century Recipe
TO MAKE A TIPSY LOAF

℄ Take a flat loaf of French bread hot out of the oven, rasp it, and pour a half a pint of red wine upon it. Cover it up close for half an hour.

Boil four ounces of macaroni in water till it is soft, and lay it upon a sieve to drain ; then put butter the size of a walnut into it, and as much cream as it will take ; then scrape in six ounces of Parmesan cheese : shake it about in the tossing pan till the mixture is like a fine custard. Then pour it hot upon the loaf ; brown it with a salamander, and serve it up.

It is a pretty dish for supper.

TIMBALE OF MACARONI

℄ Short crust pastry, four ounces of macaroni, one ounce of flour, salt, pepper and cayenne, half a pound of mushrooms, one ounce of butter, lemon juice, one tablespoonful of unsweetened Libby's milk.

Line a greased cake tin with short pastry ; boil the macaroni and strain it. Skin and cut off the tops of the stalks of the mushrooms. Melt the butter and cook the mushrooms in it ; when cooked remove them and chop them up. Add the flour to half a pint of the water in which the macaroni was boiled, and cook it till it thickens. Add the macaroni, the chopped mushrooms, condensed milk, a squeeze of lemon juice, salt, pepper and cayenne. Put all these into the tin lined with pastry ; put on a pastry top, and bake it in a fairly hot oven for about thirty minutes. Turn it out and serve very hot.

If mushrooms are unobtainable, tomatoes can be used instead, or minced beef.

MACARONI SALAD

⁋ Half a pound of macaroni, one onion, one beetroot, salt and black pepper.

Boil the macaroni, and cut the cooked beetroot into thin slices ; mix them together, and pour over it a dressing of oil, vinegar, and finely chopped onion.

MACARONI AND ONIONS

⁋ Boil some macaroni in a large pan of boiling salted water for about fifteen minutes. Cut into rings the same quantity of onion and fry it in butter till tender, without browning it. Make a white sauce of flour, milk and butter, seasoned with nutmeg and a bayleaf. Place the onions in this and let them simmer for about twenty minutes. Remove the bayleaf and add the macaroni.

Make it very hot, and serve with grated cheese.

CASSEROLE OF BARLEY

⁋ Half a pound of pearl barley, one head of celery, one carrot, a quarter of a cauliflower; dumplings, two large onions, two leeks, one turnip, two ounces of butter; salt and pepper.

Soak the barley overnight. Cook it in a large pan with two quarts of water. Put the butter in a frying pan, cut the vegetables up small and fry them in it, add the parsley, and moisten it with water. Let it simmer till all is tender.

Make some dumplings and serve them in the ragout.

FRIED HOMINY

℀ Soak some hominy overnight and cook it the next day. Put it aside to get cool, and cut it into rounds and fry it in butter till brown.

Dust with pepper and salt, and serve.

TAPIOCA CREAM

℀ One and a half pints of milk, three heaped tablespoonfuls of tapioca, two eggs, vanilla to flavour, sugar to taste, angelica.

Boil the milk with a vanilla pod (or half) to flavour it ; add sugar to taste, and put in the tapioca. Let it cook very slowly. When it is nearly cooked, stir in some finely shredded angelica. When the mixture is of the consistency of thin porridge, take it off the fire and put it aside to cool.

Beat the eggs, and when the tapioca is lukewarm stir the eggs into it. Line a mould with caramelled sugar, pour in the tapioca, and cook it in a bain-marie.

Set it aside to cool ; turn it out and serve it cold.

CREAM OF TAPIOCA SOUP

℀ Two ounces of Groult's tapioca, one onion, pepper and salt, two tablespoonfuls of cream, one clove, one and a half pints of milk.

246

Boil the tapioca in the milk (to which one pint of water has been added) until smooth ; then add the onions, clove and seasoning, and let it simmer till all are cooked. Strain it, stir in the cream after it has been re-heated, and serve.

SEMOLINA CREAM

℄ One pint of milk, two ounces of semolina, four ounces of sugar, three yolks and two whites of eggs, one ounce of butter, lemon rind, one tablespoonful of water.

Heat the milk in a double saucepan with a piece of lemon rind in it to flavour it. Add the semolina and stir it, cooking it slowly till it forms a smooth paste, and then let it cool.

Caramel sugar a mould, using two ounces of sugar to one tablespoonful of water. Remove the lemon rind from the semolina ; add two ounces of sugar, the butter, and the beaten eggs. Stir it well, pour it into the mould, cover it with greased paper, and bake it for forty-five minutes.

Let it stand for a minute or two before turning it out. Can be served hot or cold.

EASTERN SAGO

℄ Two and a half ounces of sago, one and a quarter pints of milk, two lemons, six tablespoonfuls of golden syrup, a quarter of a pint of cream.

Boil the sago in the milk in a double saucepan on a very slow fire for two hours, with the rind of one lemon. Then add the golden syrup, and, when it is cooking, the juice of the two lemons. Pour it into a wetted mould, and serve with cream.

SAGO CREAM

℃. Boil two tablespoonfuls of Goult's sago in a double saucepan with a pint of milk and the rind of half a lemon, on a low fire for two and a half hours. Sweeten it with brown sugar, and when cool pour it into a dish. Chop some candied peel and sprinkle it over the top.

CORNFLOUR À LA CRÈME
(German)

℃. This is quite unlike cornflour as it is usually served.

Half a tablespoonful of cornflour to half a pint of milk is the proportion ; not a bit more cornflour is needed, or it will be too stiff.

Mix the cornflour to a paste with a little cold milk, bring the rest of the milk to the boil, then add the cornflour and boil it for ten minutes, *stirring all the time ;* then lift the pan off the fire and *stir for twenty minutes.* This is very important. Sugar or flavouring to taste.

KEESSEL
A Russian Sweet

℃. Pour into a saucepan one pound of apricot jam, add to it a cup of water, and a quarter of a pound of cornflour first mixed with a little cold water. Let it boil, stirring it all the time till it gets thick. Pour it into a bowl and serve it cold with Devonshire cream.

XI

POULTRY AND GAME

" The Captain had spread the cloth with great care, and was making some egg sauce in a little saucepan ; basting the fowl from time to time during the process with a strong interest as it turned and browned on a string before the fire. Having propped Florence up with cushions on the sofa, which was already wheeled into a warmer corner for her greater comfort, the Captain pursued his cooking with extraordinary skill, making hot gravy in a second little saucepan, boiling a handful of potatoes in a third, never forgetting the egg-sauce in the first, and making an impartial round of basting and stirring with the most useful of spoons every minute. Besides these cares, the Captain had to keep his eye on a diminutive frying pan in which some sausages were hissing and bubbling in a most musical manner ; and there never was such a radiant cook as the Captain looked in the height and heat of these functions, it being impossible to say whether his face or his glazed hat shone the brighter."

CHAPTER XI

POULTRY AND GAME

WHEN a philosophy of fashion is written, we shall learn (unless the philosopher shirks his job and leaves the subject of food unexplored) why the changes of taste are more marked among the fowl of the air than the fish of the sea. We no longer eat swans or peacocks, though from the time of the Romans till the sixteenth century in England, these birds were the most prized delicacies at every really important banquet. We no longer eat linnets and thrushes, and the art of serving four-and-twenty live blackbirds in a pie so that when the pie was opened the birds began to sing is forgotten so completely that the nursery rhyme that recalls it is taken as pure nonsense, instead of an interesting memory—fiction instead of historical fact. But our forefathers did actually accomplish the joke and regarded it as a fitting dish for a king.

When Charles II and his Queen were entertained at dinner by the Duke and Duchess of Buckingham in 1630, Jeffrey Hudson, the famous dwarf of his day, was served up in a great cold pie—as an improvement upon the singing blackbirds.

" Four-and-twenty blackbirds " is English culinary history. The French took cooking much too seriously to perpetuate such jokes. Their bird is essentially the chicken. Their idolized Henri IV probably owed his adoration as much to his desire that every Frenchman should have a chicken for his cooking-pot as to his military prowess.

The French excel in cooking chickens, but they rarely roast or boil them whole as we do (in fact, in Paris you can go out and buy a joint of chicken as one buys a joint of meat). They cut a bird into pieces and fry or fricassee them, and serve them with various sauces. When a French cook does roast a chicken it is generally delicately stuffed, and when it is partly cooked it is basted with butter rolled in breadcrumbs, mixed with herbs and grated lemon rind, basted with butter again ; again covered with seasoned breadcrumbs, and then finished in the oven.

The average Englishman thinks of chicken as a tasteless bird, but the French method of cooking it with herbs and frying it in butter brings out all the flavour.

CHICKEN
CHICKEN SUPRÊME

❡ Chicken, butter, pepper, salt, shallot, herbs.

Cut up a chicken and fry it in butter, with pepper and salt, for twenty-five minutes. Cook the legs first, as they will take longer. Just before it is cooked add a chopped shallot, a clove of garlic, and a few herbs.

In another pan prepare a Poulette sauce. Remove and drain the slices of fried chicken, then put them into a clean casserole, pour the poulette sauce over them, and cook them for ten minutes.   Serve very hot in the casserole.

POULET À LA PROVENÇAL

❧ Chicken, onions, parsley, olive oil, bayleaf, pepper and salt.

Cut up a chicken and put it into a casserole. Take a dozen small onions and a bunch of parsley, cut them up and add them to the chicken, making a bed of onions and parsley on which the pieces of chicken lie, and a layer of onions and parsley on the top of the chicken ; add a wineglass of olive oil, a bayleaf, pepper and salt. Put it on the fire and cook it very slowly.

When cooked, dress the onions in the middle of the dish with the chicken round, and pour a brown sauce over them.

COQ AU VIN

❧ One chicken, quarter of a pound of bacon, one ounce of butter, six small onions, half a pint of red wine, quarter of a pound of mushrooms, a bayleaf, parsley, a sprig of thyme, salt, pepper, a spoonful of flour.

Cut up a chicken into eight pieces. Cut up four ounces of fat bacon into small cubes and put them with a little butter and six small onions into an earthenware casserole on the fire. When the contents are coloured brown put in the pieces of chicken with the herbs and a few mushrooms. Cover the saucepan, and cook it over a good fire. Skim off superfluous fat. When the chicken is done, pour in the wine, add the salt and pepper. Thicken the sauce with a little butter and flour before serving.

When the chicken is cooked, serve it with the sauce poured over it (the herbs taken away), and garnished with sippets of fried bread and triangular slices of lemon.

THE AMERICAN WAY OF FRYING CHICKEN

℮. Chicken, two ounces of butter, breadcrumbs, bayleaves, lemon, garlic, parsley, cloves, one shallot, vinegar, one egg.

Cut up a young chicken and soak the pieces in water to which has been added salt and a dessertspoonful · of vinegar. Change the water three times, and into the last water put a clove of garlic stuck with a clove, two bayleaves, and a slice of lemon.

Drain the chicken, sprinkle each slice with flour, then in breadcrumbs which have been mixed with the chopped shallot, parsley, pepper, salt, grated lemon peel, and a well-beaten yolk of an egg.

Put the butter in a frying pan and fry the chicken till it is pale brown. Drain it and serve.

FRIED CHICKEN

℮. Cut up a chicken and fry it in butter, with pepper and salt, for twenty-five minutes. It should be a golden brown. Cook the legs first, as they will take longer than the rest.

Just before it is cooked add a few sweet herbs, a clove of garlic and a shallot, then stir into the pan a little flour to thicken the gravy, a small wineglassful of sherry, and a little stock.

Dish the chicken and pour the sauce over it.

POULET AU BLANC

℀. One chicken, two onions, one ounce of butter, the yolks of three eggs, two lemons, a bunch of herbs, a tablespoonful of flour.

Cut the fowl into eight pieces and boil it for three-quarters of an hour with the onions, herbs, and a handful of salt.

In a small saucepan melt a piece of butter the size of an egg, stir a tablespoonful of flour into it, and make a sauce with some of the water the chicken has boiled in. Stew it for ten minutes.

Beat up the yolks of three eggs, add the juice of two lemons, stir this into the sauce very slowly till it has the consistency of cream. If necessary add a little more salt and pepper.

Arrange the pieces of chicken on the dish it is to be served in, and serve it with the sauce covering it.

FRICASSEE OF CHICKEN WITH RICE

℀. Cut up a chicken and lay the pieces in tepid water for twenty minutes ; drain and wipe them. Put into a saucepan the pieces of chicken, a piece of butter, some parsley, a bayleaf and a carrot. Cover them with cold water, put on the lid, and boil slowly till tender—for about thirty-five minutes.

In another saucepan prepare a white Béchamel or a sauce Poulette. Take out the pieces of chicken, drain them, put them into the sauce and cook them for a few minutes. (Mushrooms, parsley, or shallots can be added to the sauce.)

Have ready boiled a quarter of a pound of Patna rice, well drained ; add this to the chicken, and cook it for a few minutes more.

POULET À LA TURQUE

℄. Chicken, butter, bacon, carrots, onions, parsley, nutmeg, pepper, salt, rice, raisins, prunes.

Cover a chicken with butter, and put it into a braising pan with twelve pieces of raw bacon, carrots, onions, parsley, nutmeg, pepper and salt, and cover it with a buttered paper. Cook it for one hour.

Then cook in different pans some rice, raisins and prunes. Make a curry sauce, and when the chicken is cooked put it on a long dish, pour the curry sauce over it, and put the rice, raisins and prunes in separate groups.

CHICKEN À LA CRÈME PAPRIKA

℄. One chicken, one large onion, a quarter of a pint of tomato sauce, a quarter of a pint of milk, a quarter of a pint of cream, salt, paprika.

Cut a chicken (which should be a tender young bird) into joints. Put the pieces to soak in cold water.

Take an earthenware fireproof dish with a lid. Cut an onion into rings and lightly fry them ; put them in the casserole with a dessertspoonful of salt and one of paprika, and a quarter of a pint of tomato sauce. Put in the pieces of chicken, cover the pot, and let it cook gently for an hour, stirring it every now and then. Then add a quarter of a pint of milk, and the same amount of cream, and stir it into the sauce ; do not let it boil. Serve the chicken very hot in the dish it has cooked in, garnished with slices of lemon.

POULET À LA VALENCIENNE

ℭ. Chicken, olive oil, two cloves of garlic, onion, three red chillies, tomatoes, rice, parsley, stock.

Put a wineglassful of olive oil in a casserole with two cloves of garlic. It must not burn or it will turn bitter and the dish is spoilt. Stir the garlic until fried.

Cut up the chicken and put it in, but be sure to keep on stirring it about. Whenever a sound of cracking is heard, stir again.

When the chicken is fried a golden brown, put in some chopped onion and three chopped red chillies, and go on stirring. If once the contents catch, the dish is ruined.

Put in some tomatoes cut in quarters, and some parsley, and then add two teacupfuls of

257

rice, and mix it all up. Cover the whole with hot stock ; let it boil once and then let it simmer by the side of the fire till the rice is cooked. It must not be covered up or the rice will become like a pudding instead of the grains remaining separate.

Add a little saffron and serve it in the dish in which it is cooked. Serve with it brown bread and butter sandwiches, with chutney in between.

CHICKEN À L'ESPAGNOLE

❡ One chicken, half a pint of Espagnole sauce (page 13), half a pound of lean bacon cut in thin rashers, half a pound of small button mushrooms ; oil, bread.

Cut the chicken into joints. Make the sauce, adding some of the mushrooms cooked, and keep it hot.

Cut a piece of bread half an inch thick for each piece of chicken, and fry it in butter till nicely brown. Fry the bacon and the mushrooms.

Dip the pieces of chicken in oil and grill them. Put each piece on a crouton of fried bread, garnish it with the bacon and mushrooms, and serve it with the sauce poured over the chicken.

BLANQUETTE DE VOLAILLE À LA RUSSE

❡ Cut as many slices as are required from the breast of a roasted fowl ; remove the skin and put it on one side.

Prepare a Béchamel sauce, and when cooked cut up a small cucumber into slices about a quarter of an inch thick. Stew them in the sauce and pour it over the chicken. Add a few table-spoonfuls of cream at the last moment.

CHICKEN CUSTARD

℃ Remove all the pickings from the remains of a cooked chicken and mince them very finely ; season it with pepper and salt and moisten it with a pint of stock. Beat up the yolks of two eggs and add these to the chicken and the stock. Pour the mixture into a soufflé dish and bake.

DUCK WITH ORANGE SAUCE

℃ Duck, orange, peppercorns.

Partly roast a duck, then cut it up but leave the pieces hanging together. Put it between two plates with the juice of two oranges poured over it, salt and peppercorns. Press it between the dishes and put it in the oven to finish cooking.

Turn it over while cooking, and when cooked serve it in its own sauce.

HARE

HARE WITH PRUNES AND RAISINS

℃ Hare, stock, onions, half a pound of prunes, a quarter of a pound of stoned raisins ; salt, pepper, sugar, red wine, red currant jelly.

259

Separate the back from the front of the hare. Cut up the front portion of the hare and fry it lightly, then add stock and six chopped onions, half a pound of prunes and a quarter of a pound of stoned raisins. Season it with salt and pepper, and cook it slowly in a covered casserole for an hour and a half. Uncover it, add a pinch of sugar, a glassful of red wine, and a spoonful of red currant jelly. Cook it with the lid off and reduce. Add to it the blood and the back part of the hare, which has been roasted separately.

Pour it all into a deep entrée dish, and serve boiling hot, surrounded with fried croutons of bread.

HARE À LA POLONOISE

¶ Hare, stock, red wine, olives, capers, thyme, bayleaf, cloves, garlic, vinegar, flour, and butter.

Cut up the hare, and strain the blood into a jug ; remove the liver. Put a large piece of butter into a frying pan with some flour, and make a roux. Lard the pieces of hare and fry them lightly in the roux with half a clove of garlic, two cloves, a little thyme, and a bayleaf. Put all these into a casserole and add a quarter of a pint of port wine, a quarter of a pint of stock, and a squeeze of lemon.

When nearly cooked add the blood, pound the liver and add it also, and boil the whole for two or three minutes. Stone a dozen olives, scald them and add them to the stew with three or four capers.

FILLETED HARE WITH CHERRY SAUCE

❡ Hare, preserved cherries, potatoes, carrots, onions, thyme, bayleaf, cloves, salt, pepper and stock.

Take the fillets off the back of a young hare, lard them well and place them in a dish with some sliced carrot and onion, and a seasoning of thyme, bayleaf, cloves, salt and pepper, and leave them overnight.

Take the rest of the flesh off the hare and make it into quenelles. Put a pint of stock into a saucepan with the bones and pickings, and let them simmer for three or four hours.

Place the fillets in a pan with the vegetables, add to them the stock made from the bones, and cook it very slowly for forty-five minutes. When cooked dish the fillets on a border of mashed potatoes, put the quenelles round, and strain the sauce on to some glacé cherries. Pour the sauce and cherries over the fillets, and serve.

TURKEY

THE ITALIAN WAY OF ROASTING TURKEY

❡ Make a stuffing for the turkey of three prunes, a quarter of a pound of sausage meat, three tablespoonfuls of chestnut purée, two slices of bacon, half a cooked pear. Fry them all for a few

261

minutes in butter; chop up the liver and gizzard and add it, with half a glass of Marsala.

After the turkey is stuffed, braise it for three-quarters of an hour with salt, butter, pieces of bacon, a blade of rosemary, one carrot, one onion, one turnip, three cloves, and a clove of garlic cut in half. Roast it in the oven and serve it with the sauce poured over it.

The garlic should be removed after ten minutes.

RABBIT

FRIED RABBIT

℀ Rabbit, butter, chopped parsley.

Cut up the rabbit into small joints, and fry it very slowly in butter till it is a golden brown. When cooked pour over it some hot melted butter, with chopped parsley, well seasoned with salt and pepper. Let the rabbit and sauce simmer for a few minutes.

Serve it very hot in a silver dish with green peas and bread sauce.

RABBIT À LA TARTARE

℀ Rabbit, lemon, parsley, onion, mace, peppercorns, one egg, mashed potatoes, breadcrumbs.

Cut up the rabbit and soak it for one hour in a mixture of the following ingredients:

Two tablespoonfuls of vinegar, two dessertspoonfuls of oil, half an onion sliced, a little mace, chopped parsley, bayleaf, lemon juice.

Remove the rabbit, wipe it, egg and bread-crumb it, and fry it in boiling oil or butter till it is golden brown.

Serve it with tartare sauce and mashed potatoes.

A RAGOUT OF RABBIT

℄ Rabbit, stock, butter, onions, bread, cloves, bacon, spice and herbs, chives, parsley, carrots, turnips, mushrooms.

Remove the liver and cut the rabbit up into large pieces. Lard them with bacon, and put more slices of bacon at the bottom of an earthen-ware casserole ; season them with salt and pepper, cut up onions, carrots and turnips, and add some herbs, parsley and spice, and place the pieces of rabbit in it ; put on a lid and stew it in the oven very slowly.

Make a stock with pieces of ham, one large onion, one carrot, and one turnip sliced and put it into another saucepan, and cook till they stick slightly to the bottom ; then add a little melted butter, sprinkle it with flour, and mix it all to-gether. Moisten it with a little water, add a few chopped mushrooms, some parsley, three cloves, three chives, and a few pieces of bread. Cook it slowly, then pound the livers and add them. Pass it through a sieve when cooked and pour the sauce into a third casserole. Remove the pieces of rabbit from the first casserole, put them in the third with the sauce, cook it for a few minutes, and serve.

PARTRIDGES

PERDRIX AUX CHOUX

℃. Partridge, cabbage, butter, onion, carrot, bacon, parsley, stock.

Divide a partridge into four.

Make a brown roux of flour and butter in a casserole, and put in the pieces of partridge, with a sliced carrot and onion, a little stock, some chopped parsley, and pepper and salt, and put it into a slow oven. Cover the partridge with slices of bacon.

Divide the cabbage in quarters and boil it in boiling salted water for ten minutes. Drain it and add it to the partridge and let it cook till tender.

Remove the partridge, cabbage and bacon. Reduce the liquid to a good gravy. Strain it, and pour over the partridge, which should be dished with the cabbage.

PARTRIDGES EN PAPILLOTES

℃. Partridges, mushrooms, parsley, shallots, butter, a little flour, stock, white wine, bacon.

Cut the partridges in half and fry them lightly in butter. Before they are quite cooked take them out of the pan. Into the butter the birds have been frying in, put some chopped mushrooms, chopped parsley, and chopped shallots, a little flour, salt, and spice ; moisten it with a little stock and a little white wine. Cook this sauce, reduce it till it thickens, and spread it on the halves of partridges. Cover the birds with rashers of fat bacon. Wrap each half-bird in oiled paper, and grill them for about twenty minutes over a gentle fire.

QUAILS

Quails come from Egypt. They are a kind of dwarf partridge. The French have various ways of cooking them, but the one way of the English is really the best.

❡ Draw and truss them as if they were pheasants. Tie a vine leaf cut to the size over each breast, and cover the vine leaf with a thin slice of fat bacon. The leaf and the bacon should be tied on together neatly.

Skewer them and roast them in the oven, or better still, before the fire, on slices of buttered toast. Baste well and cook fifteen minutes.

Put gravy under the birds and serve them on the toast, with watercress and crumbs.

BRAISED PHEASANT WITH CHESTNUT PURÉE

❡ Pheasant, butter, chestnuts, milk or cream.

Put the pheasant into an earthenware pot with one and a half ounces of butter ; rub into the cavity of the pheasant some powdered herbs,

salt, pepper, and half a clove of garlic. Brown
the bird slightly in the butter, then cover the
casserole and put it in the oven, basting it from
time to time with good stock in which the bird
is cooking. Remove the clove of garlic. Cook for
forty-five minutes, and serve it with a purée of
chestnuts.

PIGEONS

PIGEONS À LA GAUTIER
with Green Sauce

❧ Pigeons, white wine, butter, lemons, bacon.

Put two ounces of butter into a casserole with
the juice of one lemon to every two pigeons ;
add salt and pepper, and let the pigeons fry
lightly. Take it off the fire.

Put into another casserole some slices of bacon;
put the pigeons on this, and pour the butter
over them ; add a small glassful of white wine,
one tablespoonful of stock, and a bunch of herbs.
Cover the pigeons with fat bacon, and cook
them in the oven for about twenty minutes.

Serve them with a green sauce. (See page 14.)

STEWED PIGEONS AND MUSHROOMS

❧ Two pigeons, one slice of bacon, stock, half
a pound of mushrooms, a cup of claret.

Fry the pigeons for a few minutes in a casserole with the bacon and a small piece of butter ;
then add the wine, the mushrooms, a quarter
of a pint of stock, and a seasoning of pepper and

salt. Cover it up and stew it very gently either in the oven or on the top of the fire until it is cooked. Watch it from time to time to see it is not too dry, and if necessary add more stock.

When cooked strain the gravy, and add a thickening of brown roux and return the mushrooms to the sauce.

Dish the pigeons and pour the sauce over.

PIGEONS À LA TARTARE

℀ Pigeons, butter, breadcrumbs.

Singe and truss the pigeons as for boiling. Flatten them as thin as possible, but do not break their skins. Smear them with melted butter, pepper and salt, and dredge them with grated breadcrumbs. Grill thirty minutes.

Prepare a tartare sauce, pour it into the dish and place the pigeons on it.

WOODCOCK AND SNIPE

A little woodcock (Bécassine).

The French regard woodcock and snipe as the most delicious of all birds, and they can offer you no greater mark of their esteem than to give you

BÉCASSES BRULÉES AU RHUM À LA BACOUAISE

Here is Brillat Savarin's own recipe for it :

℀ Prepare the birds and lard them. Put them on

267

buttered toast rubbed with garlic, and roast them in front of a good fire. When cooked the flesh should be slightly red.

The birds should then be delicately carved in four pieces, and the insides removed with a spoon, pounded, and seasoned with pepper and salt. The paste is then spread on the birds, a glass of old rum is poured over them and set fire to, and while with one hand the rum is spooned up into the flame, with the other hand a fork is used to handle the separate joints and to ensure every bit of the bird coming under the blue flame. Serve them on a napkin, garnished with fried parsley.

BÉCASSINES À LA MINUTE

℀ Put the snipe in a pan with six ounces of butter, three chopped shallots, a bayleaf, a little grated nutmeg, salt and pepper. Toss them repeatedly over the fire until they are nearly done (about ten minutes), take them out of the pan, and put in their stead a tablespoonful of breadcrumbs, a wineglass of Madeira or sherry, and the juice of a lemon. Move the sauce quickly about with a wooden spoon, put the snipe into it, and serve them when they are done.

SALMI OF WOODCOCK

℀ Two woodcocks, three-quarters of a pint of stock, one onion, two or three cloves, one anchovy, butter, flour, cayenne, salt, claret, lemon.

Half roast two woodcocks, cut them up and put them in a stewpan with the stock, an onion with two or three cloves stuck in it, one anchovy, a piece of butter rolled in flour, cayenne pepper and salt. Do not let it boil, but it must simmer for twenty minutes.

Add a glass of claret and a squeeze of lemon. The livers and entrails should be bruised in the sauce.

ROAST CAPERCAILZIE

When other birds are expensive, capercailzie is an economical bird to buy. They are usually to be obtained at a reasonable price, and they are large birds with plenty of meat on them. Cooked in the following way they are excellent :

℄ The bird must be trussed and prepared for roasting in the ordinary way as for a chicken, then inside the bird put about a quarter of a pound of beefsteak. It improves the bird, and the steak is not wasted, for it can be used afterwards for some other dish. Put some rashers of fat bacon in the breast of the bird, and bake it in a moderate oven for an hour.

When the bird has roasted for three-quarters of an hour take off the bacon, sift flour over the breast, and baste the bird well.

Serve very hot with gravy, bread sauce, fried breadcrumbs, and garnish it with watercress.

XII
FRUIT

"....a heap
Of candied apple, quince, and plum, and gourd,
With jellies smoother than the creamy curd,
And lucent syrops, tinct with cinnamon ;
Manna and dates, in argosy transferr'd
From Fez ; and spiced dainties, every one
From silken Samarcand to cedar'd Lebanon."

CHAPTER XII

FRUIT

VERY few people eat enough fruit—except perhaps the French, who, being not only culinary artists but culinary scientists, have always appreciated the value of fruit as a food. In France and in foreign restaurants the fruit is chosen with as much care as the fish and poultry, and fruit is eaten as an entremets, an integral part of the meal, instead of being a mere afterthought in the form of dessert.

In Italy fruit and cream cheese are served together and make a happy combination. Travellers in Spain, unaccustomed to Spanish cooking and the flavour of Spanish oil, welcome the generous basket of fruit that appears at every restaurant dinner—the native oranges, and almonds, and great bunches of Valencia raisins— an ample meal in themselves.

Fresh fruit should be eaten every day, and a good way to ensure it being always on the table is to use it as a table decoration. The fruits of our temperate climates—grapes, oranges, apples, peaches, apricots, plums—are very beautiful. In the winter, when flowers are expensive, a silver dish of oranges and lemons is as charming to look upon as flowers ; and there are lovely Venetian glass bowls with covers to be bought in London now, and these, filled with fruit which, seen through the glass, look mysterious and fascinating, make exquisite table decorations.

APPLES

" When God had made the oak trees,
    And the beeches and the pines,
And the flowers and the grasses,
    And the tendrils of the vines ;
He saw that there was wanting
    A something in His plan,
And He made the little apples
    The little cider apples,
The sharp, sour cider apples,
    To prove His love for man."

Apples, the most useful and popular fruit in the world, have the glamour of descent to us from the Golden Age. Traditionally, apples are the fruit that grew on the Tree of Knowledge in the Garden of Eden. The Bible doesn't say so, though most people are under the impression that the Book of Genesis mentions apples as the forbidden fruit ; it does not ; but the legends of every race made the apple tree the most significant tree in Paradise. Golden apples guarded by nymphs grew in the garden of the Hesperides. " Avalon " is simply the Isle of Apples. In the Polynesian mythology there is the tale of the Sacred Apple Tree growing in Paradise, and in ancient times the native priests, who had certainly never heard of the Bible story of Adam and Eve, taught that the forbidden fruit of the Sacred Apple Tree was somehow connected with the death of the first man and woman.

The story of the apple tree is as widespread as the story of the Flood ; and so is the belief in the healthfulness of eating apples. The English adage about apples and doctors is matched by proverbs from Arabia and Persia, and our old English custom of wassailing and blessing the apple trees at Christmas time is as old as the Roman occupation of Britain. Until the end of the last century the men and lads of Devonshire went round the orchards singing to the apple trees and firing guns in their honour.

SAVOURY APPLE SOUP À LA BOURGUIGNON

℃. Take a quart of good mutton broth or beef stock, strain it through a fine sieve, and when it boils add to it a half a pound of chopped-up apples and stew them till they are pulp. When cooked, strain it and add a small teaspoonful of ground ginger and plenty of pepper.

Make very hot and serve with a dish of rice.

APPLE SOUP

℃. One pound of apples, one lemon, sugar to taste, one ounce of Groult's potato fecule (see p. xvi), one quart of water.

Boil the water, add the apples peeled, cored and sliced, with enough sugar to sweeten ; add the juice and grated rind of a lemon. Thicken the soup with the potato flour.

A tablespoonful of vinegar will keep the apples a good colour if added with the lemon juice.

APPLE CREAM

℅ Three pounds of apples, half a pound of sugar, the whites of three eggs.

Boil the apples until soft and put them through a sieve. Mix the sugar with the hot purée. Beat the whites of eggs till they are stiff. When the purée is well mixed with the sugar, and the latter is melted, whisk in the whites of the eggs and beat it all together till it thickens.

Pile it high in a bowl and serve with cream.

CREAM OF APPLES

℅ Two pounds of apples, half a pint of milk, half a pint of cream, half a lemon, two ounces of sugar, glacé cherries, ratafias.

Peel and cut up the apples and stew them slowly with a little water and the grated rind of half a lemon, and sugar to taste.

Boil the milk and cream together, and add this gradually to the stewed apples.

When nearly cold, pour it into a silver dish and decorate with cherries and ratafias.

APPLE FOOL

℅ One and a half pounds of apples, three table-spoonfuls of cream, one and a half ounces of sugar or to taste, one lemon, four tablespoonfuls of barley, two pints of water.

Put the barley in cold water to boil. When boiling add the apples cut into slices. When both the barley and apples are soft, pass them through a sieve. Put the purée back into the pan, and add the sugar and juice of a lemon. Boil it again. Stir in the cream before serving.

APPLE MOUSSE

❡. Six or seven apples, the whites of three eggs, sugar to taste, a spoonful of rose water or orange flower water to flavour.

Put the apples into boiling water to cook. Let them get cold, and then put them through a sieve. Mix the purée with castor sugar. Whisk the whites of the eggs till they are stiff, with the flavouring and a little sugar. When well beaten, whip them into the apple purée. The mousse should be very light.

APPLES STEWED IN RUM

❡. Take one pound of juicy apples, peel, core and cut them up. Put them in a stewpan on a slow fire with half a teacupful of water and sugar to taste. Add the rind of half a lemon and a tablespoonful of rum. Stew them till they fall into a purée, then allow them to get cold, and mix with them two ounces of chopped candied peel. Add another tablespoonful of rum before serving.

Apples stewed with peach leaves give a delicious flavour to the fruit. The lemon and rum are then omitted, and the apples are served with Devonshire cream.

MIROTON DES POMMES

℃. Peel and core six apples, cut them in slices a quarter of an inch thick.

Melt an ounce of butter in a saucepan, and add to it three ounces of castor sugar, the juice of a lemon, and the grated rind of half a lemon.

Fry the apples gently in this mixture, and serve them in it, pouring over them a spoonful of white currant jelly. Garnish with dried cherries.

Red currant jelly can be used instead of white.

POMMES CONDÉ

℃. Six apples, sugar, water, lemon, apricot jam, rice, milk, angelica and cherries.

Peel and core six apples. Make a thin syrup of sugar and water, squeeze into it the juice of a lemon. Put the apples into the syrup, and boil till they are soft enough to allow a fork to pierce them easily. Then take them out and put them to drain on a sieve.

Put some apricot jam on a dish, arrange the apples on it, and fill the centre of each apple with the jam.

Boil three-quarters of a pound of rice with enough sugar and milk and a little grated lemon rind in it until it is thick, and cover the apples with it. Decorate with angelica and cherries.

POMMES À LA PORTUGAISE

℃. Apples, brown sugar, butter, cloves, lemon juice, apricot jam.

Take four to six large apples, core them and place in an earthenware dish with a cover. Put a little water at the bottom of the dish, fill up the apples with brown sugar and butter, and put a liberal supply of butter and brown sugar in the dish, with a few cloves and a squeeze of lemon juice. Put a little apricot jam on each. Cover, and bake in a slow oven for at least an hour.

DUTCH APPLE PUDDING

This is an old Dutch family recipe, little known in England. It is as simple to make as a boiled apple pudding, and is much nicer.

℃. Line a well-greased Yorkshire pudding tin with a thin suet crust. Peel and cut up sufficient apples to make a thick layer on the crust. Sprinkle with sugar and lemon juice. Cover the whole dish with another thin layer of suet crust, cover the top with golden syrup and sprinkle with brown sugar. Bake until it is dark brown.

The crust should be crisp and like toffee.

APPLES IN TAPIOCA

℃. Six large apples, three tablespoonfuls of tapioca, one pint of milk, sugar to taste, vanilla, a little apricot jam.

Peel, core and cut up the apples. Boil the milk and tapioca very slowly for some hours. Boil enough water to cook the apples with sugar to make a syrup. When it boils put in the apples, with vanilla to flavour.

When the tapioca is cooked, put half of it into a round, deep fireproof dish ; then put the apples in, and then the rest of the tapioca. Bake it in the oven. Make a syrup with the apple juice and two spoonfuls of apricot jam, and pour over the sweet to serve.

APPLE CARLOTTA

℣. Apples, breadcrumbs, sugar, butter, cloves, cinnamon, treacle.

Core and peel the apples. Butter a fireproof piedish and fill it with layers of apple slices and breadcrumbs, sprinkling each layer of apples with a little sugar, and on each layer of bread-crumbs put morsels of butter and a pinch of cinnamon. Add a few cloves. When the dish is full, pour in a syrup made of equal quantities of water and treacle. Cover it with crumbs, and bake for nearly an hour, letting the piedish stand in a tin of hot water.

APPLE SALAD

℣. Slice the tops from large eating apples, and scoop out the pulp. Mix with finely-cut celery and chopped walnuts. Fill the empty apples with the mixture and cover with a thick mayonnaise.

SWEDISH APPLE CAKE

℣. Apples, almonds, cornflour, sugar, eggs, candied peel, cream.

Core and stew two pounds of apples, which

have been cut into quarters. Butter a baking dish and put the apples at the bottom. Then make a paste of the following ingredients :

Half a pound of butter, three tablespoonfuls of cornflour, half a pound of castor sugar, half a pound of ground sweet almonds, a handful of chopped candied peel.

Cream the butter and add it to the other ingredients. Make this into a paste, and spread a layer over the apples ; then put another layer of apples, and finish with a layer of the almond paste at the top.

Sprinkle the top with chopped almonds, and bake till cooked.

This makes a delicious sweet, served with Devonshire cream.

POMMES À LA COMTESSE

❡ Make some almond paste with pounded almonds and icing sugar in equal amounts, and stir over a gentle fire until dry.

Peel and core as many apples as are required. Fill them with almond paste and bake them.

POMMES À LA JACQUERIE

❡ Peel and core as many apples as there are people, and fill them with apricot jam.

Prepare a puff paste, wrap each apple in the paste, and bake them in a moderate oven.

POMMES À LA JUBILEE

❡ Peel and core as many apples as are required. Place them in a fireproof dish, and fill them with strawberry jam.

When cold cover with whipped cream and serve in a silver dish.

POMMES À LA POLONAISE

℄ Stew some apples in a little sugar and water. Line a plate with pastry, put the apples in it as for an open fruit tart, spread over the top with orange marmalade and crushed macaroons mixed together, and bake.

ALMOND CRUSTED APPLES

℄ Apples, apricot jam, white of egg, ground almonds, castor sugar, breadcrumbs.

Peel the apples whole and core them, then fill them with apricot jam and brush them well with beaten white of egg. Then cover them with ground almonds and castor sugar mixed together in equal quantities with breadcrumbs.

Bake in a fairly hot oven.

APPLE CHEESE

℄ Six pounds of apples, six pounds of sugar, juice and grated rind of lemons.

Cut up the apples but do not peel them, and put them into a preserving pan or large saucepan. Almost cover them with water and boil to a pulp, stirring frequently. Pass them through a sieve and boil the purée for an hour with one pound of sugar for each pound of purée.

Flavour with the rind of three lemons.

APPLES WITH CREAM OF KIRSCH

℄ Peel and cut up one pound of apples, mix with three-quarters of a pound of sugar, and cook without any water. Pass through a sieve and mix with it five sheets of gelatine dissolved in a little hot water. Beat with a whisk for forty minutes. Pour this mixture into a wetted mould in which is placed a piece of muslin. Put in a cool place for six hours. Undo the muslin, turn out the shape, and pour over it a cream of Kirsch.

The mould ought to be as white as snow and very firm. It is excellent.

APRICOTS

"Who doubts you sweet
With savoury almond-stones,
Apricots ?
When you were young
You had star flowers,
Now you are little suns
Ripe in the leaves."

APRICOT BOUILLON

℄ One pound of apricots, claret, cinnamon, butter, water, arrowroot, bread.

Put one pound of apricots in a stewpan, just cover them with water, and let them cook very slowly. Extract the stones and take out the kernels. Pass the apricots through a sieve, and add to the purée sufficient claret and water to make the desired amount of soup.

Sweeten, thicken with very little arrowroot, season with a little cinnamon, and serve very hot with dice of fried bread.

APRICOT AND MARROW SOUP

❦ Stew equal weights of apricots and vegetable marrow together until quite soft, with a spoonful of tapioca. Pass it through a sieve, sweeten it to taste and flavour with lemon juice and a spoonful of brandy. Serve hot.

APRICOT SOUFFLÉ

❦ Seven or eight ripe apricots (a pound), the whites of three eggs, one teaspoonful of Kirsch, three teaspoonfuls of castor sugar.

Peel and cut the apricots in half, removing the stones. Break the stones and add the kernels to the fruit. Pulp the fruit into a purée (using a silver spoon or fork), and add the Kirsch and the kernels finely chopped. Whip the whites of the eggs to a stiff froth with the sugar ; stir the beaten whites into the apricot purée, put it in a buttered soufflé dish, and bake for ten minutes in a moderate oven.

CROÛTES AUX ABRICOTS

❦ Apricots, sugar, water, bread, butter.

Stew some fresh apricots with sugar and water till they become a compôte. Extract the stones and add the kernels to the fruit.

Fry some slices of bread—which have been cut the same size with a cutter and from which all the crust has been removed—in butter till a golden brown. Spread them with the compôte ; arrange them on a round silver dish piled up in a heap, and pour the syrup over them.

This is a favourite dish in France.

ABRICOTS CONDÉ

℃. Apricots, sugar, water, Carolina rice, milk, vanilla pod.

Stew some apricots in a syrup of sugar and water, take out the stones and add the kernels to the fruit.

Cook two tablespoonfuls of Carolina rice in a pint of milk very slowly in a double saucepan, and flavour with a vanilla pod ; add enough sugar to sweeten it.

Butter a dish, pour the rice into it and put the apricots and syrup on top. Bake in the oven until the syrup forms a caramel. Remove, and serve very cold.

APRICOT CREAM

℃. Half an ounce of gelatine dissolved in a quarter of a pint of milk, a quarter of a pint of cream, half a tin of apricots.

Whip the cream very stiff. Cut up the apricots and add to them one tablespoonful of their own syrup, and one dessertspoonful of castor sugar. Mix the apricots, cream and gelatine. Pour into a wetted mould and leave till set.

Serve with whipped cream, and decorate with the rest of the apricots round the dish.

APRICOTS À LA BOURDALOUE

℃. Three cups of milk, sugar to taste, one cup of flour, one cupful of almonds, apricots, vanilla, white of egg.

Put the milk, sweetened to taste, and the flour

on a slow fire and stir without ceasing till it thickens.

Take a cupful of almonds, blanch them and chop them up ; put them in the oven to dry. Pound them in a mortar and put them in the saucepan.

Twenty minutes before serving arrange this paste on a dish, cover it with half apricots soaked in a vanilla syrup, cover them with white of egg and castor sugar beaten to snow, sprinkle with almonds and sugar, and put in the oven to brown.

APRICOT WINE

℀ Twelve pounds of ripe apricots, one pound of loaf sugar, a pint of white wine, three gallons of water, a tablespoonful of yeast.

Remove the stones, break them and remove the kernels. Cut the apricots into small pieces in a preserving pan with the water, sugar, and half the kernels. Simmer very gently for an hour. Pour it into an earthenware jar ; when cool stir in the yeast. (If compressed yeast is used it must first be mixed smoothly with a little warm water.) Cover the vessel with a cloth and leave it for three days, then strain the liquid into a cask, add the white wine and cork lightly. Bottle after six months, and store in a cool, dry place.

The wine should be kept for a year before it is used.

APRICOT BRANDY

℀ Allow one and a half pounds of sugar to one pound of rather under-ripe apricots. Put the fruit into a pan with sufficient water to cover it ; bring it to the boil and simmer till cooked. Remove the skins. Clarify and boil the sugar and pour it over the fruit. Let it stand for twenty-four hours.

Half fill bottles with the apricots, and fill up with an equal quantity of the syrup and brandy mixed. Cork tightly and seal for a year.

BANANAS

SAVOURY BANANAS

¶ Quarter of a pound of rice, one onion, two ounces of butter, one teaspoonful of curry powder, three bananas.

Boil the rice. Melt the butter and fry the bananas in it. Keep them hot while you chop and fry the onion till it is brown. Then add the rice, sprinkle it with pepper, salt, and the curry powder ; stir it well, dish it, and garnish it with the fried bananas.

BANANAS À LA JAMAIQUE

¶ Six large bananas, strawberry jam, six slices of bread, syrup, half a pint of cream, one table-spoonful of sherry, a little milk, butter.

Make a compôte of the bananas by slicing them in half lengthways and stewing them for a few minutes in a syrup of sugar and water. Let it get cool. Then cut six slices of bread the same size as the split bananas, dip them in milk and fry them in the butter till a pale brown. Drain them well, and when crisp spread them with strawberry jam. Place them in a square silver entrée dish and put a banana finger on each slice. Whip the cream and flavour it with the sherry. Cover each banana with it.

BANANAS AND CREAM

℀. Bananas, sugar, black currant jam, rum, a quarter of a pound of cream.

Cut up as many bananas as are required, cover them with castor sugar and add a few spoonfuls of black currant jam. Leave them covered up for a few hours, then add two tablespoonfuls of rum.

Whip a quarter of a pound of cream and pile on the top.

BAKED BANANAS

℀. Skin and cut them lengthways ; put them in fireproof dish with a little apple jelly or marmalade spread on them. Pour over them a little claret and dust a little sugar on. Bake for twenty minutes or half an hour.

BANANAS AU CAFÉ

℀. Six bananas, rice, coffee, sugar candy, milk, sugar, curaçao.

Boil two ounces of Carolina rice in a double saucepan with a pint of milk very slowly until all the milk has been absorbed and the rice is well swollen. Flavour strongly with coffee and sweeten with six or nine lumps of sugar according to taste. Remove it from the fire.

Cut up the bananas, cover them with a little sugar and leave them in a basin for an hour or more, then add two tablespoonfuls of rum.

Take six or more custard glasses ; put in them alternate layers of the banana and the coffee rice, finishing with the rice, and thickly sprinkle with dark brown crushed sugar candy.

BANANAS À LA MARCELLE

℃ Cut the bananas in long slices and arrange them at the bottom of a square silver entrée dish. Pour over them two tablespoonfuls of rum or Kirsch, and leave them covered up for an hour.

Cook some chestnuts which have been peeled ; drain them and mash them through a sieve. Sweeten them and flavour them with vanilla. Mix them with a quarter of a pint of whipped cream and cover the bananas with this mixture, raking the top with a fork so that it makes a flat surface. Cover with chopped pistachio nuts.

BLACKBERRIES

BLACKBERRY FOOL

℃ One pound of blackberries, one pint of cream.

Stew the blackberries, only using enough water to cover them ; sweeten with castor sugar to taste. Put them through a hair sieve. Stir into the purée the cream. Serve cold in small glasses with shortbread biscuits.

BLACKBERRY AND APPLE SHAPE

℧ One pound of blackberries, four ounces of sugar, two cloves, one pound of apples, half an ounce of gelatine; lemon peel.

Cut up the apples and cook them with the blackberries. Add the sugar, rind of half a lemon, and cloves. Pass it through a sieve.

Dissolve the gelatine in a little hot water and add it to the purée. Fill a border mould with this mixture, and fill the centre with whipped cream.

BLACKBERRY WINE

℧ Blackberries, sugar, isinglass, one pint of white wine.

Place ripe blackberries in an earthenware vessel and pour over them enough boiling water just to cover them, and as soon as possible break up the berries with the hands. Let them stand covered till the berries rise to the surface of the liquid, which will take place in from three to four days. Now draw off the liquor into a second vessel, and to every ten quarts add one pound of sugar. Stir well and allow it to stand for ten days, when it should be strained through a jelly bag.

Next take four ounces of isinglass and steep for ten hours in a pint of white wine. Boil this next morning till it is dissolved.

Add one gallon of blackberry juice to the isinglass solution and boil together, after which it should be allowed to stand, then placed in another vessel and kept in a cool place.

BLACK CURRANTS

BLACK CURRANT JELLY

℄ Four pounds of black currants, six ounces of castor sugar.

Boil the currants for forty-five minutes. Then press them through a sieve, and boil the juice with the sugar for two and a half hours.

Pour it into little glasses. Turn out, and serve covered with Devonshire cream.

ARABIAN CURRANTS

℄ Line a plate with almond paste about half an inch thick, and make a rampart about an inch high all round.

Stew one pound of black currants in sugar and water to make a compôte, allow it to cool and add two tablespoonfuls of cassis. Pour this compôte into the almond tart and bake for a few minutes. Serve cold with sponge cakes.

BLACK OR RED CURRANT WINE

℄ One quart of water to each quart of juice, one pound of sugar to each quart of syrup.

Crush currants, rub them through a sieve; measure the juice, add the same amount of water, pour over the sugar—one pound to each quart. Let it stand all night to melt. Put it into stone bottles, and as it works over re-fill the bottles for two or three days. Put them in a warm place for three weeks; lightly cork until fermenting stops, then cork firmly.

It can be bottled in six months, but is better if left longer. This was the popular drink at G.H.Q. Montreuil during the War. It was made from this actual recipe.

CHERRIES

CHERRY SOUP

℄ Cherries, sugar, water, arrowroot, juice of half a lemon, cherry brandy.

Stone four large cupfuls of cherries and put them in a lined saucepan ; cover with a quart of cold water and bring them to the boil. Add half a cupful of sugar and continue boiling till the fruit is soft. Then pass it through a sieve.

Put the purée on the fire again and stir in a tablespoonful of arrowroot first mixed with cold water to a smooth paste. When clear remove from the fire, add the juice of half a lemon, more sugar if necessary, and a liqueur glass of cherry brandy.

CHERRY COMPÔTE

℄ Cherries, sweet almonds, sugar, Kirsch.

Stone two pounds of black or red cherries. Blanch half as many sweet almonds as cherries ; split them in half and put into the cherries.

Make a very thick syrup of three cups of water to one and a half pounds of sugar. It should boil several times. When cool add to it a tablespoonful of maraschino or Kirsch.

Put the cherries in a silver dish and pour the syrup over it. Serve with sponge cakes.

LINCOLN'S INN CHERRIES

❡ Cherries, sugar, water, two tablespoonfuls of Kirsch or maraschino, a quarter of a pint of cream, macaroons, pistachio nuts.

Stone one pound of sweet black cherries and stew them gently in sugar and water, keeping the cherries whole. Remove from the fire ; when cool add two tablespoonfuls or Kirsch or maraschino.

Take as many champagne glasses as there are people. Put a macaroon at the bottom of each glass, and nearly fill the glasses with the cherry compôte.

Whip a quarter of a pint of cream to a stiff froth, and put some on the top of each glass. Decorate with pistachio nuts.

If cream is not available, put a thick sprinkling of pistachio nuts over the cherries.

CHERRY PASTE

❡ After stoning the cherries, boil them without water for half an hour. Press them through a sieve ; reduce to a dry paste ; weigh it and add the same amount of sugar. Mix the sugar and fruit together over the fire. When it forms a ball round the spoon the paste is ready, and should be pressed into small pots.

CHERRY WINE
An old recipe

❡ When the red cherries are full ripe, strip them from the stalks and crush them as apples until the stones are broken ; then put the whole into a tub and cover it up close for three days and three nights. Then press in a cider press and put the liquor again into the tub, and let it stand closely covered for two more days. Then take off the scum very carefully and pour it off the lees into another tub, and let it stand to clear two days more; then skim and pour it off as before.

If the cherries were full ripe and sweet, put only one and a half pounds of sugar to each gallon of liquor ; stir it well together and cover close, and stir no more till the next day ; then pour it carefully off the lees as before. This process may be repeated oftener if the lees appear to be gross and likely to make it fret.

When it is settled, stop it up till seven or eight months are past, then if it be perfectly fine, bottle it ; if not, draw it off into another vessel and stop it up for some time longer.

It should not be drunk till it is a year old.

CRANBERRIES

Cranberries are a useful fruit, because they come into season about November, when other fruit is over.

Their rather bitter flavour blends well with apples or bananas in a pie or a compôte.

CRANBERRY CHEESE

℃ Cook one pint of cranberries till soft in half a pint of water.

Then pass them through a sieve and add to the purée three-quarters of a pound of sugar, two ounces of chopped seeded raisins, and two ounces of chopped walnuts. Cook this mixture over the fire until it boils, stirring it all the time and add a thinly sliced orange.

Let it simmer for twenty minutes, then pour into pots and serve cold.

DAMSON CHEESE

℃. Damsons, preserving sugar.

Pick the fruit from the stalks, and put the damsons in a covered jar in a slow oven, and cook till they are soft enough to be pressed through a fine sieve.

To every pint of this pulp allow nearly a pound of sugar. Boil the pulp and the sugar together until it is stiff, stirring it all the time.

It is an improvement if the stones are cracked and the kernels added with the sugar.

ELDERBERRY JELLY

℃. Gather the berries when they are quite ripe, on a dry day. Wash them, remove the stalks, and place them in a stoneware jar in a moderate oven till the juice flows freely. Strain the berries.

Take half a pound of apples to each pound of elderberries, slice them, and stew them with a pint of water to each half a pound of apples.

Strain them through muslin, and take equal parts of this apple water and elderberry juice and boil for fifteen minutes.

Then add three-quarters of a pound of sugar to each pint of juice, and boil till it sets.

FIGS

STEWED GREEN FIGS

❡ Green figs that are not wanted for dessert are excellent stewed. For a dozen figs make a syrup with three ounces of sugar and three-quarters of a pint of water. Boil this in an enamelled saucepan. Put the figs in the boiling syrup and stew for five minutes. Add the juice of a lemon, a glass of Kirsch, and serve cold.

MOUSSE OF FIGS

❡ Half a pound of dried figs, two ounces of cream, white of one egg.

Soak the figs, then stew them slowly, covered with water, for about two hours. Pass them through a sieve, then whip the white of the egg very stiff, and add to it the cream whipped.

Mix with the purée and serve in glasses.

CREAM OF FIGS

❡ One pound of dried figs, rind of half a lemon, a quarter of a pint of cream, three ounces of castor sugar, three-quarters of a pint of red wine and water.

Put the figs, sugar, lemon peel, wine and water into a saucepan, and let them simmer until all the juice has been soaked up, then rub through a sieve and put into custard glasses.

Serve covered with whipped cream.

COMPÔTE OF PRESERVED FIGS

℄ Half a pound of figs, two ounces of castor sugar, half a lemon, one glass of port wine, two bitter almonds.

Dissolve the sugar, and put in the figs and rind of half a lemon, and stew very gently for nearly two hours. When quite tender add a glass of port wine (claret will do) and the strained juice of the half lemon, also the almonds.

Remove the almonds before serving.

STUFFED FIGS

℄ Half a pound of figs (dried); almonds, one gill of claret, two ounces of sugar, lemon juice.

Blanch enough almonds and chop them up into fairly large pieces. Stuff the figs with them.

Heat the claret with the sugar, then add the figs and a squeeze of lemon juice, and stew them.

GOOSEBERRIES

GOOSEBERRY COMPÔTE

℄ One quart of green gooseberries, eight ounces of white sugar, one pint of water, a small wine-glassful of Kirsch, a tablespoonful of apricot jam.

Put the gooseberries, which have been topped and tailed, into boiling water in an earthenware casserole. Scald them for two minutes.

In another pan make a syrup of the sugar and water ; boil this for ten minutes, then add the gooseberries, Kirsch, and the apricot jam.

Let the gooseberries simmer till they are cooked and tender, and serve in the syrup cold.

GOOSEBERRY CREAM IN GLASSES

℃. Cover a quart of gooseberries with cold water and boil them till soft enough to pass through a sieve. Reheat the pulp, sweeten it to taste, and add an ounce of butter. Then beat up the yolks and whites of two eggs, and add them to the purée, stirring all the time but not allowing it to boil. Take off the fire when it is thick, and when nearly cold add a spoonful of orange flower water and a little spinach juice to colour it. Stir it well and pour it into glasses.

Serve with cream, and sponge cakes.

GRAPE FRUIT JELLY

℃. Soak half an ounce of gelatine in a cupful of water for twenty minutes, then dissolve it slowly in a saucepan on the fire with two tablespoonfuls of sugar. Remove it from the fire when it is dissolved, and add to it the strained juice of one grape fruit and half a lemon. Allow it to come to the boil, and then strain it through muslin.

Pour it into small moulds, and serve it, turned out, with cream cheese or salad, or chop it up and make it into a bed on which to serve cold eggs or cream cheese.

LEMON CREAM

❡ Half a pint of thick cream, half a pint of milk, four teaspoonfuls of cornflour, six ounces of sugar, juice of two lemons, a quarter of a pound of macaroons; glacé cherries and peel.

Take the cream and milk and mix them together; make a smooth batter of the cornflour with a little of the milk. Put the cream, milk and flour into a double saucepan, with the sugar, stirring all the time till it boils. Pour it into a dish, and when quite cold add to it very gradually the juice of two lemons.

Take the macaroons and line the bottom of a silver entrée dish with them; pour in part of the cream, and repeat this alternate process, finishing with a layer of cream. Decorate with glacé cherries and candied lemon peel.

LEMON SPONGE, WITHOUT EGGS
An old family recipe

❡ Half an ounce (four sheets) of gelatine, half a pint of water, four ounces of loaf sugar, lemon.

Soak the gelatine in a quarter of a pint of cold water; dissolve it in another quarter of a pint of boiling water. Then add to it the sugar and lemon peel ; let it simmer half an hour, then strain and allow it to stand till cool, but not till it sets. Add the juice of a large lemon, and whisk till perfectly white and stiff.

Pour into a wetted mould and leave to set.

MELONS

MELON À LA DOMINIQUE

ℂ. Melon, ginger, a quarter of a pint of cream, preserved pineapple.

Take an ordinary melon, peel it and cut it in half lengthways ; remove the seeds, and put the two halves together.

Prepare some hot syrup of ginger and soak the melon in it for two hours. Let it get cold.

Whip the cream very stiff, and mix into it some cubes of preserved pineapple from which the juice has been strained, and fill the melon. Put the two halves together again and serve.

It is improved by being put on ice.

MELON AND WHITE GRAPES

ℂ. Melon, sugar, water, maraschino, white grapes, white currants, pistachio nuts.

Peel an ordinary melon, cut it in half lengthways and remove the seeds. Soak it in a hot syrup of sugar and water flavoured with maraschino, for a few hours.

Peel some white grapes, and, if obtainable,

some white currants, and let them stand for some time covered with castor sugar. Add two tablespoonfuls of maraschino. Fill the melon with this, put the two halves together, and sprinkle the whole with chopped pistachio nuts.

ORANGES

ORANGE SOUP

℃. Four cupfuls of orange juice, three teaspoonfuls of arrowroot; sugar, sherry.

Heat four cupfuls of strained orange juice and thicken it with three teaspoonfuls of arrowroot, first made into a smooth paste with cold water. Stir it all the time after the arrowroot is added, and cook it until clear. Add sugar to sweeten, and after taking the soup off the fire add a tablespoonful of sherry.

Serve very cold in custard glasses with small pieces of ice in it.

ORANGE BOUILLON

℃. Four cupfuls of orange juice, one tablespoonful of cornflour, one teaspoonful of orange flower water, one teaspoonful of orange curaçao.

Heat four cupfuls of orange juice and let it come to the boil; thicken it with the cornflour and cook it till smooth. Then add one teaspoonful of orange flower water, and of orange curaçao.

Serve very cold in glasses, and sprinkle with chopped candied orange peel.

301

ORANGE JELLY

℆ Eighteen oranges, two lemons, half a pound of loaf sugar, one ounce of gelatine.

Thinly peel two oranges. Boil the sugar to a syrup in a little water and pour, when boiling, on the rind. Into another jug squeeze the juice of all the oranges and lemons, and strain it through a hair sieve. Add to this the gelatine dissolved in a little water, and the syrup.

When cold serve in small glasses.

ORANGE CUSTARD

℆ Oranges, three eggs, three-quarters of a pint of milk; sugar, salt, lemon juice.

Make a custard with the milk and the yolks of the eggs, adding a pinch of salt, vanilla to flavour, and sweeten it with white sugar to taste. Beat the whites of the eggs into a meringue, adding gradually enough sugar to stiffen it, and flavouring it with a dessertspoonful of lemon juice. Bake it for fifteen minutes in a moderate oven.

Peel the oranges, slice them and arrange them in a bowl. Pour the custard over them, and put the meringue on the top.

CARAMEL OF ORANGES

℆ Skin the oranges, cut them into thick slices free from pips and pith, and arrange them in a bowl. Pour over them a syrup made of their own juice and white sugar. Make some caramel with a quarter of a pound of loaf sugar and a gill of water, by boiling it together for about ten minutes. Pour it out to harden ; then beat it into crumbs and sprinkle it over the oranges. Cover the bowl with a little sweetened whipped cream, and on this put a few chopped burnt almonds.

BAKED ORANGES

¶ Cut a piece off the top of each orange ; mix a little sugar and lemon juice together and insert it. Put on the lids and bake in an earthenware casserole with a little water and sugar.

Serve with whipped cream.

ORANGE CREAM IN GLASSES

¶ Squeeze the juice of sweet oranges ; strain it, and to a pint of juice add the well-beaten yolks and whites of three eggs. Add enough sugar to sweeten. Put it on the fire in a double saucepan with the peel of one orange, and stir till thick without allowing it to boil. Remove the peel and pour it into glasses.

Serve with a purée of oranges flavoured with maraschino.

LINCOLN'S INN ORANGE SALAD

¶ Cut large oranges in half, allowing half an orange for each person. Remove the pulp, and mix it in a basin with some white grapes from which the seeds have been removed and also the skins. Add a tablespoonful of Sauterne to each half-orange, and a spoonful of blanched and chopped sweet almonds. Put it back in the orange shells.

Cover them with a thick mayonnaise, and sprinkle with finely chopped mint or parsley.

ORANGE MINT SALAD

℃ To the juice and flesh of four large oranges add sugar to taste and two tablespoonfuls of finely chopped mint. Flavour with a tablespoonful of sherry and one of lemon juice, and serve with leaves of fresh mint.

ORANGE MARZIPAN

℃ One pound of almonds, three-quarters of a pound of fine icing sugar ; oranges, castor sugar.

Skin the almonds and pound them to a fine paste ; boil the sugar with a tablespoonful of water, till a drop put into cold water can be rolled into a little ball with the fingers ; then remove it from the fire and add the almonds ; stir the mixture well.

Have ready half a pint of purée of oranges made from the pulp of fresh oranges passed through a sieve and mixed with sugar to taste. Mix this purée with the almond paste. Boil it up once more, stirring well to prevent it sticking to the bottom of the pan ; then pour it out to cool. Shape into balls the size of a greengage.

FRENCH ORANGEADE

℃ Six sweet oranges, six lemons, sugar to taste.

Pour a pint of boiling water over the thinly-cut rind of two oranges and two lemons. Into this squeeze the juice of all the oranges and lemons, a little ginger to taste, also sugar to sweeten, and a syphon of soda water.

GLACÉD TANGERINES OR ORANGES

℄ Two or three tangerines or oranges, a quarter of a pound of sugar, two tablespoonfuls of water.

Divide the fruit into quarters, removing the peel and pith. Put a quarter of a pound of sugar with two tablespoonfuls of water into a saucepan, melt it slowly and boil it till it is brown. Then remove the saucepan from the fire and plunge it into cold water to stop the boiling. Dip the quarters of the orange into the sugar one at a time on a fork, and lay them on a buttered dish to cool.

This is an excellent sweetmeat for afternoon tea, as well as a decoration for jellies or creams.

PEACHES

PEACHES AU VIN BLANC

℄ Peaches, sauterne, butter, sugar.

Take as many peaches as are required and cut them in half. Put them into a dish and pour over them a claret glass of sauterne. Leave them for an hour or more. Crack the stones.

Put two ounces of butter into a very clean pan ; when it boils put in the peaches and fry them lightly. Drain them carefully. Add sugar and the kernels to the wine in which the peaches have been soaked, and make into a syrup. Pour it over the peaches and serve either hot or cold.

PÊCHES À LA CARDINAL

℃. Peaches, strawberries or raspberries, chopped pistachio nuts.

Take half a tin of preserved half-peaches and fry them lightly in their own syrup, to which a vanilla pod is added. Drain them and let them get cold. Stew half a pound of strawberries or raspberries with sufficient sugar to make into a syrup. Pass it through a sieve. Arrange the peaches on a silver dish, pour the sauce over them, and decorate with chopped pistachio nuts.

The dish is improved if the peaches and the sauce are put on ice for a few hours before serving.

PÊCHES À LA BOURDALOUE

℃. Six or eight peaches, three yolks of eggs, three-quarters of a pint of milk, three and a half ounces of flour, three and a half ounces of sugar, three and a half ounces of butter, a spoonful of Kirsch, a little vanilla.

Cut the peaches in halves, remove the stones and skins, and boil them in a syrup made of sugar and water ; flavour it with Kirsch. Boil the milk separately with vanilla flavouring.

Put in a saucepan three and a half ounces of flour, an equal amount of sugar, and the beaten yolks of three eggs. Stir them all together till you have a smooth paste, and then add the boiling milk gradually, stirring all the time. When the mixture boils stir in the butter.

Pour it into a round dish, and on this cream arrange the halves of peaches. Into the syrup they have cooked in, stir in a spoonful or two of apricot jam, and pour this sauce over them to serve.

PEACH TRIFLE

℄ One tin of preserved peaches, six sponge cakes, two ounces of macaroons; cream, one wineglassful of sherry, one tablespoonful of sugar, two ounces of ratafias; milk.

Slice the sponge cakes and arrange them at the bottom of a square entrée dish, with the macaroons and ratafias. Soak them in the sherry, and if not sufficiently moist, add a little milk.

Boil up the syrup from the peaches with the sugar, and when nearly cold pour it over the cakes. Arrange the peaches on the top, and cover the whole with whipped cream.

SWEET PICKLED PEACHES

℄ Peaches, one pint of vinegar, two pounds of brown sugar, one ounce stick of cinnamon; cloves.

Skin the peaches by dipping them in scalding water for a minute, when the skin will rub off easily. Halve the peaches and remove the stones. Stick two cloves into each half-peach.

Make a syrup by boiling the sugar and cinnamon in the vinegar for twenty minutes, and cook the fruit in it until soft, a few at a time.

If pickling plums, leave out the cloves, but cut the plums and remove the stones.

PEARS

PEARS À LA CLOCHE

⁋ One pound of pears, a quarter of a pound of sugar, one gill of red wine, cloves, cinnamon.

Peel and cut the pears into quarters ; put them in an earthenware fireproof dish with a lid, with water enough just to cover them, a little cinnamon and a few cloves. Stew them very slowly, and when they are half cooked pour in a gill of red wine. The pan must be covered while the pears are cooking, and they must be gently stirred occasionally to prevent them sticking. When the pears are cooked, turn them out, serve them with their own syrup poured over them.

POIRES CONDÉ

⁋ Six pears, one and a half pints of milk, rice, sugar, a little apricot jam, a teaspoonful of Kirsch, sugar to taste, half an ounce of butter, vanilla.

Boil the rice in the milk very slowly, with sugar to taste and a little vanilla. Peel the pears ; halve them and take away the cores. Cook them in a syrup made of water and sugar.

Put the rice when quite cooked into a border mould. When it is set, turn it out into a round dish, and arrange the pears on the top of the rice. Pour over them a syrup made of a few spoonfuls of apricot jam boiled in a little water and flavoured with a teaspoonful of Kirsch.

This sweet can be served cold or hot.

CROÛTES À LA NORMANDIE

℄ Pears, sugar, water, cider, bread, butter.

Peel and cut the pears in half, and put them in a saucepan with a syrup of sugar and water, and stew them very slowly for ten minutes ; then take them off the fire and add a glass of cider, and stew till tender.

Take as many pieces of bread as there are people, and cut off all the crust, leaving them a good shape. Fry them in butter till a pale brown. and spread thickly on them the compôte, leaving sufficient fruit to serve in a mound in the centre.

Arrange the croûtes in a circle round.

PEAR CUSTARDS

℄ One tin of preserved pears ; Kirsch, jam, two whites of eggs, a quarter of a pint of cream.

Place half a pear at the bottom of each champagne glass. On it place a good teaspoonful of raspberry or strawberry jam, and pour over this one dessertspoonful of Kirsch or maraschino.

Beat up the cream with the whites of eggs very stiff, flavour it with vanilla, and pile it up in each glass. Decorate with chopped pistachio nuts or a glacé cherry.

PINEAPPLES

PINEAPPLE SOUP

℄ Two tablespoonfuls of Groult sago, one pint of water, one stick of cinnamon, cupful of chopped raisins, sugar to taste, one cupful of pineapple juice, half a lemon, pieces of chopped pineapple.

Put the sago in a pint of water and let it cook in a double saucepan till it is transparent, with a stick of cinnamon. Remove the cinnamon, and add a cupful of chopped and seeded raisins, sugar to taste, a cupful of pineapple juice, and the juice of half a lemon. Serve in glasses very cold, with small pieces of pineapple floating in it.

PINEAPPLE CREAM

❧ Half a pint of cream, one tin of preserved pineapple, half an ounce of gelatine, sugar to taste.

Dissolve the gelatine and about one and a half ounces of castor sugar in a little of the syrup. Cut up some of the pineapple finely and press through a sieve, till you have a teacupful of pineapple pureé.

Whip the cream stiffly, stir into it the pineapple purée and some pieces of pineapple finely chopped. Pour in the melted gelatine and sugar, and add a teaspoonful of lemon juice.

Pour into a wet mould and set aside to cool. Turn out to serve.

TO SERVE A PINEAPPLE WHOLE

❧ Cut off the bottom of the pineapple at the point where the sides begin to narrow downwards, and at the point where the sides between to narrow upwards cut off the top with its tuft.

Take a very sharp long knife—a saw knife is best—and take off the whole of the rest of the skin in one piece ; slip it off, and cut the pineapple into round slices without allowing them to fall apart. Stand it upright and very carefully replace it in its shell. Keep any juice that may have come away ; add a little liqueur to it and serve separately.

In taking off the cylindrical skin, great care must be taken not to break through the skin anywhere. After the knife is thrust in between the flesh of the pineapple and the skin, it should be worked gently up and down until the skin is separated from the flesh.

The skin should come off like a hollow tube.

PINEAPPLE CREAM

℄ One tin of preserved pineapple, half a pint of cream, half a pint of milk, one ounce of castor sugar, or two if made with fresh fruit, half an ounce of gelatine.

Dissolve the gelatine in the milk, and when dissolved add to it half a pint of syrup from the pineapple. Put the sugar with the cream and add both to the gelatine. Whip the mixture for twenty minutes off the fire, and pour it into a wetted mould which has been decorated with pieces of pineapple. Turn out when cold.

PINEAPPLE SOUFFLÉ

℄ A tin of preserved pineapple, a quarter of a pound of flour, a quarter of a pound of butter, a quarter of a pound of sugar, three eggs, half a pint of milk, vanilla pod.

Put the vanilla pod in the milk, bring it to the boil and stand it aside for half an hour. Melt the butter in a saucepan, stir in the flour little by little till you have a smooth mixture without lumps ; cook it for four or five minutes. Then strain the flavoured milk into it, stirring all the time, and bring it to the boil. Let it cool a little then stir in the beaten yolks of the eggs and the sugar. Then add two large tablespoonfuls of finely chopped pineapple ; lastly, add the whites of the eggs whisked to a stiff froth. Pour the mixture into a well-buttered soufflé dish, cover it with buttered paper, and steam it in a bain-marie for three-quarters of an hour to an hour.

Serve hot with the pineapple syrup as a sauce.

ANANAS AU KIRSCH

This is a very easily prepared sweet to be found on nearly every menu in every Restaurant in France

❡ Take half-slices of pineapple, either fresh or preserved. Arrange them in a long glass dish with their own juice, to which has been added a few tablespoonfuls of Kirsch.

PINEAPPLE SALAD

❡ One pineapple (or more), sugar, half a lemon.

Cut the leaves and stem off the pineapple, and very carefully pare off the rind, removing every dark speck. Squeeze all the juice from the discarded parts into the bowl or dish on which the salad will be served. Then cut the pineapple in half lengthways, and cut out the hard fibrous core in the middle ; slice the pineapple in semi-circles not more than half an inch thick. Arrange these pieces neatly in the dish, one overlapping the other in a circle ; sift powdered sugar over all, and into the juice squeeze some lemon juice to taste. Cover the bowl with a plate and let it stand in a cool place or on ice.

PINEAPPLE CUP
This is a very good French drink.

℘ Squeeze the juice from a large pineapple and add to it a breakfastcupful of well-made barley water and a wineglassful of Kirsch. Let it stand for half an hour. It can be drunk with soda water.

POMEGRANATES
Although the pomegranate (the apple of Granada) is so familiar a decorative motive in sculpture and ecclesiastical embroidery, it is the inside that is decorative and not everyone knows how to open the fruit.

A small round piece should be cut off the top and then the hard rind can be carved down by following its natural segments, which can then be pulled apart.

Pomegranates are really grown for their juice, which is the wonderful flavour of the French drink Grenadine ; it is also used with grapes in some wines. This is a delicious compôte :

COMPÔTE OF POMEGRANATES

℃. From a bowl of pomegranates pick out the large ones and halve them, removing all the seeds. Lay these halved pomegranates in a glass dish and sprinkle them with rose water.

Open and crush the smaller pomegranates to extract the juice, and add its amount in water and sufficient castor sugar to make a thick syrup.

Heat it over the fire until it thickens—let it cool and then pour it over the fruit in the glass dish.

PRUNES

Prunes, to most of us, recall our nurseries —dishes of small, rather hard shrivelled-looking black plums associated with stiff white cornflour blancmange. We were told prunes were good for us, a matter that left us coldly indifferent, and if we welcomed them it was for reasons of our own, as an occult means of foretelling our future professions, if we were little boys, or the professions of our future husbands if we were little girls ; even if we didn't much like prunes we would ask for more to avoid the mortification of " thief." And the shocking bad cooking to which the nursery prunes were and are usually subjected added a certain gambling interest to the game, for there was and is the small hard prune difficult to post-mortem, or the ragged, mangled remains of a prune that might or might not contain the stone that would bring or deny us the career we desired most. It was a list of professions obviously compiled by an unimaginative adult, for it made no provision for being either an engine driver, a clown in a circus, or " adventuress," if one were a small girl with a yearning for polar exploration.

Alternatively, " prunes " arrived at Christmas-time in a tall glass jar with a screw lid and a Bordeaux label, and were eaten raw.

But prunes properly cooked can be a sweet that may be served at any dinner party, either as a sweet or savoury. All the following recipes are delicious.

PRUNEAUX AU VIN

❦ For six or eight people buy at any good stores or grocer a pound of the very large prunes known in the grocery trade as " twenty-thirties "—from the number a pound contains. Just cover them with cold water and soak for eight hours. (Soaking these big prunes is not absolutely necessary, but it increases their size ; the cheaper smaller prunes should always be soaked for twenty-four hours before cooking.)

Pour the prunes, with the water they soaked in, into a saucepan with a vanilla pod broken in half. Vanilla pods, like these big prunes, can only be obtained at first-rate grocers.

Sprinkle in half a cupful of castor sugar and stew them on a slow fire for twenty minutes ;

then remove them from the fire, add half a cupful of claret, and simmer again for ten minutes. Remove them from the fire, and when they are cool pour into a silver dish, leaving the vanilla pod in with the prunes, and serve with sponge cakes.

MRS. BENTFORD'S WAY OF COOKING PRUNES

℄ Soak one pound of prunes in one pint of cold water, adding two tablespoonfuls of golden syrup and the very finely shredded rind of half a lemon.

Leave them to soak for twenty-four hours and then stew them gently for fifteen minutes in this liquid.

This method of cooking prunes gives them a most delicate and pleasant flavour, and served with a bowl of cream of rice this makes an excellent luncheon sweet.

PRUNE SOUP

℄ Half a teacup of sago, half a teacup of sugar, one cup of prunes, half a teacup of raisins, half a teacup of red currant juice.

Cook half a teacupful of Groult's sago in a quart of cold water till transparent. In another saucepan cook a teacupful of prunes and half a teacup of raisins, with half a teacupful of sugar. Add the fruit when cooked to the sago, with half a cupful of currant juice. Serve hot, with almond paste balls.

PAIN DE PRUNES À LA CRÈME

ℂ One pound of prunes, half an ounce of gelatine, lemon, a quarter of a pint of claret or water, a quarter of a pound of loaf sugar, cream.

Stone the prunes, crack the stones and add the kernels to the prunes. Put them in a saucepan with the rind of half a lemon, the claret and sugar, and stew until quite tender on a very slow fire. Put them through a sieve. Dissolve the gelatine in a little hot water ; add it to the strained prunes, and let it all come to the boil again. Pour it into a border mould, and when turned out the next day fill the centre with whipped cream. Decorate the prunes with blanched and split almonds.

PRUNE SOUFFLÉ

ℂ One pound of prunes, four eggs.

Soak a pound of prunes and stew them in the same water. Take out the stones when soft, and pass the prunes through a sieve. Separate the yolks from the whites of the eggs, beat up the yolks and stir them into the purée of prunes. Then whisk the whites to a stiff froth and add them. Put the mixture in a buttered dish and bake in a quick oven.

WHIPPED PRUNES

ℂ Sixteen prunes, two ounces of sugar, the whites of five eggs, a dessertspoonful of lemon juice.

Soak the prunes in enough water to cover

them for several hours. Stew them in the water they have soaked in until they are soft. Take out the stones and pass the prunes through a sieve. Then add the sugar and cook for five minutes.

Whip the whites of the eggs till they are stiff. When the purée of prunes is cold, stir it gradually into the stiff whites of egg. Add the lemon juice, and bake in a slow oven for twenty minutes.

Serve it cold with custard sauce.

CROÛTES AUX PRUNES

℞. Ripe plums, bread, sugar to taste, a little butter.

Well butter a shallow fireproof dish. Cut slices of bread about three-quarters of an inch thick and as long as the bottom of the dish if possible, and fit them together in the dish so that the bottom of the dish is covered with a layer of bread.

Take large ripe plums (or apricots) and cut them neatly in half ; take away the stones, and arrange the halves neatly side by side, their skins to the bread, as close as possible till the bread is covered ; in each half-plum put sugar and a morsel of fresh butter. Put the dish in a moderate oven ; while it bakes it must be sprinkled with castor sugar several times. When the plums are cooked, either send it in in the dish it has baked in or carefully lift out the whole croûte on to a hot plate and pour over it the juice there will be at the bottom of the dish. Serve hot or cold.

CAISSES À LA FLORENCE

℄ Prunes, bread, a little dried haddock (cooked), a little cream.

Soak the biggest prunes you have, allow one or two for each person. Take out the stones and stuff the prunes with haddock freed from skin and bone and pounded to a smooth paste with a little cream, flavoured with cayenne pepper.

Fry little oblong slices of bread in butter, put a stuffed prune on each, and heat in the oven.

QUINCE CREAM

℄ Quinces, water, gelatine, sugar, cream.

Put enough quinces in a saucepan to make a pint of juice, and to every pound of fruit put a pint of water. Stew very gently until cooked, and strain the juice from them.

Dissolve in a pint of this juice an ounce of gelatine, then add ten ounces of white sugar, and stir together over the fire for half an hour or until it jellies. Remove the scum and pour the jelly on to half a pint of cream. When cool pour into glasses and serve.

If fresh quinces are not obtainable, compote of quince or preserved quinces could be used.

WHITE QUINCE CREAM IN GLASSES

℄ Quinces, castor sugar, whites of eggs.

Gently stew some quinces till they are soft enough to pass through a sieve. Mix the purée

319

with an equal amount of castor sugar, and beat till white with two or more whites of eggs.

RASPBERRIES

RASPBERRY SOUP

℃ Two tablespoonfuls of Groult's sago, one pint of water, stick of cinnamon, half a teacupful of chopped and seeded raisins, a cupful of raspberry juice, juice of half a lemon.

Simmer until transparent two tablespoonfuls of Groult's sago in a pint of water, with a stick of cinnamon. Remove the cinnamon when the sago is cooked, and add the raisins and juice.

RASPBERRY CREAM

℃ Three-quarters of a pint of cream, half a pint of raspberry jam rubbed through a fine sieve, or half a pint of fresh raspberries stewed and passed through a sieve, half a pint of water, half an ounce of gelatine.

Dissolve the gelatine in the water, beat up the cream, add the jam or raspberries, and gelatine hot but not boiling.

Stir the cream well while adding gelatine.

RASPBERRY JELLY

℃ One pint of raspberries, two ounces of sago, one pint of red currants, half a pound of cherries.

Stone the cherries, and extract the kernels from the stones. Put all the fruit and the kernels into a pan with one pint of water. Allow them to simmer till juicy, then pass through a sieve, and add the sago and sufficient sugar to the juice. Boil again till the sago is cooked and pour into a mould. Serve when cold with Devonshire cream.

RASPBERRY SOUFFLÉ

¶. Half a pound of ripe raspberries, three eggs, two ounces of cake crumbs, two ounces of white sugar, two ounces of cornflour, half an ounce of butter, two tablespoonfuls of cream.

Beat the raspberries, cream, sugar, and corn-flour together with a wooden spoon till they are in a pulp. Separate the yolks from the whites of the eggs ; beat the yolks and beat them into the raspberries, then add the crumbs. Whip the whites to a stiff froth and stir into the mixture and bake in a hot oven in a buttered soufflé dish for twenty-five to thirty minutes. Serve very hot.

RASPBERRY AND CURRANT CHEESE

¶. One pound of raspberries, half a pound of red currants, three-quarters of a pound of sugar, two ounces of gelatine, a quarter of a pint of cream.

Put the raspberries and currants into a sauce-pan with the sugar and half a pint of water. Stir it until dissolved, then rub it through a hair sieve. Add the dissolved gelatine to the pulp, and fill a border mould with this. Turn out and serve with whipped or Devonshire cream in the centre.

WHIPPED RASPBERRIES

¶ Half a pound of raspberries, half a pound of sugar, the white of one egg.

Pick the raspberries, put them in a bowl with the sugar ; mix them together and beat in the white of an egg. Beat with a wire whisk until the ingredients are blended together. Serve cold.

RED CURRANTS

UNBOILED RED CURRANT JELLY

¶ Weigh the bowl, squeeze the fruit through a linen cloth, and to every pound of juice allow one and a half pounds of best loaf sugar. Stir till it is quite dissolved and beginning to thicken. By rubbing a finger in the mixture you will know when the sugar is dissolved. Do all this as quickly as possible, and dish before the mixture has time to thicken in the bowl. The flavour keeps fresh and delicious.

COMPÔTE OF RED CURRANTS
Served with Cream Cheese.

¶ Make a compôte of red currants by stewing them very slowly in a thick syrup.

When cooked, pour the compôte into a small china bowl and serve with " Petit Suisse " cheese.

SUMMER PUDDING

¶ Although this sweet is probably known to everyone, it is impossible to leave it out of an anthology of the best recipes, because it is one of the nicest ways of cooking red currants and raspberries.

Line a mould or basin with slices of stale bread about quarter of an inch thick, from which all the crust has been removed. Fit them together so that there are no gaps.

Boil one and a half pounds of red currants with three-quarters of a pound of raspberries. Cover them with water and sweeten to taste. Let them boil till all the juice is extracted. Pass them through a sieve ; re-heat and pour it into the mould, placing one or two pieces of bread at the top of the mould to completely encase the juice.

Leave it till the next day. Turn out and serve cold with whipped or Devonshire cream.

COLD CREAM OF TAPIOCA AND RED CURRANTS

⦿ Boil two tablespoonfuls of Groult's tapioca in a pint of milk in a double saucepan till all the milk has been absorbed. Sweeten to taste and flavour with a vanilla pod, which should remain in the saucepan all the time the tapioca is boiling.

Stew very gently one pound of red currants in a syrup of sugar and water. Take two glass dishes and pour the currants into one and the tapioca into the other. Sprinkle a very little cinnamon over the tapioca and hand the fruit and the tapioca cream together.

RHUBARB WINE

℟. Five pounds of rhubarb, one gallon of water, three pounds loaf or preserving sugar, one lemon.

Wash the rhubarb sticks, drain but do not dry them, cut them into small pieces ; put them in an earthenware crock, pound them well, and pour the water over them. Leave it for ten days covered up, stirring it well once a day. Then strain it into another crock on to the sugar. Add the juice and grated rind of the lemon. Stir it until the sugar is dissolved. Then cask it and put in a very little isinglass (less than half an ounce). Leave it uncorked for ten days, merely covering the bung-hole with several folds of a cloth, and then stop the hole up well.

Leave it for a year before bottling, when it will be fit to use.

STRAWBERRIES

" Doubtless God could have made a better berry,
but doubtless God never did."

So long as strawberries can be eaten fresh with cream, it is vandalism to cook them, but the following recipes are useful when the fruit is not at its best or is too ripe to serve fresh.

The popularity of strawberries and cream dates back to 1509, when Cardinal Wolsey set the fashion by having them at a great banquet he gave in that year.

STRAWBERRY SOUP
as made in Sweden.

❡ One pound of strawberries, teacupful of sugar, half a pint of claret, half a pint of water, almond paste balls, lemon juice.

Mash one pound of strawberries, leaving out six or seven of the best ones. Sprinkle the purée with sugar to taste, and add a teacupful of water. Let them stand for two hours, then pass through a sieve and add half a pint of claret, and half a pint of water (Sauterne can be used if claret is not available), and the juice of a quarter of a lemon. Set it on ice for three hours.

Add the whole strawberries and serve with almond paste balls.

STRAWBERRY CREAM

❡ Half a pound of strawberries, half a pint of cream, half an ounce of gelatine, three ounces of sugar, the juice of half a lemon, half a teacupful of milk.

Carefully pick half a pound of ripe sound strawberries ; press them through a hair sieve (the sieve must be perfectly clean). Add the white sugar and juice of half a lemon. After soaking the gelatine, melt it in the milk and strain it on to the purée of strawberries. Then whip the cream and mix it into the strawberry pulp. Put it into a mould, and if possible keep it on ice till it is time to turn it out and serve it. If no ice is available, stand the mould in a bowl of cold water.

COLD STRAWBERRY SOUFFLÉ

℄ Half a pound of strawberries, one table-spoonful of red currant jelly, four eggs, three-quarters of a pint of milk, two ounces of sugar, one ounce of cornflour, a quarter of a pint of cream, liqueur glassful of maraschino, two ounces of butter, vanilla.

Mix the cornflour with a little of the cold milk. Heat the milk in a saucepan, add the vanilla, sugar and cornflour, stirring all the time until it boils and thickens. Take it off the fire.

Rub the strawberries through a sieve and stir the purée into the cornflour, add the butter, then stir in the yolks of the eggs and the cream, and whisk it over a very slow fire till the eggs set.

Melt the gelatine in a little water, add the red currant jelly, and strain it into the mixture. Whip the whites of the eggs very stiff and add them, and last of all the maraschino.

Paper a soufflé dish and put in the mixture. Dissolve a little red currant jelly, and when nearly cold pour it over the top of the soufflé to form a skin, and put the soufflé on ice in the refrigerator.

Remove the paper before serving.

DUTCH FRUIT SALAD

This is an expensive concoction nowadays, but it is so good that it is worth recording.

℄ Into a tall earthenware jar empty a bottle of brandy and a bottle of rum, and into this put any ripe fruit—slices of oranges, bananas, pine-apple, apples, plums, currants, strawberries, raspberries, grapes, apricots, peaches, pears, melons, figs—and to every pound of fruit, which of course must be peeled, skinned, stoned, or stripped, put three-quarters of a pound of sugar. Into this jar can be put any liqueur, or any fruit that happens to be available. It will keep for months, and is quite extraordinarily nice.

A SALAD OF FRESH FRUIT
Served in a Cantaloup Melon.

℄ Put the freshly gathered fruit, after preparing it, in a basin and sprinkle lots of sugar over it—half a pound to every pound of fruit. Leave it to stand for some hours till it makes its own juice.

Remove the inside of a cantaloup melon, throw away the seeds and mix the fruit with the salad.

Pour all the fruit and juice into the empty melon ; add two liqueur glasses of maraschino and serve.

327

XIII
ALMONDS

" Open-work Almond Tarts with butter, velvet pastries perfumed with musk and stuffed deliciously, saboun biscuits, small cakes, lime tarts, honey-tasting jam, those sweets called mouchabac, little souffléd patties, called louc-met-el-cadi, and those others named assabih zeinab, which are made with butter and mingled with milk and honey."

CHAPTER XIII

ALMONDS

THE genius who first paired almonds with raisins is possibly responsible for them being comparatively neglected in connection with other dishes, at least in England, where almond paste is used only on very rich cakes—an unnecessary limitation. Other countries know better. In Sweden almond paste balls are always served with the fruit soups that are such a favourite dish there, and " turron " or almond paste is the national sweetmeat of Spain. At Seville Fair there are rows of stalls where " turron " is sold in great slabs, some of it full of nuts or ginger, and it is brown, or white, or pink, or any colour of the rainbow. In fact, unless you have seen almond paste at Seville Fair you can hardly be said to have seen almond paste at all.

The possibilities of almonds are varied ; they can be used to change a commonplace dish into a delicacy.

Nowadays ground almonds can be bought from all the big grocers and can be used if preferred in all the following recipes in place of whole almonds.

This will save both time and labour.

ALMOND SOUP

℄ Two ounces of almonds, one and a half pints of new milk, a quarter of a pint of cream, one tablespoonful of flour, one root of celery, one onion, one ounce of butter.

After blanching the almonds, chop them up and boil gently for one hour in a pint of milk with the onion and the celery. Then remove the onion and the celery. Make a smooth paste with the butter and flour, stir in half a pint of milk gradually, flavour it with pepper and salt, mace and a little cayenne. Put this into the soup and stir it over the fire till it boils, let it boil for a few minutes, then add the cream, and when it boils again remove it from the fire and serve it at once. Only the white part of the celery should be used.

CREAM OF ALMOND SOUP WITH FRENCH BEANS

¶ Melt half an ounce of butter in a saucepan, and stir in half an ounce of flour. Mix well and add, stirring all the time, half a pint of white stock and half a pint of milk ; add two ounces of ground sweet almonds. Let it all come to the boil and then allow it to simmer for fifteen minutes.

Put into the soup a handful of dried cooked French beans, and finally add another half-pint of milk in which the yolk of an egg has been mixed.

Stir all the time until taking it off the fire, and serve with fried croutons of bread.

ALMOND BALLS FOR SWEDISH FRUIT SOUPS

¶ One dozen sweet almonds, two eggs, three-quarters of a cupful of flour, one teaspoonful of baking powder.

Blanch the almonds and pound them to a paste. Beat the eggs and add them to the almonds, with the flour, and also a teaspoonful of baking powder. Mix and roll the paste into balls about the size of a greengage, and drop these into boiling soup five minutes before serving.

For Savoury Fruit Soups the almond paste, before being made into balls, should be seasoned with pepper and salt, and half a teaspoonful of chopped parsley should be added.

ALMOND CREAM

℘ Four ounces of sweet almonds, one pint of good milk, the whites of two fresh eggs, four ounces of sugar, orange flower water.

Blanch the almonds and pound them into powder. Boil the milk, with the whites of the eggs and the sugar, over a slow fire and stew it for about a quarter of an hour, stirring it incessantly. When the cream begins to thicken, add the almonds and bring to the boil eight to ten times. Pass it through a fine sieve, and add five or six drops of orange flower water. Serve it cold in a china dish with a little caramel round it.

Another Recipe for
ALMOND CREAM

℘ Half a pint of cream, two ounces of almonds, one ounce of sugar, half an ounce of leaf gelatine; almond essence.

Blanch and skin the almonds, chop them and brown them in the oven. Melt the gelatine and sugar in three tablespoonfuls of water. Whip the cream, adding a few drops of almond essence, then stir in the sugar and gelatine, and the almonds when cold. Pour into a wet mould and set in a cold place. Turn out to serve.

MENCHIKOFF

ℭ. A quarter of a pound of nuts or almonds, a quarter of a pound of fresh butter, a quarter of a pound of castor sugar, a quarter of a pint of cream.

Blanch and pound the almonds, and mix with the sugar and butter till a cream ; add the cream flavoured with vanilla.

Turn into the mould lined with biscuits, press well, cover, and leave till the next day in a cool place.

BAKED ALMOND PUDDING

ℭ. Two ounces of ground almonds, two ounces of chopped candied peel, a quarter of a pint of milk, two ounces of breadcrumbs, two eggs, two ounces of sugar.

Beat the sugar and butter to a cream ; add to it the crumbs, the milk made warm, and the almonds. Mix well, and then add the peel and the eggs well beaten.

Butter a pie dish, and pour in the mixture and bake till firm—about fifteen minutes.

ALMOND RICE

ℭ. One quart of new milk, four even table-spoonfuls of Carolina rice ; lemon rind, essence of almond, two ounces of ground almonds, and fifteen lumps of loaf sugar.

Put the milk in a double saucepan ; add to it the rice, three pieces of very thin lemon rind, the sugar, and half a teaspoonful of essence of almonds. Boil very slowly for four hours, stirring occasionally. Five minutes before removing from the fire add two ounces of ground almonds. Stand for a few minutes in cold water, and when cool pour into a silver dish and sprinkle with powdered cinnamon, and decorate with whole almonds.

ALMOND ICING MADE WITH GROUND ALMONDS

℄ One and a half pounds of ground almonds, one pound of castor sugar, one raw egg, lemon juice, and a few drops of orange flower water.

Pound the almonds and the sugar, and the egg and a few drops of orange flower water.

Flavour the whole with lemon juice.

XIV
CREAMS, CUSTARDS AND JELLIES

" Make your transparent sweetmeats truly nice,
With Indian sugar and Arabian spice ;
And let your various creams encirclèd be
With swelling fruit just ravish'd from the tree.
Let plates and dishes be from China brought,
With lively paint and earth transparent
    wrought."

CHAPTER XIV

CREAMS, CUSTARDS
AND JELLIES

IN England a cream means a sweet in which cream is one of the chief ingredients, or else a sweet which looks and tastes as if there were cream in it. But fresh cream is almost unobtainable in France, so eggs are used instead, and the French word " crème " means the same as the English word " custard."

The little French custard creams are flavoured with vanilla, violets, roses, coffee, tea, almonds or pistachio nuts, and served in little pots. They look very charming handed on a china tray for everyone to choose the flavour they prefer ; according to their flavouring they are different colours.

There are these four ways of cooking all custards :

(*a*) By letting the mixture thicken in a saucepan on the fire.

(*b*) By baking it in the oven.

(*c*) By cooking it in a bain-marie.

(*d*) By steaming it.

The first way is perhaps the best of all, but a great deal of experience is required to know the exact moment when the pan must be removed from the fire. If it is taken off too soon the custard will be too thin, and if it is left a second too long the custard will curdle.

Custards made in this way are never so thick as they are when they are cooked in the other ways, but their flavour is more delicate.

Here are the directions for the different methods of making the custards :

(*a*) When the ingredients are well mixed, pour the mixture into a double saucepan and stir it incessantly until it thickens. Then remove the pan from the fire and pour the custard into the glasses to cool.

(*b*) Pour the mixture into little fireproof pots and bake them in a moderate oven for about ten minutes, or until they are just set. The oven must not be too hot or the ingredients will separate.

(*c*) Strain the mixture into the little fireproof pots or cups, and stand them in a pan of boiling water. The little pots must be immersed in water for two-thirds of their depth. Let the water boil for five minutes, then cover the pan with its lid and leave the pots in it for another ten minutes, during which the water must not actually boil.

(*d*) Pour the mixture into the little pots ; put them into the steamer, and steam them for ten or fifteen minutes.

This is a recipe for Coffee Custards :

¶ Add a quarter of a pint of strong black coffee to three-quarters of a pint of milk. Put in eight lumps of sugar, and make this coffee and milk very hot. Well beat the yolks of three eggs, pour the hot milk and coffee on the yolks, stirring it all the time. Pour the mixture into the little fireproof cups, or into a soufflé dish, and cook it in one of the four ways already given.

BROWN BREAD CREAM

℄ Brown bread, butter, sugar, claret, eggs, almonds, glacé cherries, cinnamon.

Mix in a basin a quarter of a pound of butter with two ounces of castor sugar ; add to it the yolks of four eggs singly.

Soak two ounces of brown bread in a little claret, pass it through a sieve and add it to the cream.

Pound two ounces of sweet almonds and add these also, and half a tablespoonful of chopped glacé cherries and a pinch of cinnamon. Mix well and add the four beaten whites of the eggs.

Pour into a wetted mould and steam in a bain-marie for several hours. Serve cold, turned out in a silver dish.

BURNT CREAM

℄ One pint of cream, yolks of four eggs, castor sugar.

Well beat the yolks of four eggs. Boil a pint of cream for a minute in a milk saucepan ; take it from the fire, add the beaten yolks, and boil it up again. Pour it into a flat dish—in which it must be served—and stand it aside to cool. When it is cold cover it thickly with castor sugar and brown it with a salamander. Serve it very cold.

341

CALVES FOOT JELLY

℄ One ox foot cut into three pieces, one nap broken up (see p. xvi).

Wash the ox foot well and soak it for an hour in cold water. Put it into a ten-inch saucepan and fill it up with cold water to about three inches from the top. Put it on the fire with the lid only half on ; bring it to the boil. Add a teacupful of cold water and bring it again to the boil, and let it boil slowly and continuously for six hours. Then strain it and lay it aside till next day. Take off all the meat and gristle from the foot and nap, and lay it aside for nap pie.

Next morning remove all the fat from the stock, which must be a stiff jelly, wiping it with a dishcloth wrung out in boiling water. Turn it into a preserving pan. Put in one pound of brown sugar, seven lemons (the rind thinly cut off and the juice squeezed in), also the remains of one of the lemons after the juice has been squeezed out. All the seeds must be kept out. Add two dessertspoonfuls of cassia buds, twelve cloves, twelve white peppercorns, one ounce stick of cinnamon, and the whites and shells of four eggs and as many extra shells, either boiled or not, as possible. Stir it constantly till it boils. Boil it quickly for five minutes, then set it aside for ten minutes, well covered. Then pour it into a jelly bag wrung out of boiling water. If not perfectly clear, run it through the bag a second time. Add two glasses of sherry or marsala, and put it into moulds. It is important to keep the bag close to the fire while the jelly is running through.

NAP PIE

℧ Slice the meat and gristle (see p. xvi). Fill a pudding dish with layers of this meat, bacon, and hard-boiled egg. Flavour it to taste. Pour in any sediment left from the stock of the jelly, and if the meat is very stiff and gluey some water may be necessary. Cover it with water paste and bake it one hour. If the paste is not liked, twenty minutes will be enough to bake the meat.

CARAMEL JUNKET

℧ One pint of milk, rennet, salt, vanilla, two and a half ounces of sugar, half a teacupful of water.

Make a caramel syrup of the sugar and water. Let the syrup cool till it is just warm. Warm the milk ; add the syrup to the milk, and then put in the rennet and make the junket, with a pinch of salt and vanilla to flavour it. Pour it into a flat bowl to eat, and when it is set stand it in a cold place or on ice.

A little sweet whipped cream, put on it when cold, is an improvement ; and so is the addition of a sprinkling of chopped almonds or other nuts.

COFFEE SOUFFLÉ

℧ Three-quarters of a pint of strong coffee, a quarter of a pint of milk, three eggs, a quarter

343

of a packet of gelatine, four or five ounces of sugar, salt, and vanilla.

Put the made coffee with the milk, half the sugar, and the gelatine, into a double saucepan. Beat up the yolks of the eggs with the rest of the sugar and a pinch of salt, and stir this into the coffee. Whisk the whites of the eggs to a stiff froth. When the coffee mixture thickens take it off the fire (it must not boil) and add the whites of the eggs and vanilla to taste. Pour into a wet mould and set aside to cool. Serve cold with whipped cream.

CHOCOLATE CREAM IN GLASSES

This is a delicious sweet.

℃, Heat a pint of milk in a double saucepan, with twelve to fourteen lumps of sugar and a vanilla pod. Before it boils pour into it a smooth paste made of two ounces of cocoa, two level tablespoonfuls of cornflour, and sufficient cold milk to make it into the consistency of cream. Stir this well into the milk and keep on stirring till it thickens. Cook it for another five minutes, stirring all the time. Remove it from the fire, take out the vanilla pod, and stir it all the time till cool. Then pour it into custard glasses till they are three-quarters full.

When cold, pile Devonshire or whipped cream on the top.

Serve very cold.

CHOCOLATE CREAM

℃. Two ounces of cocoa, half a pint of milk, two eggs, a quarter of pound of castor sugar or to taste ; sponge fingers or ratafia biscuits, whipped cream, vanilla.

Dissolve the chocolate in the milk. Stir the yolks of two eggs with the sugar until white and thick. When the chocolate is well boiled, pour it into the eggs *very* slowly so that it does not curdle. Then put it on the fire and stir it till it thickens, but it must not boil.

Place a few sponge fingers or ratafia biscuits on a dish, pour the chocolate over slowly while it is hot. When cold cover it with whipped cream.

A little vanilla should be added to the chocolate, and the yolks of the eggs must be well beaten. The chocolate need not be thickened.

CHOCOLATE SOUFFLÉ

℃. One and a half ounces of Van Houten's cocoa, one ounce of butter, one ounce of flour, a quarter of a pint of milk, two ounces of castor sugar, half a teaspoonful of vanilla, four eggs.

Melt the butter, add to it the flour and cook it for five minutes. Add the milk and the cocoa, also the sugar and vanilla, stirring all the time; until it boils and thickens. Take it off the fire, let it cook, and add the yolks of the eggs singly, beating each well ; lastly, stir in the whites, which have been beaten very stiffly.

Put it into a well-greased soufflé dish, and

bake it for twenty minutes in a moderate oven.

More or less cocoa can be added to suit the taste.

CHOCOLATE CARAMEL

℄ One pint of milk, two ounces Van Houten's cocoa; sugar, three eggs, vanilla pod, caramel.

Line a mould with caramel made with brown sugar and water. Boil the cocoa with the milk and sweeten it to taste. It will require a good deal of sugar. When cool add the eggs well beaten. Pour this mixture into a mould and steam it till set.

Turn it out while hot, and if into a glass dish put a wet cloth under the dish to prevent it breaking. Serve it cold with Devonshire cream.

MOUSSE AU CAFÉ

℄ Eggs, coffee, castor sugar, gelatine, and cream.

Put into a basin the yolks of four eggs, and add to it a quarter of a pint of very strong coffee freshly made, then mix in from two or four ounces of sugar according to the taste. Heat this without letting it boil ; let it get cold, and add to it the beaten whites of the four eggs, and a quarter of a pint of whipped cream.

Serve it in glasses with petits fours.

COFFEE CREAM

℄ Half an ounce of isinglass, three-quarters of a pint of milk, a quarter of a pint of cream, the yolk of an egg, three ounces of coffee, three ounces of sugar.

Pour a quarter of a pint of water on to the coffee, and when it boils strain it on to the isinglass, which has been soaked in a quarter of a pint of milk. Add the sugar and dissolve it over the fire, and set it aside to cool.

Make a custard with the remainder of the milk and the yolk of the egg, and add the custard to the coffee. Whisk the cream and pour the coffee to it, stirring it all the time. Pour it into a mould.

VELVET CREAM

¶ One ounce of gelatine, three-quarters of a pint of sherry, peel and juice of two lemons, five or six ounces of loaf sugar, one pint of cream.

Soak the gelatine in the sherry for an hour or more ; then boil it with the peel and juice of two lemons and five or six ounces of loaf sugar, until the flavour is well out of the lemon peel.

Strain it, and when nearly cold mix it with one pint of cream.

CREAM SPONGE
An old family recipe.

¶ Half a pint of cream, half a pint of milk, two ounces of gelatine, three tablespoonfuls of castor sugar, juice of two lemons.

Dissolve the gelatine in three tablespoonfuls of hot water. Whip all the ingredients together until stiff, and pour it into a wetted mould.

CRÈME DE MENTHE JELLY

℃. Six lemons, half a pound of sugar, one ounce of isinglass, one and a quarter pints of water, three large leaves of peppermint geranium, or two or three drops of essence of peppermint.

Squeeze the juice of six lemons, add to it the grated rinds, and let the mixture stand for some hours.

Boil the sugar in a quarter of a pint of water to a syrup, pour it into a basin to cool, and then strain the lemon juice into it.

Dissolve the isinglass in a pint of water, and let it simmer slowly till it jellies. Stir in the lemon and sugar, and put in three large green leaves of the peppermint geranium and half a teaspoonful of spinach green colouring.

Strain it through a jelly bag, and serve it cold.

CUSTARD MERINGUE

℃. Four eggs, one pint of milk, sugar to taste, vanilla or other flavouring.

Separate the yolks from the whites of the eggs, and make a custard with the yolks and the milk and sugar. Boil the custard slowly, stirring it well ; then pour it into a fireproof dish.

Well whip the whites of the eggs ; when they are whisked into a stiff froth sift plenty of fine white sugar over them, and cover the custard with this meringue. Sift more sugar over it, and put it into a slow oven to bake till the meringue is coloured. Serve at once.

DIABLE BLEU

This is what it was called on the menu of a tiny restaurant in the Boulevard St. Germain. Curiosity called for it, and when it proved to be a very good orange jumble with whipped cream on it, we asked the waiter why it was called by such a melancholy name. " Pour la réclame, mademoiselle," was the excellent answer.

This is the recipe :

℃. A quarter of a pound of almonds, two ounces of flour, three ounces of butter, a quarter of a pound of sifted sugar, grated rind and juice of two oranges.

Blanch and shred the almonds very finely ; mix all the ingredients together. Have a buttered baking tin ready and put the mixture on to it in teaspoonfuls far apart, as the jumbles melt and spread out as they cook. Bake in a fairly slow oven.

Serve them cold, spread with whipped cream on each.

GERANIUM JELLY

℃. Fill an earthenware jar with apples ; rub them but do not cut or peel them. Set the jar in a pan half filled with water, and let them simmer all day until the juice is extracted. No water should be put with them. When the apples are reduced to pulp, strain them through a jelly bag, and add a little water to extract the utmost from the apples. To each pint of juice allow one pound of sugar, and boil together in a preserving pan with a handful of sweeted scented geranium leaves. Heat the sugar in the oven and do not add it to the juice until the pulp has boiled for twenty minutes. Cease stirring when all the sugar is melted, and let the liquor come to the point of rapid boiling for one minute only. Take it off the fire and immediately fill the moulds or pots, which should be already standing in boiling water. Remove the geranium leaves and tie down the pots. This should be served in jelly glasses with Devonshire cream.

MACAROON SOUFFLÉ

℄ Half a pint of milk, grated rind of half a lemon, one ounce of sugar, eight macaroons, four eggs, almonds.

Bring to the boil half a pint of milk, into which has been added the grated rind of half a lemon and an ounce of sugar. When it boils remove the lemon peel and add eight crushed macaroons. Cook it for a few minutes. Remove it from the fire and add the yolks of four eggs mixed with a little milk, then add the well-beaten whites of the eggs and strew the top with blanched and chopped almonds, and bake it.

This makes a delicious cold sweet with half an ounce of gelatine dissolved and added to it to set it ; then leave out the whites of the eggs.

MERINGUES WITH PISTACHIO NUTS

℄ Make meringues in the usual way by mixing the well-beaten whites of eggs with icing sugar, but add a tablespoonful of blanched and chopped pistachio nuts to every four meringues.

CRÈME DE PAQUES

❡ One pint of cream, yolks of three eggs, two ounces of raisins, three or four ounces of sugar, a quarter of a packet of gelatine, two tablespoonfuls of cold water, three tablespoonfuls of brandy, rum, and maraschino, vanilla to flavour.

Stone the raisins and stew them in a little cooking brandy till they are soft and have soaked up the brandy. Beat up the yolks of the eggs with the sugar, add a pinch of salt and vanilla to flavour, and make a custard with one pint of cream or half a pint of milk and half a pint of cream. Add the gelatine, soaked in a little cold water, to the hot custard. Strain the custard into a wet mould ; when it has cooled a little stir in the rest of the brandy, rum and maraschino, then put in the raisins. Set it aside to cool.

RATAFIA CREAM

❡ Four eggs, one lemon, two ounces of ratafias, about a quarter of a pint of milk, a quarter of a pint of cream, liqueur glass of maraschino, a quarter of a pound of fresh strawberries.

Whisk together the yolks of four eggs and the whites of three, with the grated rind of a lemon. When it froths add the milk and the ratafias, which must have been soaked in milk until soft, and pounded. Put the mixture through a sieve, and then stir in half the cream, then the maraschino.

Butter a border mould, put the mixture into it to steam for thirty minutes. Set it aside to cool. When cold turn it out, decorate it with fresh strawberries dipped in maraschino, and with the rest of the cream whipped and put on the strawberries.

RHENISH CREAM

¶ One ounce of gelatine, four ounces of sugar, one lemon, half an orange, yolks of two eggs, glassful of sherry; cream.

Dissolve in a pint of hot water an ounce of gelatine, then add the sugar and the grated rind of one lemon and half an orange, with the juice of both. Beat the yolks of two eggs and add them, and also a glass of sherry. Stir it till it is almost boiling ; it must not quite boil.

Pour it into a wetted mould, and serve it with whipped cream.

SALLY'S CREAM

For four generations this has been known in the compiler's family as " Sally's Cream," after the cook who made it, but as she brought it with her from Arundel Castle it probably is known under another name in the Duke of Norfolk's kitchen.

It is the most delicious of creams.

¶ One pint of cream, the peel and juice of a lemon, a quarter of a pound of sugar, ratafia biscuits, almonds, and cherries, sponge cakes.

Make the cream (with the lemon rind in it) scalding hot in a double saucepan, but do not let it boil. Add the sugar ; then make it hot again, adding the juice of the lemon, but it must never boil. Remove it from the fire and stir it all the time till it is nearly cold.

Put into a glass or china bowl seven or eight sponge cakes cut in slices. Soak them in rum with a little milk, and pour the cream over them.

Decorate it with ratafia biscuits, split almonds, and glacé cherries.

SAUTERNE JELLY

❡ Half a packet of gelatine, one gill of cold water, three-quarters of a pint of boiling water, three-quarters of a pint of Sauterne, half a pound of white sugar, three tablespoonfuls of lemon juice.

Soak the gelatine in the cold water ; dissolve it in the boiling water ; add the Sauterne, sugar and lemon juice, and enough green colouring to make it a pretty colour. Strain it into a shallow vessel, and when it is cold cut it into squares and serve.

SUSSEX CREAM

❡ One pint of milk, four eggs, one ounce of gelatine, half a wineglassful of sherry, five ounces of sugar, a quarter of a pound of macaroons ; glacé cherries, half an orange, cream.

Soak the gelatine in cold milk. Boil the milk and add the yolks of the eggs, the grated rind of the orange, the sugar and the macaroons. Stir it all the time until thick, then add the gelatine and the sherry. Strain it and cool it. Add the cream and the cherries.

Pour it into a wetted mould. Turn it out when set, and serve it on a silver dish.

TUTTI FRUTTI

℃ Half a pint of cream, crystallized fruits, desertspoonful each of maraschino, rum and curaçao.

Flavour the cream with the liqueurs and whip it well ; fill little glasses with it (a pint of cream will be enough for eight people), and set it on ice. Freeze it for over an hour.

Cut into small shreds some crystallized fruits, soaked in the liqueurs, to make a wreath round the top of each glass. Different fruits should be chosen and mixed, as the creams will be prettier if decorated with many colours—red, and green, and yellow, and pink.

WINE JELLY

℃ Half a packet of gelatine, half a pound of sugar, half a pint of sherry, four tablespoonfuls of orange juice, three tablespoonfuls of lemon juice, a little over three-quarters of a pint of boiling water.

Soak the gelatine in cold water, then dissolve it in boiling water ; and the sherry, orange and lemon juice, and the sugar.

Strain it into a wet mould and set it aside to cool.

Creams and Jellies of Apples, Almonds, Apricots, Bananas, Chestnuts, Figs, Red Currants, Black Currants, Gooseberries, Lemons, Pineapple, Peaches, Pears, Prunes, Oranges, Quinces, Raspberries, and Strawberries, are arranged under the fruit from which they take their name.

SANDWICHES AND SAVOURIES

" I like to eat my meat in good company, Sir."
" So do I, and the best company for meat is bread. A sandwich is better company than a fool."

CHAPTER XV

SANDWICHES AND SAVOURIES

FORTUNES are made in the City of London out of sandwiches, yet to the average household a sandwich is merely two slices of bread and butter and a piece of ham palmed off in a hurry on those who desire to picnic, but the proper accompaniment of a sandwich is not the schoolboy's ginger beer or railway station coffee, but a glass of champagne, or some of the excellent white French wines which at present are cheaper than beer.

If a busy City millionaire can lunch on sandwiches and desires nothing better, why shouldn't sandwich lunches be popular in Mayfair ? There is as much art in making sandwiches as in preparing a French menu, and many hostesses who offer their friends indifferently cooked but pretentious lunches could, with far less trouble, gain an epicurean reputation if they were content with the simplicity of wine and sandwiches.

In New York new and expensive sandwich shops are springing up in the most fashionable streets. Possibly the popularity of the sandwich meal is accounted for by the domestic service problem, as a sandwich supper after the theatre is such a convenient innovation. And Prohibition does not apparently deprive the sandwich of its natural accompaniment of wine.

These sandwiches are not limited to mere slices of cold meat ; all the most elaborate sauces and salads are drawn upon to make them interesting and appetising. Fish, fowl, cheese, fruit, vegetables, are used in every permutation and combination. And undoubtedly they will become as fashionable here as in America, for the sandwich habit is adaptable to every household in every circumstance and emergency.

Two of the secrets of successful sandwich making are to use plenty of butter, and to grate ham, tongue, chicken, etc., instead of using the meat in slices.

Never put mushrooms into sandwiches ; they are not safe to keep to eat cold.

One of the best and least known mixtures for filling sandwiches is green butter, and it is particularly good between slices of Veda bread (see p. xv). This is how it is made:

GREEN BUTTER

℃. Well wash and bone two ounces of anchovies. Boil a large handful of very green parsley, just cover it with water and leave the lid off the pan it boils in. Boil for about five minutes and then immediately put the parsley under the cold-water tap. Strip the parsley from the stalks and chop it very fine (a parsley cutter only costs a few pence and saves a lot of time). Beat the parsley, the anchovies and a quarter of a pound of butter together into a paste, and pot it.

This will keep for a week.

Other good sandwiches are :—

DELHI SANDWICH

℃. Six anchovies, three sardines, one teaspoonful of chutney, one egg, one ounce of butter, one small teaspoonful of curry powder.

Free the sardines and anchovies from bones. Pound them with the seasonings, the chutney and butter. Beat up the yolk of the egg and stir this in, with a pinch of cayenne. Heat the mixture, stirring it into a smooth paste.

This is excellent spread between toast. The toast should be made in rather thick slices, split in two, and the soft sides buttered.

SOLE SANDWICH

℃. Fillets of cold sole, seasoned with cayenne pepper and salt, between slices of brown bread and butter make a delicious sandwich.

CHEESE SANDWICH

℃. Beat two eggs with two ounces of grated Parmesan cheese ; cook it until thick, and allow it to get cold. Spread the bread with anchovy paste and then spread it with the cheese mixture.

RUSSIAN SANDWICH

℃. Chop watercress very finely and mix it to a paste with butter, and spread it on toast ; sprinkle it with salt and paprika. Cover it with caviare seasoned with lemon juice.

MOCK CRAB SANDWICH

℃. Rub the yolk of a hard-boiled egg to a smooth paste with a tablespoonful of oil ; add a teaspoonful of salt, sugar, and made mustard, and

a dash of cayenne. When well mixed add a
a quarter of a pound of grated cheese and a tablespoonful of vinegar seasoned with onion juice.
Mix well and spread between slices of bread.

CREAMED CHICKEN SANDWICH

℆. Mix a cupful each of chopped, cooked chicken
meat and celery with very thick Béchamel sauce;
season it with onion juice and salt, and add the
stiffly beaten whites of two eggs. Cook it in a
double saucepan, but do not let it come to the
boil. Add a little lemon juice. Pour it into a mould
to get cold.

Turn it out and cut into thin slices for the
sandwiches.

CHICKEN SALAD SANDWICH

℆. Mix grated chicken and ham with cold
mayonnaise and spread between bread.

EASTERN SANDWICH

℆. Mix grated chicken and chopped almonds
with cream, and season with salt and paprika
and spread between bread.

MOCK CHICKEN SANDWICH

℆. Mix chopped hard-boiled eggs and grated
veal; season it with salt, pepper and mushroom ketchup rubbed to a paste with butter
and spread between bread.

DEVILLED FISH SANDWICH

℆. Mix chopped cooked fish and hard-boiled
eggs, moisten it with cream and season it with

minced parsley and Worcester sauce and spread
between bread.

COLD DEVIL SANDWICH
¶ Mix scraped meat and celery with tartare
sauce, and spread between bread.

CRÈME D'HARICOTS SANDWICH
¶ Mix baked beans, seasoned with horseradish,
onion juice and made mustard, with minced
parsley and celery. Pound it to a paste, and
spread between bread.

CREAMED HADDOCK SANDWICH
¶ One cooked dried haddock, three tablespoonfuls of cream, one ounce of butter, a tablespoonful of minced parsley, a little milk, cayenne,
salt, pepper.
Flake the flesh from the bones of the fish.
Make the cream, butter, pepper, parsley and
cayenne into a paste, and mix it with the flaked
haddock. Spread between slices of bread or
toast.

LOBSTER SANDWICH
¶ Pound the meat of a small lobster to a paste
with a little cream and butter, a chopped
anchovy, salt and pepper. Add two or three
tablespoonfuls of chopped watercress, and mix
thoroughly. Spread between slices of bread.

DEVILLED CHEESE SANDWICH
¶ Grate some cheese and pound it to a paste
with butter, season it with tarragon vinegar,

and made mustard and spread between slices of bread.

CHEESE AND EGG SANDWICH

¶ Grate some cheese and mix with the yolk of a hard-boiled egg, rubbed to a paste with butter. Season it with salt, pepper, and mustard and spread it between slices of bread.

SUMMER SANDWICHES

¶ Mix chopped olives and cream cheese, and spread it between brown bread and butter.

CHICKEN LIVER AND CHESTNUT SANDWICH

¶ Pound some cooked chicken livers with some boiled chestnuts, mix it with melted butter, and season it with salt, pepper and lemon juice. Spread it between slices of bread.

GREEN FOIE GRAS SANDWICH

¶ Mix pate de foie gras with scraped chicken meat, and lettuce leaves dipped in French dressing and spread between bread.

SALADE D'ECRIVISSE SANDWICH

¶ Mix pounded shrimps seasoned with lemon juice and pepper, with mayonnaise and spread between bread.

SAVOURY LETTUCE SANDWICH

¶ Mix tartare sauce and lettuce leaves and spread between bread.

CUCUMBER SALAD SANDWICH

℁ Mix sliced cucumber with mayonnaise and spread between bread.

DEVILLED HAM SANDWICH

℁ Mix minced boiled ham with tartare sauce and spread between bread.

DEVILLED SALMON SANDWICH

℁ Mix salmon pounded to a paste with butter and seasoned with salt, pepper and Worcester sauce, with sliced cucumber dipped in French dressing and spread between bread.

AMERICAN SALAD SANDWICH

℁ Mix chopped pimentos with mayonnaise, lettuce leaves and cream cheese, and spread between brown bread.

FIFTH AVENUE MIXTURE SANDWICH

℁ Mix cold cooked spinach and chopped hard-boiled eggs, with tartare sauce, and spread between bread.

TOMATO CREAM SANDWICH

℁ Six anchovies, half a pound of tomatoes; mustard and cress, whipped cream (two table-spoonfuls), cayenne pepper.

Skin the tomatoes. Chop up the anchovies very fine. Pound the tomatoes with the anchovies, season it with pepper and cayenne and stir in the cream.

Slice finger rolls, butter them, spread them with this mixture and decorate them with mustard and cress.

TOMATO AND SARDINE SANDWICH

❧ Half a pound of tomatoes, one tin of sardines, lemon juice, castor sugar, one ounce of butter, pepper and salt.

Bone the sardines, pound them with one ounce of butter and rub it through a sieve. Season it with pepper and salt. Skin the tomatoes and cut them in very thin slices. Spread buttered bread with the sardine mixture, lay on this the thin slices of tomato, and complete the sandwich.

DEVILLED ALMOND AND ANCHOVY SANDWICH

❧ Three ounces of sweet almonds, three ounces of butter, one teaspoonful of anchovy paste, cayenne pepper, half a teaspoonful each of minced parsley and onion.

Blanch the almonds and pound them ; mix them with the butter, and add the parsley, onion and anchovy paste. Season the mixture with cayenne, and spread between split pieces of toast.

NORWEGIAN SANDWICHES

❧ Six anchovies, one hard-boiled egg, minced parsley, smoked salmon, one ounce of butter.

Pound six anchovies to a smooth paste with an ounce of butter, and spread both pieces of buttered toast with this. Lay a thin slice of smoked salmon, sprinkled with chopped hard-boiled egg and the parsley, between them.

OLIVE AND ANCHOVY SALAD SANDWICH

¶. Allow three olives for each anchovy ; chop them, pound them together, season it with pepper. Spread the sandwich with this and then with mayonnaise sauce. Sprinkle it with minced capers.

EGG AND MANGO CHUTNEY SANDWICH

¶. One teaspoonful of mango chutney to one egg, watercress.

Hard boil the eggs ; chop them finely with mango chutney and some watercress, and spread the sandwiches with the mixture.

CAVIARE TOAST SANDWICHES

¶. Make the toast rather thick, split it, butter the soft side, spread it with caviare seasoned with lemon juice, and sprinkle it with hard-boiled egg chopped very finely.

EGGS AND ANCHOVY PASTE SANDWICH

¶. Three eggs, half an ounce of butter, one dessertspoonful of anchovy essence; salt , pepper.

Hard boil the eggs ; pound the yolks with butter, stir in the anchovy essence, add pepper to taste, and mix it well. Spread between slices of bread or toast.

LIVER SANDWICH

℃. Calves' liver grated and pounded with butter and cream, and seasoned with pepper and salt.

And if a more substantial luncheon dish is required, here is an excellent recipe for a hot " sandwich " :

HOT HAM SANDWICH

℃. Cold ham, bread, two ounces of butter, grated Parmesan.

Cut the bread very thin and as nearly as possible to the size of the slices of ham, and cut one more piece of bread than there are slices of ham.

Start the sandwich with a piece of bread and put it in a frying pan, then place a slice of ham upon it, after this a slice of bread and again a slice of ham until sufficiently big, beginning and ending with a slice of bread. Sprinkle grated Parmesan between the slices and on the outside, also season it with pepper and salt.

Fry it a golden brown in butter, and serve it very hot.

And for a sweet Sandwich :

HONEY AND OATMEAL SANDWICHES

℃. Take two handfuls of oatmeal, and bake it in the oven till it is a pale brown.

Spread the buttered bread with honey, sprinkle the oatmeal over it, and make into sandwiches.

The Savoury is a British institution. French dinners usually end with the sweet. In this book Savouries will be found under their ingredients —Mushrooms, Eggs, Chestnuts, Prunes, etc. They are indexed under " Savouries."

Here are some good Savouries that do not come under other headings :

CHEESE WAFERS

❡ Grate ordinary cheese with an equal quantity of Parmesan, and season it with pepper and salt. Moisten the mixture with a little cream. Spread this mixture between unsweetened ice wafers and bake it in the oven till crisp—about seven minutes or ten if the cream is omitted.

INDIAN CROUTONS

❡ Spread finely chopped curried ham or meat between small rounds of thin fried bread, and serve with a drop of hot cheese on the top of each crouton.

AMERICAN SAVOURY

❡ Cut two-inch (or larger) cubes of bread and hollow out the centre. Mash some cooked chicken liver with cream and the yolk of an egg, and season it with salt, paprika, and lemon juice. Fry the bread shells in butter, fill them with the mixture, and sprinkle them with minced parsley. Serve them very hot.

COD'S ROE ON TOAST

❡ Half a pound of dried cod's roe, mace, lemon, butter, salt, pepper and cayenne.

Soak the roe well in water, and then pound it with some butter, and season it with a little mace, pepper and salt.

Put a lump of butter in a saucepan and when melted add the pounded mixture and a squeeze of lemon juice. Make it very hot and spread it thickly on croutons of fried bread.

KIDNEY TOAST

ℂ One veal kidney, one egg, half an onion, minced parsley, salt and pepper.

Cook the kidney and the onion separately. When cold, mince both separately and pound them together in a mortar with the chopped parsley, pepper and salt.

Stir the well-beaten egg into the mixture and make it very hot, and spread it thickly on fried croutons of bread.

CHEESE CREAMS

ℂ Half an ounce of grated Parmesan, one table-spoonful of cream, the whites of three eggs, chopped parsley.

Whip the whites of the eggs to a stiff froth, then stir in the grated cheese and the cream. When well mixed, put into little fireproof pots, stand these in hot water, and steam the creams for a quarter of an hour. Serve with tomato sauce.

LA FONDUE
A Swiss Dish
A speciality of Fribourg and the pays de Vaud

ℂ Take a kilogram of Gruyère cheese; cut it in thin slices and melt it over the fire with a litre of white wine. When reduced to a cream mix it with a little of Groult's fécule, and add a liqueur glass of Kirsch.

It should be served very hot.

STUFFED BACON

¶. One egg, one small cooked onion, breadcrumbs, one tablespoonful of cream or milk, two tomatoes, four mushrooms, bread, as many slices of very thin bacon as there are people.

Mince the following ingredients, and make them into a paste :—the egg, onion, tomatoes, mushrooms, a few breadcrumbs, and the cream, pepper and salt. Spread this on the very thin slices of bacon and roll up each slice very firmly and skewer them.

Fry them and serve them on croutons of fried bread.

HOME-MADE WINES AND CUPS

" Cyder bring and cowslip wine,
   Fruits and flavours from the East ;
Pears and pippins too, and fine
   Saffron loaves to make a feast ;
China dishes, silver cups,
   For the board where Celia sups."

CHAPTER XVI

HOME-MADE WINES AND CUPS

IN older days the harvest of the hedges was valued; nowadays the elderberries, the sloes, the hips and haws, the brambles are wasted, and so are dandelions and daisies: but the elderberry wine and sloe gin that were in every good housewife's stillroom only a little while ago, have virtues that should not be forgotten—moreover they are very easily made, so are currant or rhubarb wines, and wines made from other fruits or herbs or flowers. Anything vegetable will ferment ; Nature has not passed a nineteenth amendment to her constitution. Nowadays, when excellent French wine is to be had for two shillings a bottle, it is a pity that the northern nations do not emulate the southern races and drink more wine. The light wines of France or Spain are more wholesome than spirits or than the strangely concocted cocktails with weird names that come from America.

Why is it that drinking is so much more poetical than eating ? Why may poets write sonnets about wine and not about food ? Not at any rate about specific food such as fried soles and rice pudding—not, that is, if they wish to be taken seriously. This distinction, this sharp dividing line between the prosaic and the lyrical is not of fashion nor of nationality, it is as old as literature : nor is it to be attributed to any kink in the artistic temperament, nor to any imagined affinity between genius and insobriety. Homer wrote lyrically about " sweet honey-hearted wine," but the rebuke of Antinous to Odysseus, whom he accuses of being " wounded with the honey-sweet wine " that " taken in great draughts and drunk out of measure darkened the mind and the heart of Eurytion, so that he wrought foul deeds and began the war between the Centaurs and mankind," is far more poetical than any modern temperance literature, and no less convincing.

BARLEY WATER
As made at the Bachelors' Club by Mr. Hammond

℄ Put the outside peel of two lemons into two quarts of water, with eight lumps of sugar, and boil for ten minutes. To this add two dessert-spoonfuls of Robinson's Patent Barley previously mixed to a smooth paste with a little cold water. Continue to boil it for five minutes and allow it to cool. Serve with slices of lemon.

In the compiler's opinion it is a great improvement to add the juice of the two lemons when the barley water is cool. Double the amount of sugar is then required.

Another Recipe for
BARLEY WATER

℄ Wash three tablespoonfuls of pearl barley in a quart of water, and change the water several times. Then put a fresh quart of water with the barley into a saucepan. Bring it to the boil and allow it to simmer for ten minutes. Strain it and add sugar to taste, and the juice of two lemons.

BISHOP
An Oxford Recipe

℃ Lemon, cloves, half a pint of water, cinnamon, mace, allspice, ginger, port wine, sugar.

Take a lemon and make incisions in the rind. Stick cloves in these incisions and roast the lemon in front of a slow fire. Put into a saucepan half a pint of water with a little cinnamon and the same amount of cloves, mace, allspice and ginger. Boil it till it is reduced to a quarter of a pint. Empty a bottle of port wine into another saucepan and set fire to it while it is in the saucepan, to burn a little of the spirit out of it. Add the roasted lemon and the spiced water. Stir altogether and let it stand near the fire for ten minutes.

Rub some sugar on the rind of a lemon, and put it into a bowl with the juice of half a lemon. Pour the wine on it, grate in a little nutmeg, sweeten it to taste, and serve it with the lemon and spice floating in it.

A roasted Seville orange stuck with cloves can be used instead of a lemon.

CHABLIS CUP

℃ Pour a quarter of a pint of boiling water over four or five lumps of sugar, and add a little thin lemon rind. Let it stand for thirty minutes before adding a bottle of Chablis, a sprig of verbena, half a pint of water and a wineglassful of sherry. Mix it and allow it to stand for fifteen minutes. Strain it, add a bottle of seltzer water, a few strawberries, and some ice.

BRAMBLE TIP WINE

A Yorkshire recipe—most excellent

❧ Pick the tips of the shoots of the blackberry vines, taking just about an inch of the tender ends. To a gallon measure of these tips add four pounds of sugar, and boil them together in a gallon of water for an hour. Strain the mixture and let it stand and ferment for about a fortnight. Then it can be bottled.

This is a very popular wine in Yorkshire and the north of England, and has a flavour like sherry.

CIDER CUP

❧ Put at the bottom of a jug a slice of toasted bread, and grate over it half a nutmeg, and a little ginger. Add six lumps of sugar, and some very thin lemon rind. Then add two wineglassfuls of sherry, the juice of a small lemon, two bottles of lively water, and three pints of cider.

Mix it well and serve it with ice and borage.

CLARET CUP

❧ Put into a bowl the very thin rind of a lemon, a little sugar, and a wineglassful of sherry. Add a bottle of claret, sugar to taste, a sprig of lemon-scented verbena, one bottle of aerated water, and a grated nutmeg. Strain and ice.

MULLED CLARET
A French Recipe

℃. Boil a quarter of an ounce of mixed cinnamon, bruised ginger, and cloves in a wineglass and a half of water, with three ounces of castor sugar. When it becomes a syrup pour into it a pint of claret, and stir it until nearly boiling. It must not actually boil. Serve it immediately.

ELDERBERRY WINE

The elder tree is generally found near human habitations, because in olden days it was planted as a protection from evil spirits. The tree itself was a protection, for the Norse mother of the good fairies, Hulda, lived under its roots, hence its name. The superstition, with the habit of planting the tree near a dwelling-place, probably came across the North Sea with the Danes, but the respect for the elder tree's efficacy persisted well into the Middle Ages. It was the custom to make crosses with elderberry juice on the hearthstone to ward off witches and warlocks. Such crosses are to be seen on the fireplace in the " solar " in Stokesay Castle to this day. In some parts of Northern Europe it is considered polite, if not prudent, to ask the permission of an elder before cutting it, and until quite recent years there was a distinct reluctance in rural England and Scotland to cut down an elder tree in any circumstances. But nobody ever suggested that the tree had any objection to its fruit or flowers being used. Both elder-flower water and elderbery wine have always been highly prized.

℃. Gather the berries on a dry day, clean from the stalks and put them into an earthenware pan. Pour two gallons of boiling water to every three gallons of berries. Press the berries into the water. Cover them closely and leave them till the next day. Then strain the juice from the fruit through a sieve, and when this is done squeeze from the berries any remaining juice.

Measure the juice and add to every gallon three pounds of sugar, three-quarters of an ounce of cloves, and one ounce of ginger. Boil it for twenty minutes, removing the scum as it rises. Put it when cool into a well-washed and dry cask, or into large stone bottles.

Entirely fill the cask, and pour very gently into the bung-hole a large spoonful of new yeast mixed with a very small quantity of the wine.

MILK LEMONADE
A good old Recipe

℃. Take a pint of boiling water and add to it six ounces of sugar, a quarter of a pint of sherry, and the same amount of lemon juice. Finally add three-quarters of a pint of cold milk. Stir it well, and pass it through a jelly bag.

HAWBERRY WINE
A Yorkshire Recipe

℃. Put one gallon of hips and haws, gathered when ripe and red, in a pan with a gallon of boiling water. Leave it for a fortnight to ferment, stirring it every day. Then drain off the liquor, pressing the berries well, and boil the liquor for fifteen minutes. Then strain and measure it, and to each gallon of liquor add three pounds of sugar, one ounce of whole ginger bruised, and a quarter of an ounce of cloves.

Boil it all again for fifteen minutes, then strain and bottle when cold.

HERB WINE
A wine with a romantic story attached to it

The story goes that a long time ago some monks in a monastery by the sea were very poor, and, having borrowed money for their needs from a usurer, were being pressed by him for payment. In their great distress one of the brothers had a vision, or dream, that help was coming to them from the sea. But the only thing that came to them from the sea was a wrecked boat from which they rescued a half-drowned man. They revived him, took him in and sheltered him, and explained their desperate poverty, but shared with him what they had, though their hospitality made their own plight worse. When he was a little restored he went into their garden, which was only full of herbs, and he said there was no need for them to be so miserable, as he would show them how to make money out of their herbs, and he brewed herb wine for them. They sold it, and it was so appreciated that they made themselves a big distillery, brewed it in large quantities, paid off their usurer, and their financial crisis was at an end.

This is the actual recipe for this very herb wine :

ℭ, Take a quantity of fresh herbs—mint, thyme, sage, agrimony, marjoram, basil, etc. Soak them in water ; the quantity must vary according to the size of the bunch of herbs, but to a gallon of water add three pounds of sugar. Boil the herbs with the sugar till the strength and flavouring of the herbs are extracted, then let it get cold, strain it, and cover it up. After three weeks strain it again, and bottle it.

RAISIN WINE
which will keep for years

ℭ, Allow eight pounds of raisins to one gallon of water. Boil the water first and allow it to get cold. Then fill the cask alternately with water and raisins, pressing the raisins well down. Partly close the bung, and stir it every day, and keep the cask full by adding boiled cold water.

In six or seven weeks, when the fermentation is over, press in the bung and leave it for twelve months. Then draw it off into a clean cask, and fine it with isinglass tied in a muslin bag and suspended in it.

RUMFUSTIAN

℃ Take the yolks of two eggs and beat them with a tablespoonful of sifted sugar. Put them into a large jug, and add one pint of old Burton ale, one wineglassful of sherry, and one wineglassful of gin, a little spice and lemon rind. Allow it all to come to the boil, then remove it from the fire, pour in the eggs and whisk it well.

Serve it hot with grated nutmeg.

SLOE GIN

English port used to be manufactured from sloes, which make an excellent drink

℃ Mix together an equal quantity of sloes and white sugar. Prick the sloes, and half fill the bottles with the sugared fruit and fill up with gin. Cork tightly and the gin will be ready in about three months.

A VERY REFRESHING SUMMER DRINK

℃ Take six ounces of lump sugar and rub them well against the rind of a lemon. Put the sugar thus tasting of lemon rind, and the juice of one and a half lemons into a jug. Dissolve the sugar and pour in a bottle of cider and three wineglassfuls of sherry. Grate in half a nutmeg. Put it on ice, and serve it with sprigs of borage.

TEA CUP

℄ Boil a quart of tea made of three-quarters of Indian with a quarter of green tea, and mix it with a bottle of Apollinaris water, the very thin rind of a lemon, a little sugar, borage and ice.

Place on ice and add a wineglassful of curaçao.

WASSAIL
A very old cup which used to be drunk at Jesus College, Oxford

℄ Put into a jug half a pound of castor sugar, and pour over it one pint of warm beer ; grate into it a little nutmeg and ginger, then add four glasses of sherry and five other pints of beer. Stir it well and sweeten it to taste. Allow it to stand for three hours, then add to it three or four slices of toasted bread and a few slices of lemon.

Bottle it, and drink it in a few days.

See also under Fruit and Flowers :

Apricot Brandy.
Apricot Wine.
Blackberry Wine.
Cherry Wine.
Cowslip Wine.
Daisy Wine.
Dandelion Wine.
Marigold Wine.
Rose Wine.
Woodruff Wine.

XVII
COOKING FOR CHILDREN

" Bunches of grapes," says Timothy.
" Pomegranates pink," says Elaine,
" A junket of cream and a cranberry tart
  For me," says Jane.

CHAPTER XVII

COOKING FOR CHILDREN

MANY children listen to the story of Cinderella with their sympathy for the heroine warped by the reflection that at any rate she was given the free run of the kitchen when the family departed for the ball. Most children prefer the kitchen to the nursery or drawing-room. If the cook is an Irishwoman, she will welcome the society of five or six children in the kitchen at all hours, if she is any other nationality she will probably prefer them one at a time or not at all. But it is a pity when a child is debarred from all contact with the practical affairs of the home during its impressionable years, and anyway, the time to interest children in cookery is when they are under twelve, when their education cannot or should not be all book work, and when it is undiluted bliss to be allowed to shell peas, to pick currants, and whisk eggs. By the time they are eighteen the glamour of life will be re-oriented. But when we are very young there is romance in the oven and the singing kettle.

A child in a kitchen is an alchemist learning the properties of those mysterious elements—fire and water. A saucepan is a crucible in which anything may happen. Cooking is sheer magic to the child, the purest white magic. A child watches the kneading of flour and water into dough and the transmutation of the pale dough into crusty loaves and brown cakes with the delighted wonder with which the cherubim and seraphim must have looked on at the creation of the world.

It is easy to give children the natural primitive pleasure of making things themselves. They can make or help to make their own toffee and ginger beer : they can cut out their own gingerbread duck and whales. Not all the following recipes are intended to be made by children themselves. The " ostrich-egg " calls for some skill, and the point of others is their surprise. But they have been chosen because they will appeal to children by providing that combination of the familiar with the unexpected which is the real zest of pleasure to children all over the world.

TO MAKE AN OSTRICH EGG

℄ Get a pig's bladder, boil it and cleanse it thoroughly. Break about a dozen eggs, separating the whites and yolks. Half-fill the bladder with some of the white, and plunge it into hot water and allow it to boil, shaking the bladder so that the whites form a coating to the lower part of the bladder. Then beat the yolks and pour them in to the centre of the bladder, shaking it so that the yolks, as they cook, form a ball in the middle. Lastly, pour in the rest of the whites, so that the yolks are covered and a complete egg is formed.

Cut away the bladder and serve the enormous ostrich egg in a Béchamel sauce.

WHITE STRAWBERRY JAM

This is a delicious sweet, fit for a luncheon party, but children will not get the full joy of seeing red jam turn white unless they are allowed to make it themselves

℀. Four ounces of strawberry jam, four ounces of red currant jelly, whites of two eggs beaten separately very stiff.

Mix the whites of the eggs with the jam and whip the two together without ceasing till the mixture becomes white.

Serve in a glass dish and hand sponge cakes separately.

FRUIT IN CHEMISES

℀. Choose fine bunches of red and white currants, large ripe cherries, and strawberries or raspberries.

Beat up the white of an egg with half as much cold water ; dip the fruit into this so that it is well covered. Drain for a moment, and then roll in castor sugar until it is entirely coated. Shake gently and lay on sheets of white paper to dry, either in a warm room or a sunny window. It will take from three to four hours.

This has the appearance, when finished, of the most expensive confectionery.

The sugar that is used must be very dry.

BRANDY SNAPS

¶ A quarter of a pound of treacle, one ounce of flour, one ounce of butter, half a teaspoonful of ginger, a quarter of a teaspoonful of allspice.

Mix the flour and spices in a basin. Melt the butter and treacle over the fire and pour it on to the flour and mix it thoroughly. Grease a baking sheet, and on to it put teaspoonfuls of the mixture far apart. Bake it slowly. They will spread out and become thin.

After taking the sheet from the oven, let it stand for a minute, then loosen the cakes with a knife, turn them over, and curl them round a greased stick, when they will harden at once.

CHOCOLATE FUDGE

¶ One pound of best granulated sugar, four penny bars of chocolate, half a teacupful of milk, a piece of butter the size of a walnut.

Put the sugar in a double saucepan and mix it with the milk to form a thick paste. Grate the chocolate into it, and add the butter. Put it on a slow fire and do not let it come to the boil till the sugar and the chocolate are melted. Then let it boil for five minutes, stirring it hard all the time. Take it off the fire, beat it till it is thick, and pour it on to buttered soup plates or dishes.

Cut it into squares before it gets cold.

OMELETTES IN SAUCERS

Children can make omelettes for themselves very simply. This is the recipe :

¶. Well butter a saucer. Beat up an egg in a cup, season it with salt, add a little chopped parsley. Pour the beaten egg into the saucer and put the saucer in the oven for a minute or two till the egg is set.

This makes quite a nice little omelette, and the child can put into it a little puffed rice or other harmless ingredient—it will amuse the child and won't hurt the omelette.

MERINGUES

¶. Six fresh eggs, three-quarters of a pound of icing sugar.

Separate the whites of six fresh eggs very carefully from the yolks. Whisk them to a very stiff froth and gradually whip in three-quarters of a pound of icing sugar.

Line an oven tray with thick white paper and lay the mixture in tablespoonfuls on the paper. They should keep the shape of the spoon. Sift more sugar over them and put them in a gentle oven. Bake them till they are a pale brown, then gently remove them from the paper, and when quite cold scoop out some of the inside and fill them with vanilla-flavoured whipped cream.

The whole success of meringue making depends upon the oven being just right, and they must be looked at from time to time.

GINGERBREAD

The joy of the old-fashioned gingerbread, sold at every English fair was, of course, the fact that it was fashioned into enchanting shapes of animals and human beings ; for choice, kings and queens in gilded crowns. But the expression, " the gilt is off the gingerbread " has outlived, in England, the custom of giving gingerbread so romantic a form.

In Holland, for weeks before St. Nicholas' Day, December 6th, the windows of every baker's shop are filled with gingerbread in every strange device from figures of the children's Saint himself to that of little animals, donkeys, rabbits and bears. Some of these cakes are two feet long, and of all sizes.

Even the most blasé modern child feels the fascination of these fantastic delicacies, and they are very easily made.   Here is the recipe :

℃, Two pounds of flour, a quarter of a pound of brown sugar, one ounce of ground ginger, two ounces of candied peel, half an ounce of carraway seeds, half an ounce of cinnamon, a quarter of a pound of butter, two ounces of hot treacle.

Mix the dry ingredients well together, then cream the butter and mix well, add the hot treacle. Knead it into a thick paste. If it is too stiff, moisten it with a very little milk. The paste must be very smooth. Roll it out thin and cut it into any shape, making any design upon it with the back of a knife. The shape of the gingerbread need be limited only by the skill or fancy of the artist. Fishes are easy to draw, so are birds, and pigs, and elephants, and humans in Anglo-Saxon attitudes.

Bake them till they are crisp all through.

A GINGERBREAD HOUSE

A " Gingerbread House " is an old-fashioned Christmas treat that is worth making for the delight of nurseries where the children are not too blasé; if the children are allowed to help to make it no child will be too modern to enjoy it.

The pattern for the little house must be cut out first in paper. Each of the four sides of the house must be made separately, and the sections of the roof, which should have two gables if it is to be firm ; therefore the front and back walls of the house must have two points to support the sections of the roof. Thus :—

Then doors and windows must be drawn on the paper, according to the architectural tastes of the designer. When the four walls and the four sections of the roof are cut out in paper, the paper must be laid on the rolled-out paste, which must be carefully cut out. Then it is baked. When it is cooked and hard the little house must be fitted together and cemented with white of egg. It should stand on a pastry board or any convenient equivalent. A little chimney should be added, and a gingerbread wall round a little garden. Then there must be icing on the roof for snow, and icing in the little garden, in which bunches of raisins will stand as trees. This " snow " will help the gingerbread wall or railings to stand up. At the door of the cottage should be a little gingerbread woman.

The old-fashioned way of illuminating the house was to put a night-light inside. But in these days, when Christmas trees are lit with electric light, probably something could be done with an electric lamp in the little house, for a night-light was apt to give the gingerbread a smoky flavour—not that the children who ate it minded that, for the end of the little house is to be demolished and eaten.

SURPRISE FRENCH ROLLS

℃. Take some French rolls of bread, cut a slit in the side. Remove some of the crumb from the centre, and insert strawberry or raspberry cream mixed with whipped or Devonshire cream.

EGGS IN OVERCOATS

℃. Six eggs and the whites of two more, six large potatoes, six tablespoonfuls of minced ham, two tablespoonfuls of chopped parsley, three tablespoonfuls of butter, four tablespoonfuls of cream ; salt and pepper.

Bake the potatoes ; cut a piece off the top of

each and scoop out the inside. Mash it with a little hot milk. Add the minced ham, parsley, cream and butter, salt and pepper, and bind the mixture with the well-beaten whites of two eggs. Line the potato skins with the mixture.

Poach six eggs lightly, put a poached egg into each potato, cover each potato with the mashed potato mixture, and bake till this is brown.

CREAM TOFFEE

℄ One pound of sugar, half a pound of golden syrup, one tin of condensed milk, one and a half ounces of butter, one gill of water.

Melt the sugar in the water, stirring until it is quite dissolved ; add the other ingredients, and let it boil until it forms a moderately hard ball when dropped in cold water.

GINGER BEER

℄ One ounce of bruised ginger, two pounds of white sugar, two ounces of cream of tartar, one lemon sliced.

Put all these into a large earthenware pan and pour over them two gallons of boiling water. When nearly cold, put one teaspoonful of yeast spread on toast. Bottle in twenty-four hours, and tie down the corks.

WINTER STRAWBERRIES AND CREAM

℄ Cut up six bananas into small rounds ; put them into a glass dish and spread over them a thick layer of strawberry jam. Mix well together into a purée. Whip a quarter of a pint of cream very stiffly and cover the bananas with it.

FRUIT PASTES

❡ Almost any fruit can be used for this sweet-meat—oranges, apples, pears, cherries, plums, raspberries, etc.

Peel the fruit if it has a strong skin, like oranges or apples, and boil it in sugar till it makes a thick marmalade. Let it get cool and mould it into thin cakes. Dry these in the oven.

Before these pastes are dried they will take the impression of any seal and may be moulded into any shape and have any ornament or design stamped upon them. A small decorated butter pat might be used, such as are used in dairies to stamp a quarter of a pound of butter, or some such domestic equivalent as the lid of a china box with a raised Wedgwood design upon it.

FIGURED ORANGES

❡ Choose large oranges with smooth skins ; on their rinds draw faces and figures, flowers or beasts ; a ring of little dancing elves is effective. Draw the figures in ink, which will wipe off quite easily if the first attempts are not succesful, and when the drawing is satisfactory, cut out the figures very carefully with a small knife, only removing the yellow surface of the peel and leaving the white rind underneath intact.

Then cut a small piece out of the rind at the top of the orange, large enough to insert a coffee spoon. Scoop out the inside of the orange, free the pulp from pips and fibre, mix the pulp and juice with sugar and refill the orange skin with it, or the orange can be filled with jelly.

To preserve the oranges put the whole oranges into water and boil them till they are soft, and then cut a hole in the top and scoop out the inside. Then make a syrup with sugar and water, fill the oranges with this syrup and boil it for three-quarters of an hour. Take them out to cool, leave them for a few days, and then boil them again for twenty minutes. Repeat this process until the orange rind is candied.

XVIII
FLOWER RECIPES

" Excellent herbs had our fathers of old,
Excellent herbs to ease their pain :
Alexanders and marigold,
Eyebright, orris, and elecampane,
Basil, rocket, valerian, rue,
(Almost singing themselves they run),
Vervain, dittany, call-me-to-you,
Cowslip, melilot, rose of the sun,
Anything green that grew out of the mould
Was an excellent herb to our fathers of old."

CHAPTER XVIII

FLOWER RECIPES

NOWADAYS we admire flowers so much for their beauty and fragrance that we forget their flavour, unless we are very young, with the habit of tasting everything in the garden. But originally our English gardens were herb gardens, and were cultivated mainly for utilitarian reasons.

Sugar is a comparatively modern innovation ; our forefathers depended upon flowers for sweetness in a very literal sense, for honey was the only form of sugar obtainable. Plants that we regard as weeds were valued either for their savour or for their healing properties ; and flowers themselves have fallen out of fashion as ingredients in the kitchen.

The Romans crowned their bowls of wine with roses and put roses in their wine to add to its fragrance. There is a story that the Spartan soldiers, after the battle of Cirrha, refused the wine offered them because it was not perfumed with roses.

Flowers are still used by the Chinese in the tea factories of Canton for flavouring their scented teas. Orange Pekoe is scented with orange blossoms—about forty pounds of petals to one hundred pounds of tea. The dry tea and the fresh flowers are mingled for a day and a night, then the flowers are winnowed out. Sometimes a petal or two is left and can be found in the tea when it is unpacked in England. Other delicious teas are scented with jasmine or oleanders, gardenias, peonies and roses. These flower-scented teas are deemed very precious by the Chinese ; they keep them for their own use. Jasmine-scented tea is sometimes exported, but the teas scented with peonies and roses rarely leave China, probably because they do not keep long, possibly because the Chinese won't waste the refinements of sweet peonies and oleanders on foreign devils who don't know how to drink tea and have lost the taste for roses and gardenias.

Yet some flowers are delicious if properly used. These recipes are perfectly practical, and can be made by anyone who likes their flavours. And the rose has a special and pretty significance for those who dine wisely or unwisely. The rose was the flower of Venus, the goddess of Love, and the story goes that Cupid bribed with white roses Harpocrates, the god of Silence, not to betray some episode Venus wished to keep a secret. Since then the white rose has been the emblem of silence. In ancient days a white rose was painted or carved on the ceilings of banqueting halls and dining-rooms as a gentle reminder to guests that conversations held under the hospitable roof were private and not to be repeated elsewhere.

The white rose on the dining-room ceiling

lingered on through the Middle Ages, and even to-day the round plaster ornament in the centre of ceilings is technically known as a " rose," but its original meaning has been forgotten.

CAMOMILE TEA

℄ Camomile tea is very good for the complexion. It is so much drunk by American women after lunch instead of coffee that it is now obtainable at most fashionable English hotels. At the Carlton it is generally made in an infuser teapot.

A teaspoonful of the dried flowers is allowed for every cup of water. The boiling water is poured on the flowers as on tea.

CHRYSANTHEMUM SALAD

℄ Clean and wash in several waters about twenty chrysanthemum flowers picked from the stalks. Blanch them in acidulated and salted water ; drain them and dry them in a cloth.

Mix them well into a salad composed of potatoes, artichoke bottom, shrimps' tails, and capers in vinegar.

Arrange this in a salad bowl, and decorate it with beetroot and hard-boiled egg. A pinch of saffron may be added to this salad for seasoning.

The dark yellow chrysanthemums are best. In Yokohama the flowers already prepared are sold in the greengrocers' shops.

COWSLIP PUDDING

℀. Take a quarter of a peck of cowslips and rob them of their stalks and seeds. Cut them up and pound them. Add two ounces of grated biscuits or bread and three-quarters of a pint of milk. Bring them to the boil, then remove it from the fire, and when cool add four well-beaten eggs which have had a little milk and rose water added to them.

Sweeten to taste. Mix it well and pour into a buttered dish and bake it. Sprinkle it with powdered sugar, and serve.

COWSLIP WINE

℀. To every gallon of water allow three pounds of lump sugar, the rind of two lemons, and the juice of one. Also the rind and juice of one Seville orange, and one gallon of cowslip pips.

Boil the sugar and water for thirty minutes, and remove the scum. Pour the boiling syrup on the lemon and orange rinds, and the juice of both. When just warm add the flowers picked from the stalks and seeds. To nine gallons of liquor add three-quarters of an ounce of German yeast. Leave it for a few days, and then put it into a cask which has been well scalded out and cleaned. Add a bottle of brandy to every four and a half gallons of wine.

Leave it for two months, then bottle off and use.

Made in April or May, it should be ready to drink in June or July.

DAISY WINE
A Yorkshire Recipe

℃. Over four quarts of daisy blossoms, picked off the stalks, pour one gallon of boiling water. Let it stand all night ; then drain the liquid off and boil it for ten minutes. When it is lukewarm add one yeast cube, dissolved in a little warm water, two lemons and two oranges sliced, a cupful of raisins and three pounds of white sugar. Cover the crock with a cloth and let it stand three weeks to ferment. Skim it, strain and bottle it. In about a month it will be ready to use.

DANDELION WINE
As made in Bucks.

℃. Pick the heads of the dandelions only ; spread them out on sheets of paper to get rid of insects. To each gallon of flower heads add one gallon of water, two oranges, one lemon, one ounce of root ginger crushed ; tie the ginger in a muslin bag. Put into a pan and bring it all to the boil, and boil it for twenty minutes. Then strain it and add four pounds of sugar. If not clear, add the white of an egg, and to make it work put in half an ounce of yeast on a slice of bread. Leave it a week, strain and bottle it loosely at first, then tighter.

It should stand for six months before using.

PURÉE OF DANDELION

℃. Dandelion leaves, butter, one tablespoonful of milk, flour, bread.

Pick a large quantity of dandelion leaves from the young roots. Wash them clean and boil them in a large pan with plenty of water. Drain them thoroughly and pass them through a sieve.

Put into a saucepan butter and flour for thickening, very little milk, and the dandelion purée, and season with salt and pepper. Heat it through, and serve it with fried bread.

HAWTHORN CORDIAL

¶ Take a basketful of hawthorn flowers ; rob them of all their leaves and stalks, and fill a large bottle with the flowers without pressing them down. Pour in with them as much brandy as the bottle will hold. Cork it down, and after three months strain off the brandy.

EGGS COOKED WITH MARIGOLD

¶ Marigolds, eggs, nutmeg, pepper, salt, slices of bread, milk.

Blanch and chop some marigold flowers ; poach as many eggs as are required, and while they are cooking sprinkle them thickly with chopped marigolds and season them with nutmeg, pepper and salt. They should be poached very slowly.

Fry some slices of bread first steeped in milk. Strew the croutons with powdered marigolds ; serve the eggs on the top with fried parsley, and garnish them with fresh marigold flowers.

MARIGOLD CORDIAL

℃. One peck of marigold petals, one and a half pounds of stoned raisins, seven pounds of castor sugar, two pounds of honey, three gallons of water, three eggs, six oranges, four tablespoonfuls of German yeast, one ounce of gelatine, one pound of sugar candy, one pint of brandy.

Take a peck of marigold petals and put them into an earthenware bowl with the raisins. Pour over them a boiling liquid made of the sugar, honey, and three gallons of water. Clear this liquid while it is boiling with the whites and shells of three eggs, and strain it before putting in the flowers. Cover up the bowl and leave it for two days and two nights. Stir it well and leave it for another day and night. Then strain it and put it into a six-gallon cask which has been well cleaned, and add to it one pound of sugar candy and the rinds of six oranges, which have been peeled and stripped of all white pith. Stir into it four tablespoonfuls of German yeast and cover up the bung-hole. Leave it to work till it froths out ; when the fermentation is over pour in a pint of brandy and half an ounce of dissolved gelatine. Stop the cask and leave if for several months.

NASTURTIUM SALAD

℃. Take a good-sized lettuce, six nasturtium leaves, some of the nasturtium seeds, and a handful of the flowers for decoration.

Cut up the lettuce and the leaves, mix the seeds with the oil and vinegar dressing, and pour over it.

Arrange the flowers round.

CANDIED PRIMROSES

℄ Gather the primroses when dry, and pull the flowers from the green calyx. Make a syrup of icing sugar and water, and boil it until when a little is dropped into cold water it is crisp.

Then put in the primroses for a minute. Take them out and dry them on a sieve. Leave them in a warm place to dry, then sprinkle them with icing sugar. Gently open the flowers and sift any superfluous sugar from them, and keep them in a dry place.

PRIMROSE VINEGAR

℄ Boil six pounds of castor sugar in four gallons of water for ten minutes, and take off the scum. Shake into it a peck of primroses, and when cool spread some yeast on a piece of toast and put it in the liquid. Let it ferment all night, then put it into a barrel and keep it in a warm place till it has done working. There must be an air hole in the top of the barrel. In several weeks the vinegar may be bottled.

COMPÔTE OF ROSES

℄ One pound of rose petals, four pounds of castor sugar, one cupful of water, juice of half a lemon, a few drops of concentrated eau de roses.

Boil the rose petals in boiling water ; strain and dry them. Add to them one pound of castor sugar, and pound them together.

Put three pounds of sugar into a saucepan with a cupful of water, and boil it to a thick syrup. Add the juice of half a lemon and stir in the pounded roses and sugar. Bring it to the boil ; take it off the fire, and add a few drops of concentrated eau de roses. Mix well, and pour it into jars.

ICE CREAM OF ROSES

℄. One pint of cream, two handfuls of fresh rose petals, yolks of two eggs, sugar.

Boil a pint of cream and put into it when it boils two handfuls of fresh rose petals, and leave them for two hours, well covered. Then pass this through a sieve, and mix with the cream the well-beaten yolks of two eggs, and sugar to taste. Add a little cochineal, and put it on the fire, stirring it all the time, but do not let it boil on any account.   Put it on ice.

ROSE WINE

℄. One gallon of rose water, sugar, rose petals, spices.

Place one gallon of still cold rose water in a glazed vessel. Put a quantity of rose petals into it, and place it in a copper so that it is surrounded by hot water. Allow it to cool, and then press the petals into the liquid. Repeat this procedure until the liquid has gained considerable flavour from the petals.

To every gallon of liquor put three pounds of loaf sugar and mix it well. Now place it in a cask, and put in a piece of toast covered with yeast to ferment it. Allow it to stand for thirty days. Wine and spices may be added to it.

A similar process may be used for making wine from the following flowers :

Carnations, Wallflowers, Violets, Primroses, and any other heavily scented flowers.

Mr. Marcel Boulestin's Recipe in his book
" Simple French Cooking "

OMELETTE AUX FLEURS DE SALSIFIS

℄ This omelette is not easy to make, not because it is difficult to do it well, but because it is not easy to get the necessary flowers.

Salsifis flowers are not usually sold in shops ; in fact they are only to be found in the vegetable garden in the late spring. The best salsifis for this purpose is the one imported from Spain, which has black roots and yellow flowers.

Nip them literally in the bud, and wash them well in several waters to get rid of the kind of milk which oozes from them when you break them. Then dry them in a cloth for a few minutes, after which cook them in butter till they are brown, with salt and pepper. Mix them with the beaten eggs, and make your omelette in the ordinary way. Do not be surprised to see the buds open in the hot butter. It affects them more quickly than the sun. Some show a few already yellow petals ; it is a pretty sight ; also the taste is delicious.

VIOLET TEA

❡ Pour half a pint of boiling water on to one teaspoonful of dried violets ; leave it for five minutes. Strain it, and sweeten it with honey.

This is very soothing to people suffering from bronchitis.

MARMALADE OF VIOLETS

❡ Half a pound of violet flowers, one and a half pounds of sugar, half a cup of water.

Take half a pound of violet flowers picked from their stalks and crush them in a mortar.

Boil the sugar and water to a syrup, and when boiling add the flowers. Allow it to come five or six times to the boil on a very slow fire. Stir it with a wooden spoon, and pour it while hot into little pots.

VIOLET NOSEGAYS

❡ Take fresh violets ; tie them in bunches of ten or twelve flowers with cotton.

Boil some sugar until it pearls or bubbles. Try a little in a spoon and blow hard upon it. The bubbles should leave the spoon and float in the air like soap bubbles. Then let the sugar cool. Dip into it the bunches of flowers ; drain them and put them on a sieve. When dry cut out some papers and put round the flowers to look like nosegays, and serve cold.

SYRUP MADE OF WHITE ACACIA

℃. Place in a jar in alternate layers two ounces of white acacia flowers freshly gathered, and three ounces of castor sugar. Put them in a cool larder for six hours, and then pour over them a quart of boiling water. Leave it to infuse for twenty-four hours. At the end of this time dissolve five ounces of sugar in less than a quarter of a pint of water. Drain off, without squeezing the flowers, the liquid in which they have been soaking. Mix it with the syrup prepared in the saucepan, which should be boiling ; when cold pass through a fine sieve.

WOODRUFF WINE

Always drunk in Germany on May Day

℃. Put a pint of white wine and two of red into a jug with sufficient sugar to sweeten it. Cut an orange, without peeling it, into thick slices and add it to the wine ; then throw into it some bunches of woodruff well washed and drained. Cover the jug and leave it till the next day.

XIX
CAKES

"There is a cake for any man
If he will watch the fire."

CHAPTER XIX

CAKES

POETS and historians continue to vaunt the heroic qualities of King Alfred, yet his merits leave his own nation quite cold; because the schoolroom story that he burnt the cakes impresses young minds with the strong conviction that " he must have been a silly ass "; and the hero of the story is undoubtedly the cake.

One of the minor mysteries of food is the dignity conceded to the British cake with which we celebrate the most important joyful and poetical occasions of life. At weddings and christenings, birthdays, Christmas festivities and Easter holidays, the Cake, " black as the devil, heavy as sin, sweet as young love," covered with almond paste, and encrusted with devices of white sugar, is part of the fun. By its solid virtues it has acquired a romantic place as the centre of the hospitable rites of a romantic people.

But there are other cakes, or tea would not be the delightfully variegated meal it is. And it is the nicest meal of the day, whether it is taken in the nursery with a two-year-old host making milk and honey flow with a lavishness that rouses wonder why, on paper, the process should sound poetical; or in a North country inn with eleven or twelve different sorts of cakes on the table; out of doors or merely in the drawing-room. Philosophers might say the charm of the meal lay in the informal opportunity for recreative conversation; pedants may contend that all hangs on the country of origin of the tea itself, and upon whether the hostess lets the kettle boil; but all children, and all sensible people, know that the fascination of tea really depends entirely upon the cakes.

SPONGE CAKE

℄. Six eggs three-quarters of a pound of castor sugar, half a pound of flour, lemon juice to flavour.

Beat the yolks and whites of the eggs separately. Stir the sugar slowly into the beaten yolks, then gradually add the flour; lastly stir in the well-beaten whites of the eggs and lemon juice to taste. Bake about three-quarters of an hour in a moderate oven.

RAISIN CAKE

℄. One pound of flour, half a pound of butter, half a pound of seeded raisins, half a pound of sugar, two eggs, half a pint of milk, one dessert-spoonful of baking-powder, and the rind of half a lemon.

Rub the butter into the flour. Add the sugar, baking-powder, raisins and the grated lemon rind. Beat the eggs separately, and add the yolks first, then the whites, and enough milk to make into a dough.

Bake in a well-greased tin for about an hour and a half.

CHOCOLATE CAKE

❡. A quarter of a pound of chocolate powder or cocoa, a quarter of a pound of butter, two and a half ounces of flour, a quarter of a pound of sugar, two eggs, one teaspoonful of baking-powder.

Heat the chocolate in the oven. Add it to the flour and sugar. Melt the butter and mix it with the whole. Whip the whites and yolks of the eggs separately; add the yolks first and then the whites, and bake in a moderate oven in a well-buttered tin.

The cake should be removed from the oven as soon as it is cooked inside. Over-baking will make it too dry, and this cake should always be a little moist when it is cut into.

GINGER CAKE

❡. Three pounds of flour, three pounds of treacle, three-quarters of a pound of butter, three-quarters of brown sugar, three teaspoon-fuls of carbonate of soda, five eggs, two ounces of ground ginger, one pound of peel, one pound of sultanas, one teaspoonful of cream of tartar.

Mix the butter and sugar. Add the flour, then

the treacle; then stir in the beaten eggs and the other ingredients. Bake the cake for about two hours in a slow oven.

This is a large cake, but it keeps well, and it is extremely good.

GUEST CAKE

℀. One pound of flour, seven ounces of butter, half a pound of brown sugar, one pound of sultanas, half a pound of candied citron peel, half a pint of milk, one teaspoonful of carbonate of soda, three teaspoonfuls of vinegar.

Mix all the dry ingredients first. Then mix the milk, carbonate of soda and vinegar separately, and while it is effervescing pour it into the centre of the dry mixture. Stir it well with a fork, and put it into a greased tin and bake in a moderate oven for two hours. If possible do not open the oven door while the cake is baking.

A RICH CHRISTMAS CAKE

℀. One pound of flour, one pound of butter, three-quarters of a pound of sugar, a quarter of a pound of sweet almonds, half a pound each of seedless raisins, candied peel, sultanas and currants, six eggs, a large teaspoonful of mixed spice, and also of baking-powder, and one glass of sherry.

Beat the sugar and butter together, then add the flour with which the baking-powder and spice have been mixed, and after that the fruit

416

and chopped and blanched almonds. Beat the whites and yolks of the eggs separately; add the yolks first, beat the mixture well, then add the whites and mix well.

Only fill the baking-tin, or tins (which must be well buttered first), three-quarters full, and bake in a moderate oven for two or three hours. The next day cover the cake with almond icing, made with half a pound of ground almonds and the same amount of icing sugar, kneaded well together, flavoured with vanilla, and with enough white of egg to moisten it. Roll it out into a paste and spread it over the top of the cake.

GIRDLE CAKES

❡ Take a pound of flour and mix with it a teaspoonful of carbonate of soda, a little salt, half a teaspoonful of cream of tartar and enough sour milk to make it a dough; a small lump of butter mixed with the flour makes the scones richer. Mix very lightly, and handle the dough as little and lightly as possible.

Place the dough on a floured board, take a small piece at a time and shape into a flat round scone.

Heat the girdle on the cooking-stove and have it ready by the time the scones are shaped.

Sprinkle it with flour to test the heat, and either leave the flour or grease the girdle before placing the scones on it.

Brown on both sides and serve hot, cut in

half and buttered. They will take about ten minutes to brown.

HUNGARIAN CHEESE CAKE

℄ One York cream cheese, (i.e. approximately six to eight ounces) a quarter of a pound of butter, a quarter of a pound of sugar and four eggs.

Beat the butter to a cream, mix in the cheese, crumbled small, then add the sugar and the beaten yolks of the eggs, and lastly the stiff snow of the whites. Add a few sultanas and flavour with vanilla.

Line a cake tin with a nice short pastry crust, and fill it with the cheese mixture. Brush the top with the yolk of another egg to colour it, and bake in a moderate oven.

HAZEL NUT CAKE

℄ A quarter of a pound of finely ground hazel nuts, three and a half ounces of sugar, three eggs, two tablespoonfuls of dry breadcrumbs, and a quarter of a teaspoonful of baking-powder.

Beat the yolks of eggs and the sugar for twenty minutes, add the nuts, the breadcrumbs, the baking-powder and the whites of the eggs, whipped to a stiff snow.

Fill a buttered cake tin with the mixture and bake for half an hour (or more) in a slow oven. When cold the cake can be iced over with coffee icing.

The cake is also very good if it is made with walnuts.

ALMOND BISCUITS

℄ Half a pound of flour, four ounces of butter, four ounces of white sugar, one egg, a few blanched almonds.

Cream the butter and sugar, then add the flour and mix with the beaten egg. Roll out the paste a quarter of an inch thick and cut it into small rounds. Brush these over with white of egg and sprinkle the biscuits with little pieces of chopped almond. Bake them in a hot oven.

SHREWSBURY BISCUITS

℄ A quarter of a pound of butter, a quarter of a pound of castor sugar, half a pound of flour, one egg, the grated rind of one lemon, and a little salt.

Cream the butter and sugar with the back of a wooden spoon, then add the beaten egg and half the flour. When this is well mixed, add the lemon rind grated finely, and the rest of the flour and the salt. Roll the mixture very thin and cut it into small biscuits. Bake them in a moderate oven. They are pale fawn colour when cooked. Be careful not to grate the white of the lemon rind.

XX

THE ALCHEMIST'S CUPBOARD

" A Master Cook ! why, he's the man of men
For a professor: he designs, he draws,
He paints, he carves, he builds, he fortifies ;
Makes citadels of curious fowl and fish.
Some he dry dishes, some moats round with
    broths,
Mounts marrow-bones, cuts fifty-angled cus-
    tards ;
Rears bulwark pies, and for his outer works
He raiseth ramparts of immortal crust ;
And teacheth all the tactics at one dinner.
What ranks, what files to put his dishes in ;
The whole cut military. Then he knows
The influence of the stars upon his meats,
And all their seasons, tempers, qualities ;
And so to fit his relishes and sauces,
He has Nature in a pot, 'bove all the chemists
Or airy brethren of the rosy cross.
He is an architect, an engineer,
A soldier, a physician, a philosopher,
A general mathematician."

CHAPTER XIX

THE ALCHEMIST'S CUPBOARD

ONCE upon a time a celebrated alchemist made a large fortune by selling his secret recipes for curing all the ills the sun shone upon. If he had lived nowadays he would have made an even larger fortune, for he would have made, and bottled, one specific, given it a mysterious name and a horrible smell, advertised it widely, sold it for sixty times its cost, and kept his secret to himself. But as he lived six hundred years ago he was more guileless, and sold the secrets themselves. However, he was not so guileless that he did not ensure his reputation against their failure. When his clients complained that their hearts still ached, or that their children continued to cough, or that their enemies prospered, he would gravely point out that they obviously had not taken the right precautions with the component parts of his prescription—that the valerian or black briony had been gathered, or planted, under a waxing moon instead of by the light of the moon on the wane, and that the black horse from whose tail they had filched three hairs must have been a shade too old, or been the foal of a miserable mother. In fact, the alchemists were not such fools as modern scientists make out, and no more irritating than people who give recipes without mentioning the idiosyncrasies of ingredients. Grocers are apt to recommend as " the best on the market " the particular brand upon which they get the largest commission ; so the following lists of what is wanted in an ideal kitchen in the way of stores, also pots and pans, will be useful to housekeepers who want the best results without having to experiment for themselves.

The following list has been compiled as a guide for those who want to obtain the best value for their money when buying cooked food or preparations. Nearly everyone buys, in one crisis or another, preserved tongues, in tins or glass, bottled or tinned fruits, soups, etc. There are hundreds of different brands on the market, and the general public are sometimes misled into buying things under the guileless impression that what is most widely advertised is " the best," whereas many things which have stood the test of years and have never been surpassed are often not as much advertised as newer and possibly quite inferior brands. Naturally each grocer recommends to his customer whichever make he happens to stock, and, also naturally, grocers are apt to stock whichever brand it pays them best to sell, i.e. the goods upon which they get the largest commission. So advertisements and grocers are not infallible guides.

It is not necessary to buy the most expensive things on the market, but it is necessary to buy things of good quality, and this list, and the one for the kitchen store cupboard, has been drawn up in an attempt to help people by combining quality with economy and cheapness.

Every kitchen store cupboard should contain :

Worcester Sauce	Lea and Perrin's.
Harvey's Sauce	Lazenby.
Tomato Catsup	Heinz.
Mushroom Ketchup	Army and Navy Stores.
Parisian Essence	

Essence of Anchovy ⎫
Anchovy Sauce   ⎬ Burgess.
Anchovies   ⎭

Olive Oil — ⎧ Lucca or Provençal.
The Barto Valle, sold by Jackson's is an Italian oil from a Southern vineyard. Provençal oil is more refined and generally more suitable to the English palate.

Chilli Vinegar   ⎫
White Wine Vinegar   ⎪
Tarragon   „   ⎪
Fines Herbes   „   ⎬ Maille's.
Ravigote   „   ⎪
Eschalot   „   ⎪
French Mustard „   ⎭

Mustard — Colman's Extra Genuine.

Mignonette Pepper

Black Peppercorns — ⎧ The Mangalore have the more distinct flavour, but are much more expensive than the ordinary ones.

Ground White Pepper

Hungarian Paprika — ⎧ The Army and Navy Stores seem to be the only grocers who import this direct from Hungary.

Searcy's Oriental Salt
Cayenne Pepper

Celery Salt	{ Only obtainable at Harrod's and
Onion Salt	{ other big grocers.
Household Salt.	
Chutney	Ahmuty's or Daw Sens of Calcutta.
	{ Vencatachellem is the best, but
	{ there is difficulty in obtaining it
Curry Powder	{ owing to a family quarrel. A good
	{ second choice is Veerasawny's
	Nizam.
Capers	
Bay Leaves	
Cloves of Garlic	
Dried Mint	
„ Marjoram	
„ Thyme	These should all be bought in
„ Basil	bottles from one of the big grocers.
„ Sage	
„ Mixed Herbs	
Allspice	
Ground Cinnamon	The Ceylon.
Cloves	The Penang.
Mace	„ „
Mixed Spice	
Nutmeg	The Penang.
Vanilla Pods	The finest are the Bourbon.
Cinnamon Sticks	
Ground Ginger	Jamaica.
Whole Ginger.	„
Carraway Seeds	The Dutch are best.
Jordan Almonds	{ These come from Spain ; for cook-
	{ ing the Valencia are all right.
Ground Sweet	{ These are always used now in
	{ cooking, and save a great deal of
Almonds	{ trouble.
Whole Chillies	The Toulouse are the best.
Pistachio Nuts	Sicilian are the best.
Orange Flower Water	French (from Grasse).

Rose Water	French (from Grasse).
Ratafia	
Prunes	{ The Californian 20-30, attainable at Harrod's and the big grocers.
Figs	The Smyrna are the best.
Currants	{ The Vostizza are the best, but the Colonial fruit is good in colour, though not so fine in flavour as the Greek.
Sultanas	
Raisins	Valencia.
Angelica	The round is best.
Glacé Cherries	
Mixed Candied Peel	{ The Army and Navy Stores is famous for this.
Crystallized Violets	
,, Rose Leaves	
Icing Sugar	
Granulated Sugar	Tate's.
Loaf Sugar	,,
Demerara Sugar	
Moist Brown Sugar	{ This comes from Barbadoes and is known as Moscovado Sugar.
Dark Sugar Candy	
Cocoa	{ Van Houten's. It can be obtained loose by the pound at Rapson's in Lamb's Conduit Street, and is much cheaper than in tins. The Dutch cocoa is quite different from the English, because it is cooked at a higher temperature and is mixed with an alkali.
Chocolate	{ Bakers' unsweetened, to be obtained at Jackson's. Bakers' unsweetened chocolate or Van Houten's cocoa are much the best preparations of the kind for making chocolate puddings and creams.

Rennet	Hansen's Danish tablets or Clark's Junket Powder are on the whole more satisfactory than the liquid.
Red Currant Jelly	So much used in the making of sauces and hashes.
Apricot Jam	Used in the cooking of apples.
Condensed Milk	Libby's unsweetened.
Golden Syrup	Lyle's, or if a darker one is liked—Hudson's " Dark."
Carolina Rice	The unpolished should be used.
Patna Rice Ground Rice	The Army and Navy Stores have the finest at a cheaper price than elsewhere.
Macaroni	The Italian is the best. It comes from Naples. A smaller kind comes from Genoa.
Spaghetti	Groult puts up a good French macaroni and spaghetti, but the French flour used in the making of these is not as good. The Italian flour is similar to the Hungarian flour.
Cornflour	Brown and Polson's.
Semolina	
Cream of Hominy	
Flour	Finest Whites, which is a mixture of Foreign and English.
Sago Crème de riz Tapioca Chestnut Flour Potato "	Groult's preparations are excellent.
Pearl Barley	Scotch.
Cream of Barley	Robinson's or Groult's.
Arrowroot	The Bermuda is best, but too expensive for ordinary use ; the St. Vincent is therefore nearly always used.

Lentils	Egyptian split.
Haricot Beans	{ The Rangoon, because the Dutch, though the best, are not easy to obtain.
Baking Powder	Borwick's or Royal.
Gelatine	Nelson's or Coignet's.
Meat Glaze.	The Army and Navy home-made.
Parmesan Cheese	

Wines and Liqueurs required in cooking :

Chablis	Marsala	Port
Claret	Maraschino	Sherry

This list has not been compiled as an advertisement for the firms mentioned ; the authors' only object has been to be of use to the public. If a certain partiality for the Army and Navy Stores is apparent, it is because the authors have discovered that, in spite of their modernization, old-fashioned excellencies still linger in the Kitchen Department there. For instance, each Madeira Cake made there actually contains Madeira wine.

THE BEST PREPARATIONS
What to buy and Where to buy them

❡ In spite of all attempts to imitate every successful preparation on the market, certain things have held their own and remain the best in defiance of all modern competition. For instance, Lea and Perrin's Worcester Sauce, and Harvey's Sauce, which are both used in Cumberland and other sauces, are unsurpassed.

In the first chapter of this book are given recipes for making all the well-known sauces, such as Sauce Robert, Diable Sauce, Tartare Sauce, etc., but for those who prefer to buy them ready-made the most reliable brand is " Escoffier."

TONGUES

℩. There is an old superstition on the part of the public that tongues and other food preserved in glass is safer and more wholesome than the same food in tins. This is quite a fallacy.

When buying tinned foods the purchaser is ensured that the food is thoroughly sterilized, for the tins are airtight, and if fermentation takes place the tin expands, that is, it blows out in blisters and is at once detected. On, the other hand, there is no such safeguard when the container is glass. The rubber band that is part of the cap when a glass is used may perish and let in the air, and decomposition may set in without any visible trace. Another consideration is that tinned foods are a good deal cheaper than the same thing in glass.

Both Petty Wood and Shippam's put up excellent tongues at a reasonable price. The Petty Wood two-pound " Epicure " tongue is 6s. The Army and Navy Stores' preserved tongues are also to be recommended ; they are prepared in their own kitchen. All their cooked foods are excellent and reasonable in price.

SOUPS

There is no soup at the price to compare with Campbell's. It is sold in 8d. tins, which, with the addition of the necessary quantity of milk, makes enough for four people ; or if only a small cup for each person is wanted, one tin will make enough for six people. Campbell's " Tomato " and " Oxtail " soups are sold by most good grocers, but Selfridge's is one of the few shops at present that keep the Asparagus soup, the Green Pea, and the Celery soups, which are less known but equally good.

Of the more expensive soups we should recommend those made by the Army and Navy Stores and those sold by Fortnum and Mason and Jackson. The Army and Navy are cheaper.

HAMS

ℭ Every English county has its own special way of curing hams, and Yorkshire has acquired a reputation of curing more hams than ever Yorkshire produced. But the Suffolk sugar-cured hams are not so well known, but are un-equalled for flavour and delicacy. They are difficult to find in London, but are obtainable at the Army and Navy Stores, and possibly elsewhere. The black Bradenham hams which come from Buckinghamshire are more widely known.

Virginia peach-fed hams, so prized by American gourmets, are to be bought at Cadbury, Pratt and Co.'s and Selfridge's.

CHEESE

ℭ Everyone knows about Stilton, Gruyère, Wensleydale, Gorgonzola, etc., but the peculiar merits of the Blue Cheshire Cheeses are not so well known. Not all Cheshire cheeses will turn blue. The cheeses that are kept for this purpose are usually chosen from the spring dairying, when the cows are feeding on buttercups, and are on the market in the early autumn. This is probably the reason why they are not so popular as the Stilton, though they have a more delicate flavour, but they are too early for the Christmas market, when expensive foods are more generally bought. Hudson Brothers keep them in their season, and other provision merchants.

Fortnum and Mason sell a particularly good cream cheese called Thornbury's Gloucester.

SMOKED BEEF AND SMOKED BACON

℃ These are American prepared meats, and the beef is necessary for Pink Hash, for which the recipe is given on page 196.

They are to be obtained at Jackson's, Piccadilly, and Selfridge's.

SARDINES

℃ French sardines are the best, but some of the famous French firms sell their stock so quickly that the sardines have not time to mature in the oil, and at the moment Penandross make is to be recommended, as well as the first-rate brands of Rodel and Pinaud.

BLACK OLIVES

℃, Black olives, which make such delicious hors d'œuvres, can be obtained at Parmignani, of 42 Old Compton Street, Soho, at 1s. a pound.

PALM HEARTS

℃, These delicacies, which make excellent salads, are not so well known as they deserve to be. They are naturally rather an expensive luxury, as they are only obtained when palm trees are cut down, and each tree has only one heart. They are to be obtained at Hediard's, Place de la Madeleine, Paris.

TINNED FRUIT

℃, By far the finest pears, peaches and apricots on the market is the San José brand. They are also the most expensive. They are the finest because they are the most carefully graded, and the fruit is preserved in a rich syrup. They come from California. The Colonial brands of fruit now coming on the market—Australian, New Zealand, and South African—are all good and will undoubtedly be popular, but the growers have not yet learned to grade the fruit perfectly. Other good tinned fruits on the market at reasonable prices are those put up by Libby, especially their blackberries. Soft fruits, such as strawberries and raspberries, are coming from Switzerland, under the name " Lengbourg." An excellent and cheap brand of raspberry is the " Irvington Club " brand from California, which can be obtained from Rapson's, Lamb's Conduit Street.

JAMS AND MARMALADES

❦ Tiptree's jams are still the best, and can now be obtained everywhere. Cooper's Oxford marmalade, for those who like a thickly cut and bitter marmalade, is the best of its kind. The same firm sell a damson cheese with almonds in, which is unlike anybody else's.

AMERICAN SPECIALITIES

Sweet Corn	The "Duchess" brand is very good.
Clam Bouillon	{ Clam is a fish much prized in America. Bouillon is sold at Selfridge's.
„ Chowder	Selfridge's.
Maple Syrup „ Butter „ Sugar	} The "Pride of Canada" is a good brand.
Pickled Peaches „ Pears „ Apricots „ Figs	These are much served on the Continent and in America with hot and cold meat. Miss Ellen North's are perhaps the best, but a new brand, the "Iris," is very good.
Pea Nut Butter	{ This can be bought at Jackson's and Selfridge's.

CHINA TEAS

❦ There is no doubt that the reason China teas are not as universally popular as Indian, is because people have not yet learnt how to use them. There are three great points to be observed in the making of China tea :

1. That China tea weighs lighter than Indian, therefore more tea in bulk should be used than is used if it were Indian.

2. That the water with which it is made must be poured on to the tea the moment it boils. If it is allowed to boil for even a minute after this the flavour of the tea is spoilt.

3. China tea must be allowed to stand at least five minutes.

There are nearly seventy different kinds of China teas and many blends. Mr. Leonard Hudson, of Hudson Brothers, who was trained as a tea planter, blends most of the teas put up by Hudson Brothers, and their teas are excellent. They sell chiefly Keemun's and Kintuck's, but they have all the finest Lapseng Souchongs, though Messrs. Peek Bros. and Winch specialize in the Lapseng Souchongs with the tarry flavour, which are usually called Caravan teas, because they were carried overland by camel caravans from China to Russia, where they were drunk by the rich long before they were known elsewhere in Europe. These " Caravan Teas," being spared the long sea voyage, have their delicate flavour unimpaired.

The scented Chinese teas, which are so much drunk by the Chinese themselves, are very little exported. The most exquisite of all, perhaps, the Jasmine tea, can be bought at Hediard's, in the Place de la Madeleine, Paris, and small quantities of it, and also of the Chloranthus and the Bitter Orange, are occasionally to be found in London, but it is very expensive, usually about 15s. a pound.

That famous blend of scented China tea, the Earl Grey mixture, was originally blended by a grocer called " George Charlton," who had a shop in the Charing Cross Road. He made it for the Earl Grey of 1830, and it was drunk in all the great Whig houses of that day. It is now to be had at Jackson's, Piccadilly. Jackson's bought the recipe on the death of Charlton, and became the sole proprietors, but they forgot to register the name, and the tea has been copied by other grocers, but Jackson's is the genuine Earl Grey mixture. It costs 5s. a pound, and should not be bought in large quantities, as, once exposed to the air, it quickly loses its flavour. Jackson's put it up in half-pound tins.

THE COOKING UTENSILS WHICH ARE NECESSARY FOR EVERY KITCHEN

A Kettle.
A Steamer.
A Set of Aluminium Saucepans with long handles.
A deep Frying Pan with a wire basket to fit it.
An ordinary Frying Pan.
A Fish Kettle.
*An Omelette Pan.
A Double Saucepan (aluminium).
*A Wire Sieve.
A Colander.
*A Conical Strainer.
*A Gauze Strainer.
A Fish Slice.
*An Egg Whisk.
*A Wooden Pestle.
*A Wire Salad Basket.

*A French Chopping Knife.
*A French Fillet Knife.
*A French Office Knife.
 A Palette Knife.
 A Mincing Machine.
 A Small Wooden Chopping Board.
 A Pastry Board.
 A Pastry Roller.
 A Pair of Scales.
 A Set of Wooden Spoons.
 A Pair of Scissors.
 Set of Skewers.
 A Grater.
 A Funnel.
 An Aluminium Measure.
*A Piping Bag and Tubes.
 A Fish Slice.
 A Pepper Mill.
 A Basting Spoon.
*A Set of Cake Tins.
*A Coffee Grinder.
*A Tin Coffee Machine.
 Castle Pudding Tins.

The utensils marked with a * are best obtained in Soho
M. Saulnier, of 35c Old Compton Street, keeps French
utensils made of the strongest and best materials.

He has just patented a new sieve with seven meshes, which
can be obtained nowhere else ; a small size for private houses
costs about 9s.

The Algerian Coffee Stores in Old Compton Street provides cheap and good coffee utensils.

OTHER USEFUL UTENSILS WHICH
ARE NOT INDISPENSABLE FOR EVERY
KITCHEN

A Bain-Marie.
An Ice Cream Freezer.
The Reliance or the White Mountain are two of the best

cheap makes in the market. The Auto-Vacuum Freezer is quite good, and is useful for keeping the ice cream in after it is made, but the machine does not make such smooth ice as the other two.

A Vegetable Slicer.

Monsieur Saulnier has a very good one which slices vegetables for Julienne Soup, Cucumbers, and Potatoes for Pommes Soufflé. It costs 6s. 6d.

Another one for slicing potatoes for Pommes Gaufrette costs 4s. 6d.

A Salamander.

As the firms and shops mentioned in the above lists have not paid anything to have their names inserted the authors have been free to publish what they chose.

INDEX

INDEX

441

INDEX

INDEX

445

INDEX

449

INDEX

450

INDEX

454

INDEX

INDEX

INDEX